G000123215

FREEHAND 9

FOR WINDOWS AND MACINTOSH

Sandee Cohen

 Peachpit Press

macromedia®
PRESS

Visual QuickStart Guide

FreeHand 9 for Windows and Macintosh

Sandee Cohen

Peachpit Press

1249 Eighth Street
Berkeley, CA 94710
510/524-2178
510/524-2221 (fax)
800/283-9444

Published by Peachpit Press in association with Macromedia, Inc.

Find us on the World Wide Web at: http://www.peachpit.com
Peachpit Press is a division of Addison Wesley Longman

Copyright © 2000 by Sandee Cohen

FreeHand 9 exercises and updates: Tom Baer
Editor: Nancy Davis
Cover design: The Visual Group
FreeHand 9 Visual QuickStart Guide design: Sandee Cohen
Production: Tom Baer and Kate Reber
Technical Editor: Joanne Watkins
Index: Steve Rath

This book was created using: FreeHand 9 for illustrations, QuarkXPress for layout, and Ambrosia SW Snapz Pro for screen shots. The computers used were Macintosh PowerPCs. The fonts used were Minion Condensed, and Futura Condensed, from Adobe, and two specialty fonts created using Macromedia Fontographer.

ISBN 0-201-35489-6

9 8 7 6 5 4 3 2 1

Printed and bound in the United States of America

DEDICATED TO

My cousin Marcia who said in 1986, "Oh,
Sandee, you're creative, you should get a Mac."
I wouldn't have this career if she hadn't told
me that!

THANKS TO

Tom Baer who did the magnificent job of writing and illustrating all the new features for FreeHand 9 and putting the whole book together. I look forward to seeing his next book which will be totally his own. Good luck, Tom, may you write a bestseller.

Paul Tomzack who started the revision process way back last year.

Nancy Ruenzel publisher of Peachpit Press.

Nancy Davis my editor at Peachpit Press who got Tom and me through the process without a hitch.

Marjorie Baer the executive editor at Peachpit Press.

Kate Reber of Peachpit Press who can tell line screen with her eyes closed and made sure the book printed right.

The staff of Peachpit Press I may not have met you all, but you make me proud to be a Peachpit author.

Steve Rath who does the best index in the business.

Brian Schmidt the FreeHand 9 product manager. Yes, Brian, you gave me exactly what I wanted in the new Envelope tool. It's perfect!

Joanne Watkins of Macromedia, who provided the technical edit. Thanks, Joanne, I wish I had your eagle eye and encyclopedic memory.

Olav Martin Kvern author of *Real World FreeHand*. Not only is it the best "advanced" FreeHand book; it's a lot of fun to read. No one who writes PostScript code should be able to write a book as good as his.

Michael Randasso and the staff of the New School for Social Research Computer Instruction Center.

Pixel who insists that she gets mentioned.

David Lerner of **Tekserve** who personally helped me get my PowerBook back up and running at the last moment of the project. If you need Macintosh equipment, repairs, or accessories, try Tekserve (www.tekserve.com).

TABLE OF CONTENTS

INTRODUCTION

Welcome to Macromedia FreeHand. If you are like most people who are just starting out with the program, you may find it a little overwhelming. This Visual QuickStart Guide has been written to help you sort out the many different features.

What you can create with FreeHand

FreeHand is one of the most versatile graphics programs for the computer. At its simplest, FreeHand is a vector drawing program. It allows you to create varied artwork such as drawings, logos, and illustrations.

FreeHand also lets you add scanned artwork from programs such as Macromedia Fireworks or Adobe Photoshop. This makes it an excellent layout program to create ads, book covers, posters, and so on. FreeHand has a multiple-page feature that allows you to create newsletters and flyers, as well as multipage presentations with differently sized pages.

Finally, FreeHand uses the newest Flash 4 technology to turn FreeHand artwork into animations. FreeHand also lets you save your files in formats that can be posted directly onto the World Wide Web.

How this book is organized

The first few chapters provide overviews of the program. You may find that you do not create any artwork in those chapters. Do not skip them. They contain information that will help you later.

The middle chapters of the book contain the most artistic information. This is where you can see how easy it is to create sophisticated artwork using FreeHand.

The final chapters are about printing, preferences, and using your artwork with other applications and the Web. Some of this information refers to technical printing terms. If you are not familiar with these terms, speak to the print shop that will be printing your artwork.

Using this book

If you have used any of the Visual QuickStart Guides, you will find this book very similar. Each of the chapters consists of numbered exercises that deal with a specific technique or feature of the program. As you work through each exercise, you gain an understanding of the technique or feature. The illustrations for each of the exercises help you judge if you are following the steps correctly.

Instructions

Working with a book such as this, it is vital that you understand the terms I am using. This is especially important since some books use terms somewhat incorrectly. Therefore, here are the terms I use in the book and explanations of what they mean.

Click refers to pressing down and releasing the mouse button on the Macintosh, and the left mouse button on Windows. You must release the mouse button or it is not a click.

Press means to hold down the mouse button, or the keyboard key.

Press and drag means to hold the mouse button down and then move the mouse. In later chapters, I use the shorthand term *drag*; just remember that you have to press and hold as you drag the mouse.

Menu commands

FreeHand has menu commands that you follow to open dialog boxes, change artwork, and invoke certain commands. These menu commands are listed in bold type. The typical direction to choose a menu command might be written as **Window > Panels > Style**. This means that you should first choose the Window menu, then choose the Panels submenu, and then choose the Style command.

Keyboard shortcuts

Most of the menu commands for FreeHand 9 have keyboard shortcuts that help you work faster. For instance, instead of choosing New from the File menu, it is faster and easier to use some keys on the keyboard.

Keyboard shortcuts are sometimes listed in different orders by different software companies or authors. For example I always list the Command or Ctrl keys first, then the Option or Alt key, and then the Shift key. Other people may list the Shift key first. The order that you press those modifier keys is not important. However, it is very important that you always add the last key (the letter or number key) after you are holding the other keys.

The keyboard shortcuts for the menu commands are listed in Appendix B. There are several reasons for not including those shortcuts right in the book. Most importantly, many of the keyboard shortcuts for the Macintosh platform differ from those for the Windows platform. This means that the shortcut for **File > Save As** would have appeared in the text as Command-Shift-S/Ctrl-Shift-S. Rather than clutter the exercises, they are listed in Appendix B separated by platform.

Customizing keyboard shortcuts

FreeHand 9 also lets you customize the program with whatever keyboard shortcuts you want to use. This means that you can add a shortcut to a menu item that does not have one. Or you can switch keyboard shortcuts to commands you are more familiar with. So if you are used to working with programs such as CorelDRAW or Adobe Illustrator, you can change the FreeHand shortcuts to be the same as those programs.

Because of the customizing it is very possible that your version of FreeHand might not have the same shortcuts as mine. So rather than confuse you by printing shortcuts you may not have, I have put them at the end of the book where you can refer to them if you want.

Learning keyboard shortcuts

While keyboard shortcuts help you work faster, you really do not have to start using them right away. In fact, you will most likely learn more about FreeHand by using the menus. As you look for one command, you may see others that you would like to explore.

Once you feel comfortable working with FreeHand, you can start adding keyboard shortcuts to your repertoire. My suggestion is to look at which menu commands you use a lot. Then each day choose one of those shortcuts. For instance, if you do a lot of blends, you might decide to learn the shortcut for the Blend command. For the rest of that day use the Blend shortcut every time you need to make a blend. Even if you have to look at the menu to refresh your memory, still use the keyboard shortcut to actually apply the blend. By the end of the day you will have memorized the Blend shortcut. The next day you can learn a new one.

Cross-platform issues

One of the great strengths of FreeHand is that it is almost identical on both the Macintosh and Windows platforms. In fact, at first glance it is hard to tell which platform you are working on. However, because there are some differences between the platforms, there are some things you should keep in mind.

Modifier keys

Modifier keys are always listed with the Macintosh key first and then the Windows key second. So a direction to hold the Command/Ctrl key as you drag means to hold the Command key on the Macintosh platform or the Ctrl key on the Windows platform. When the key is the same on both computers, such as the Shift key, only one key is listed.

Generally the Command key on the Macintosh (sometimes called the Apple key) corresponds to the Ctrl key on Windows. The Option key on the Macintosh corresponds to the Alt key on Windows. The Control key on the Macintosh platform does not have an equivalent on the Windows platform. Notice that the Control key for the Macintosh is always spelled out while the Ctrl key for Windows is not.

Platform-specific features

A few times in the book, I have written separate exercises for the Macintosh and Windows platforms. These exercises are indicated by **(Mac)** and **(Win)**.

Most of the time this is because the procedures are so different that they need to be written separately. Sometimes features exist only on one platform. Those features are then labeled as to their platform.

Interface features

Most of the illustrations of the interface were cropped so that the platform is not too obvious. When necessary, I have put both the Macintosh and Windows elements on one page. If you need a more detailed look at the Windows interface, please see Appendix A, where I have shown side-by-side examples of the different interface designs.

Learning FreeHand

With a program as extensive as FreeHand, there will be many features that you never use. For instance, if you are an illustrator, you may never need any of FreeHand's text or layout features. Or you may never need to create charts or graphs. And if you are strictly a print person, you may never need to do any exporting as Web animations. Do not worry. It may be hard to believe but even the experts do not use all of FreeHand's features.

Find the areas you want to master, then follow the exercises. If you are patient, you will find yourself creating your own work in no time.

And don't forget to have fun!

Sandee Cohen (SandeeC@vectorbabe.com)
March 2000

B efore you can start working, you need to prepare your document. This preparation is very important to make sure your document is the correct size and you are working in the way that is most comfortable for you.

In this chapter you will learn how to

Launch FreeHand.

Start a new document or continue working on an old document.

Change the size of your pages.

Change the orientation of your pages.

Add pages to your document.

Move pages together.

Change the page magnification.

Add a bleed area to your work page.

Save your work as a document or a template.

Close your document.

Quit FreeHand.

FreeHand 9

❶ *Double-click the **FreeHand 9 icon** to launch the program.*

To launch FreeHand (Mac):

In the Finder, open the FreeHand folder and double-click the FreeHand 9 icon ❶.

To launch FreeHand (Win):

Use the Start menu to open the FreeHand application ❷ or in the Explorer, double-click the FreeHand icon.

TIP You can double-click the icon for a previously saved FreeHand document. This launches FreeHand and brings you directly to that document.

❷ *(Win) Use the **Start menu** to launch the program.*

Launch FreeHand

If you double-click the FreeHand icon instead of a saved document, you see the FreeHand menus and palettes on your screen, but you will not have an actual document open. (If you are working with FreeHand for Windows, you will see the Wizard screen. See the instructions at the end of this chapter for working with the Wizard.)

To create a new document:

To start working, you create a new document. To do so, choose **File > New**.

FreeHand 9 allows you to customize all the commands in the menus. (*For instructions on how to customize your menus, see Chapter 22, "Customizing FreeHand."*)

You now have an untitled document window open. (*For a detailed listing of all the features in the document window, see Appendix A.*)

Inside the document window is the rectangular work page where you create your work. A plain white area called the *pasteboard* surrounds the page ❸. Objects in the pasteboard do not print unless a bleed has been set (*see page 10*).

To change the units of measurement:

Use the the pop-up menu at the bottom of the document window ❹ to choose the units of measurement for the document.

TIP You can still enter sizes in other units and FreeHand will convert them into the unit you have selected for your document:

- For picas, type *p* after the number.
- For inches, type *i* after the number.
- For millimeters, type *m* after the number.
- For kyus, type *k* after the number.
- For centimeters, type *c* after the number.
- For pixels, type *x* after the number.
- Type *p before* the number for picas.
- Type *p after* the number for points.

or

- Type *pt after* the number for points.

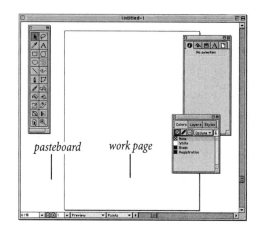

❸ *The* **work page** *sits inside the* **pasteboard** *area.*

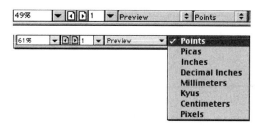

❹ *Use the* **Units of Measurement pop-up menu** *to change the units of measurement.*

❺ *In the Document Inspector, open the* **Printer Resolution pop-up menu** *to change the resolution for your document.*

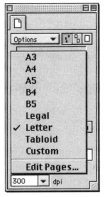

❻ *There are* **eight preset page sizes,** *plus* **Custom,** *which lets you enter the exact measurements for any size work page.*

❼ *When you choose Custom from the* **Page Size pop-up menu,** *you can enter your exact measurements in the x (horizontal) and y (vertical) fields.*

Once you have a new document open, check the settings in the Document Inspector.

To display the Document Inspector:
To open the Document Inspector, choose **Modify > Document**, or **Window > Inspectors > Document**. (*For a detailed listing of all the Inspectors, see Appendix A.*)

To change the printer resolution:
1. Make sure the Document Inspector is open.
2. Use the pop-up menu or drag across the field for the Printer resolution ❺ and enter the resolution for the type of printer you will be using.

As you create documents, you may need to change your work page to a different page size.

To select a new work page size:
1. Make sure the Document Inspector is displayed.
2. To change the size of the work page to one of the preset page sizes, choose the page size from the pop-up menu ❻ in the Document Inspector.

If none of the preset sizes is right for your job, you need to create a work page with custom measurements. For instance, if you are creating business cards, you would want your work page to match the trim size of the card.

To create a custom-size work page:
1. Choose Custom from the Page Size pop-up menu of the Document Inspector.
2. Click in the field next to the *x* and type the horizontal measurement of your page.
3. Click in the field next to the *y* and type the vertical measurement of your page ❼.
4. Press Return on the keyboard to apply the sizes to the work page.

Printer Resolution; Work Page Size; Custom-Size Page

You may decide that you want to reverse the horizontal and vertical sizes of your document.

To change the orientation of a page:

1. Make sure the Document Inspector is displayed.
2. Click the Wide icon next to the Page Size pop-up menu. This swaps your horizontal and vertical measurements ❽–❾.

TIP If the Tall icon is selected, FreeHand does not accept measurements that would make a page wider than it is tall. Similarly, while the Wide icon is selected, you can never specify a page that is taller than it is wide.

Once you have set your page size, you may need to create additional work pages. For instance, if you are creating a series of layouts for your client to choose from, you would need multiple pages.

To create additional work pages:

1. Make sure the Document Inspector is displayed.
2. Choose Duplicate from the Options pop-up menu. This creates a new work page exactly the same size as the first page ❿.

   or

   Choose Add Pages from the Options menu. The Add Pages dialog box appears. Type the number of pages you want. Use the pop-up menu to pick the page size. Choose the Tall or Wide icon for the proper orientation ⓫.
3. Click OK or press Enter or Return on the keyboard. The pasteboard shows the additional pages.

TIP You can also option-drag pages on the pasteboard using the Page tool to duplicate them and everything on them.

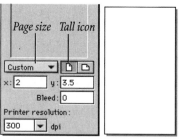

❽ *A custom-size page with the* **Tall orientation.**

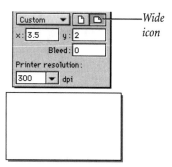

❾ *A custom-size page with the* **Wide orientation.**

❿ *Choosing Duplicate from the* **Options pop-up menu** *of the Document Inspector creates a new work page the same size as the page selected.*

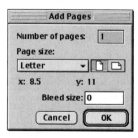

⓫ *The* **Add Pages** *dialog box lets you specify how many pages you want to add, their size, orientation, and bleed size.*

⓬ The **Page tool** *in the Toolbox allows you to move and resize pages on the pasteboard.*

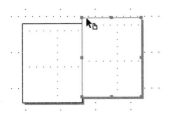

⓭ The **Page tool** *lets you select pages directly on the pasteboard and move them into position. The page icon shows that you are moving the page.*

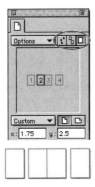

Magnification icons

⓮ **Moving the page thumbnails** *in the Document Inspector changes the layout of the pages on the pasteboard.*

⓯ **The Page tool icons** *change to show what function they are going to perform.*

When you work with multiple pages, you might want adjacent pages to touch each other so that you can spread the artwork from one page to the other. You can move pages using the Page tool or the page thumbnails in the Document Inspector.

To move pages with the Page tool:

1. Choose the Page tool in the Toolbox ⓬.
2. Click to select a page. The page selection handles appear, indicating the page is selected.
3. Hold the Shift key to select additional pages.
4. Press and drag to move the selected pages ⓭.
5. Release the mouse button when the page is in position.

TIP Hold the Shift key to constrain the motion to 45-degree angles.

To move pages with the page thumbnails:

1. In the Document Inspector, click the middle or large Magnification icon. Numbered boxes appear in the rectangular area of the Document Inspector that are thumbnails of your document pages ⓮.
2. Drag one of the page thumbnails next to one of the other thumbnails. The work page on the pasteboard moves to reflect the new layout ⓮.

TIP You can also resize your pages and switch them between vertical and horizontal orientation with the Page tool.

Putting the page cursor near the inside of one of the handles on a highlighted page changes the icon to the resizing icon. Bringing it just outside changes it to the rotation icon ⓯.

To see more thumbnail pages at once, you may need to change the thumbnail magnification within the Document Inspector.

To change the page icon magnification:

1. Click the first Magnification icon **⑯**. This shrinks the thumbnails to the smallest size.

TIP Try the smallest magnification setting for documents with four or more pages.

2. Click the middle Magnification icon **⑰** to expand the size of the thumbnails to the second size.

TIP Try the middle magnification setting for documents with two or three pages.

3. Click the third Magnification icon **⑱**. This expands the size of the thumbnails to the largest size.

TIP Double-click the thumbnail in the Document Inspector to go to that page and fit the page in the window in one step.

If you want artwork to print right to the edge of a page, you actually need to extend or *bleed* the artwork outside the edge of the page. In order for artwork to print when it extends off the page, you must set a bleed size. The bleed is added to the page size you have already set up.

To set a bleed size:

1. Make sure the Document Inspector is open.

2. At the bottom of the Document Inspector, enter your desired bleed size. Press Return or Enter.

3. A light gray line appears around your work page. This is the bleed area **⑲**.

TIP Use the bleed area to hold elements that should print outside the live area of your artwork **⑳**.

TIP You do not have to create crop marks or registration marks. FreeHand's print options with PostScript printers lets you insert those automatically (*see page 240*).

⑯ *The* **Magnification icon** *(circled) for the* **smallest size** *setting shows the most thumbnails at once.*

⑰ *The Magnification icon (circled) for the* **middle size** *setting works for two or three pages.*

⑱ *The Magnification icon (circled) for the* **largest size** *setting works for single page documents.*

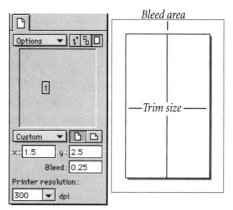

⑲ *The light gray line outside the work page indicates the* **bleed area.**

⑳ *The notes and gray background in the bleed area print. The print shop then cuts off the bleed area to the final trim size.*

Page Icon Magnification; Bleed Size

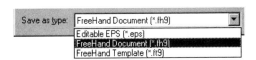

㉑ *The* **Save** *dialog box lets you choose to save your document as a* **FreeHand Document**, *a* **FreeHand Template**, *or an* **Editable EPS**.

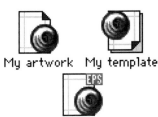

㉒ *The difference between the icons for a* **FreeHand Document** *(top left), a* **FreeHand Template** *(top right), and an* **Editable EPS** *(bottom).*

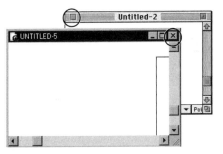

㉓ *The* **Close box** *for a Macintosh window (top) and Windows window (bottom).*

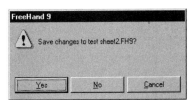

㉔ *The standard* **Save Changes** *dialog box.*

Now that you have created your pages in the correct size, you will want to save your work. This is not too different from the usual way of saving. There are three document types or formats to choose among.

To save a document:

1. Choose **File > Save**. The Save dialog box appears.

2. From the Format (Mac) or Type (Win) pop-up menu, choose the file format you want **㉑**. If you are just working on ordinary artwork, save it as a FreeHand document.

3. To protect your document from inadvertent changes, save it as a FreeHand template.

TIP To make changes to a template, open it and make the changes. Save the document with the same name as the original template.

4. To bring your document into other applications such as Adobe PageMaker or QuarkXPress, save it as an editable EPS.

TIP You can tell the difference between a FreeHand document, a FreeHand template, and an editable EPS by their icons **㉒**.

To close a document:

1. Choose **File > Close** or click the Close box **㉓**.

2. If you have not saved the document, FreeHand prompts you to save it with a dialog box **㉔**.

3. Click Save to save your changes, Don't Save to close it in the last saved version, or Cancel to leave the document open.

To revert to the last saved version:

Choose **File > Revert**. In the dialog box that appears, click the Revert button to restore your last saved version.

TIP You can also revert to the last saved version by closing the document without saving any changes and then reopening it.

Save; Close; Revert

To quit FreeHand:

1. Choose **File > Quit** (Mac) or **File > Exit** (Win).

2. If there are unsaved documents, the Review dialog box opens **㉕**. Click Review to see each of the open documents along with the Save Changes dialog box. Click Quit Anyway (Mac) or click Exit (Win) to close all documents, discarding any unsaved work. Click Cancel to remain in the application.

TIP You can turn the Review feature on or off by changing the Preferences settings (*see page 250*).

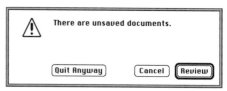

㉕ *The* **Review dialog box** *prompts you to save or discard any changes you have made in your documents before quitting/exiting FreeHand.*

As mentioned earlier in this chapter, when you are working on the Windows platform, FreeHand provides a Wizard which lets you easily get to work.

To use the Wizard (Win):

1. Launch FreeHand from the Start menu to see the Wizard screen **㉖**.

2. Click one of the five icons to select the way you prefer to begin.

• Click New to begin a new document.

• Click Previous File to open the last file you worked on.

• Click Open to open a previously saved document.

• Click Template to open one of the pre-made templates that ship on the FreeHand CD.

• Click FreeHand Help to access the FreeHand online Help information.

3. Click the checkbox if you do not want to see the Wizard again when you launch FreeHand from the Start menu.

㉖ *The* **Wizard screen** *allows you to choose from various different functions.*

VIEWS AND PRECISION

FreeHand offers many different features that control what you see on the screen. While these features do not affect the final output or printing of your artwork, they are important in how quickly and efficiently you work.

In this chapter you will learn how to

Use the Preview, Fast Preview, Keyline, Fast Keyline, and Flash anti-alias modes.

Work with the Page Rulers.

Work with Guides.

View and set the Grids and Relative Grid.

Use the Snap To settings.

Zoom using the Magnification menus and Magnifying tool.

Create and edit Custom Views.

Show and hide the panels.

Zip and Unzip panels.

Work with tabbed panels.

Work with docked panels.

❶ *The* **Preview mode** *shows the fills, strokes, and other elements that will print.*

Once you have a document open, there are different ways to display your artwork. The Preview mode ❶ is the standard view while working; it shows all your elements as they will print.

To view artwork in the Preview mode:

Choose **View > Preview**. If Preview is checked, you are already in the Preview mode.

or

Choose Preview from the pop-up menu at the bottom of the document window ❷. The pop-up menu always shows the mode you are currently working in.

❷ *The* **View mode pop-up menu** *switches between the view modes.*

In the Fast Preview mode ❸, you see your elements but blends and gradients are shown in a rough form. This makes the screen redraw faster.

To view artwork in the Fast Preview mode:

Choose **View > Fast Mode**. If Fast Mode is checked, you are already in the Preview mode.

or

Choose Fast Preview from the pop-up menu at the bottom of the document window.

❸ *The* **Fast Preview mode** *shows the elements without smooth blends and gradients.*

In Keyline mode ❹, you see only the outlines that define the shapes of paths. In the Fast Keyline mode ❺, you see fewer steps between blends. The keyline modes make it easier to select objects and speed up the redraw of the monitor as you move around a document.

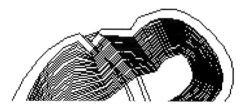

❹ *The* **Keyline mode** *shows only the outlines that define the shape of objects.*

To view artwork in the Keyline modes:

Choose **View > Preview**. If it is checked, selecting it will uncheck it and take you into the Keyline mode. If you are in the Fast mode, this takes you into the Fast Keyline mode.

or

Choose Keyline or Fast Keyline from the pop-up menu at the bottom of the document window.

❺ *The* **Fast Keyline mode** *shows fewer steps between blends.*

The Flash Anti-alias mode adds a slight blur to the edges of objects ❻. This is similar to the artwork in Macromedia Flash. Some people find it easier to view their artwork in this mode.

To view artwork in Flash anti-alias mode:

Choose **View > Flash Anti-alias**.

> *or*
>
> Choose Flash Anti-alias from the pop-up menu at the bottom of the document window.

TIP The Flash Anti-alias mode affects only the onscreen display of the artwork. It does not change how the file prints.

Flash anti-alias off   *Flash anti-alias on*

❻ *The* **Flash Anti-alias mode** *smooths the edges of the objects.*

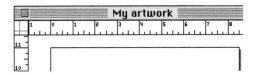

❼ *The* **Page Rulers** *run along the left and top sides of the document window.*

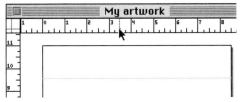

❽ *To create a* **horizontal guide**, *place your pointer on the top ruler and drag down into the page.*

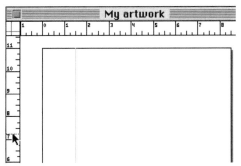

❾ *To make a* **vertical guide**, *place your pointer on the left ruler and drag to the right.*

FreeHand's two page rulers extend along the top and left sides of your document window **❼**. With page rulers you can see the sizes of objects and work more precisely.

To see the page rulers:

To make the rulers visible, choose **View > Page Rulers > Show**. When Page Rulers is checked the rulers are visible. If you choose Page Rulers when it is checked, you turn off the rulers.

Once the rulers are visible, you can use them to create guides on your page. Guides can be used to divide the page into different areas as well as help you align objects.

To create guides by dragging:

1. Choose **View > Guides > Show**. (If Show is already checked, then do not choose the command.)

2. Move your pointer so that it touches either the top (horizontal) ruler or the left (vertical) ruler.

3. For a horizontal guide, press and drag the pointer down into the page **❽**.

TIP You must drag your arrow from the ruler onto the page, not the pasteboard.

4. For a vertical guide, press and drag the arrow to the right into the page **❾**.

TIP As you drag from the rulers a line appears that shows where your guide will be when you release the mouse.

5. Release the mouse. If you are in Preview mode, you see a colored line on your page; in Keyline mode, it is a dotted line (Mac).

TIP If Snap to Guides is selected, guides will be placed only at fixed multiples of the measurement units set for the document (*see page 18*).

TIP To turn a path into a guide, you need to place the path on the Guides layer (*see page 28*).

Page Rulers; Create Guides

To move a guide by dragging:

To move guides you have already positioned, use the Pointer in the Toolbox; just drag the guide into position.

To delete a guide by dragging:

To delete a single guide, use the Pointer to drag the guide off the page onto the pasteboard.

You can also create, move, and delete guides from the Guides dialog box.

To add guides precisely:

1. Double-click any guide or choose **View** > **Guides** > **Edit**. The Guides dialog box appears **⑩**.

2. Click Add to open the Add Guides dialog box **⑪**.

3. Choose Horizontal or Vertical.

4. To set a specific number equally spaced guides, click Count and enter the number.

5. To set a specific distance between guides, click Increment and enter the spacing.

6. Use the First and Last fields to specify where the guides should start and end.

7. Use the Page range to set the pages on which the guides should appear.

8. Click Add to return to the Guides dialog box.

9. Click OK in the Guides dialog box. The new guides are inserted on the page.

TIP If you want the guides in front of the artwork, you need to change the order of the Guides layer (*see page 28*).

page back/forward buttons

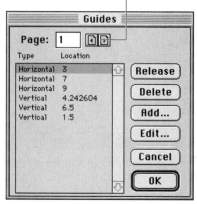

⑩ *The* **Guides dialog box** *gives you a list of all the guides on each of the pages as well as their positions in the unit of measurement for the document.*

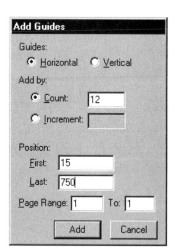

⑪ *The* **Add Guides dialog box** *allows you to create multiple guides at regular intervals down or across your work pages.*

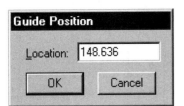

⓬ *The* **Guide Position dialog box** *allows you to relocate guides precisely.*

To reposition guides using the Guides dialog box:

1. Double-click the guide or choose **View > Guides > Edit** to open the Guides dialog box.

2. Select the guide from the list.

3. Click Edit. This opens the Guide Position dialog box **⓬**.

4. Enter a new location in the field and click OK to return to the Guides dialog box.

5. Click OK to close the Guides dialog box and institute the changes.

To delete guides using the Guides dialog box:

1. Double-click the guide or choose **View > Guides > Edit** to open the Guides dialog box.

2. Select the guide or guides from the list.

3. Click Delete (**Mac**) or Remove (**Win**). This deletes the guide from the list.

4. When you have finished, click OK.

TIP Hold down Shift or Command (**Mac**) or Ctrl (**Win**) to select multiple guides in the Guides dialog box.

TIP Guides need not be straight lines parallel to the sides of the page. *Any* path can be turned into a guide by selecting it and then double-clicking on Guides in the Layers panel.

TIP The Release button in the Guides dialog box turns the selected guide into a regular path.

You can lock guides to prevent them from being moved.

To lock guides:

Choose **View > Guides > Lock**. If you choose Lock when it is checked, you unlock the guides.

TIP You can also lock guides using the Layers panel (*see page 31*).

As you move objects, you may want them to *snap to* the guides. This makes it easy to know your objects are aligned correctly.

To turn on Snap To Guides:

Choose **View > Snap To Guides**. If Snap To Guides is checked, the feature is already turned on. When you move an object and it jumps onto a guide, the Snap To Guide cursor appears next to the pointer **13**.

TIP The Preferences let you control the snap to distance. This is how close the object has to come before the guide pulls the object onto it (*see page 248*).

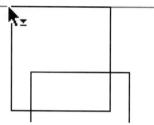

13 *The small triangle and line next to the pointer is the* **Snap To Guide cursor**. *This means that the object being moved will jump into place along a guide.*

Another feature that helps you work precisely is the document grid **14**.

To view the document grid:

Choose **View > Grid > Show**. If you choose Show when it is checked, you turn off the grid.

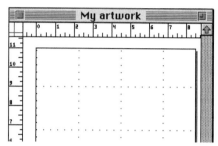

14 *The* **Document Grid** *consists of nonprinting dots evenly spaced along your work page. It helps you align elements precisely.*

You can change how far apart the intervals of the grid are spaced.

To change the document grid intervals:

1. Choose **View > Grid > Edit**. The Edit Grid dialog box appears **15**.

2. In the Grid size field, type the distance you want between the imaginary lines of your grid.

3. Click OK or press Return.

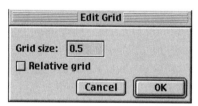

15 *The* **Edit Grid dialog box** *lets you change the increments of the invisible grid in the units of measurements for your document.*

Aligned to grid   *Not aligned to grid*

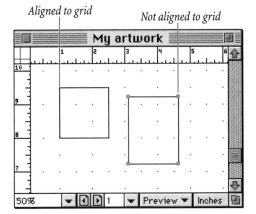

16 *When an object is drawn with Snap To Grid on, its sides fall on the grid intervals. When an object is drawn with Snap To Grid off, its sides fall between the intervals.*

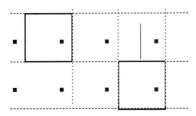

17 *Turning on the Relative grid means that when the object is duplicated, it stays aligned (indicated by dotted lines) to the position of the original rather than the document grid (indicated by square dots).*

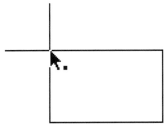

18 *The dot next to the pointer is the **Snap To Point cursor**. This indicates that the object being moved will snap to a point so the two rectangles meet at their corners.*

You can set objects so that their edges or bounding box always falls on the grid. This is called setting an object to *snap to* the grid.

To turn on Snap To Grid:

Choose **View > Snap To Grid**. If you choose Snap To Grid when it is checked, you turn off the feature.

TIP The grid does not have to be visible for objects to snap to it.

TIP If Snap To Grid is on, you cannot draw objects between the grid intervals **16**.

FreeHand also has a relative grid. This allows you to use the selected object as the start of the document grid. This lets you copy an object and keep the copy aligned to the original **17**.

To work with a relative grid:

Check Relative Grid in the Edit Grid dialog box (see previous page). This makes any selected object the start point for a grid on the page.

FreeHand also lets you snap to points. This lets you move an object so that one of its points lies precisely on the point of another.

To turn on Snap To Point:

Choose **View > Snap To Point**. If Snap To Point is already checked, you turn off the feature when you select the command.

TIP When you move an object and it snaps to a point, the Snap To Point indicator will become part of the cursor **18**.

TIP FreeHand (Mac) also offers a series of snap-to sounds that play when the object snaps to a guide, a line in the grid, or a point. These sounds are controlled in the Preferences settings (*see page 254*).

TIP Snap To Point overrides Snap to Guides which in turn overrides Snap to Grid.

Snap To Grid: Snap To Point

When working in your document, you may find that you need to see different magnifications. There are several ways to zoom in and out of your document.

To zoom using the View menu:

Choose **View > Fit All** to see all the pages in your document.

Choose **View > Fit to Page** to see the entire page you are working on.

Choose **View > Fit Selection** to zoom in on selected artwork.

Choose **View > Magnification** to choose one of the preset magnification amounts.

To zoom using the Magnifying tool:

1. Click the Magnifying tool in the Toolbox **19**.

2. Click the Magnifying tool on the object you want to zoom in on. Keep clicking as many times as you need to get as close as necessary to the objects you are working on.
   or
   Drag the Magnifying tool diagonally across the area you want to zoom in on. When you release the mouse button, you zoom in on the area **20**.

TIP Press the Command/Ctrl and Spacebar to get the Magnifying tool without leaving the tool that is currently selected in the Toolbox.

TIP Press the Option/Alt key while in the Magnifying tool to zoom out from objects. The icon changes from a plus sign (+) to a minus sign (-) **21**.

19 *Choose the* **Magnifying tool** *from the Toolbox to control how much of the page is displayed.*

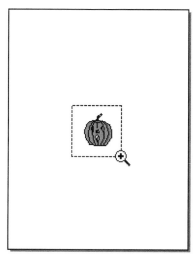

20 *Use the* **Magnifying tool** *to zoom in on a specific object by dragging a marquee around that object. The dashed-line marquee shows the area being selected.*

21 *Hold the* **Option/Alt key** *while in the Magnifying tool to zoom out from an object.*

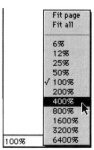

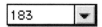

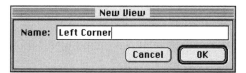

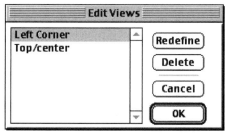

㉒ *The* **Magnification** *pop-up menu lets you choose one of the preset magnifications.*

㉓ *Double-click or drag across the number in the* **Magnification pop-up menu** *to enter an exact magnification amount.*

㉔ *The* **New View** *dialog box is where you can name a* **custom view***.*

㉕ *The* **Edit Views** *dialog box is where you can redefine or delete custom views.*

To use the Magnification pop-up menu:

1. Choose one of the preset magnification settings from the Magnification pop-up menu at the bottom of the document window **㉒**.

2. Choose Fit Page to zoom in or out so that the page fits completely inside the window.

3. Choose Fit All to fit as many pages as is possible in the window.

TIP When you choose one of the magnification settings, FreeHand uses the center of your page as the center of the zoom.

To enter exact magnification amounts:

1. Double-click or drag across the number in the Magnification pop-up menu **㉓**.

2. Type in the percentage at which you would like to view your page. (You do not need to type the % character.)

3. Press the Return/Enter key.

You can also set custom views for a specific magnification and page position. Once you have created a custom view, you can then edit it.

To create and choose a custom view:

1. Choose the magnification and page position you want for the view.

2. Choose **View > Custom > New**. The New View dialog box appears **㉔**.

3. Type a name for the view and then click OK.

4. Choose **View > Custom**. The views you create are listed in the menu.

To edit a custom view:

1. Change your magnification and position to the way you want your new view to look.

2. Choose **View > Custom > Edit**. The Edit Views dialog box appears **㉕**.

3. Select the view you want to change, click Redefine and then OK to set the new view.

Magnification Menu; Custom Views

As you are working, you may want to hide onscreen elements such as the Toolbox.

To hide onscreen elements:

To hide all the toolbars, choose **View > Toolbars**. This command toggles between hiding and showing all the toolbars including the Toolbox.

To hide all the Inspectors and other panels, choose **View > Panels**. This command also toggles between hiding and showing the panels.

To hide the Toolbox, choose **Window > Toolbar > Toolbox**.

TIP Choose from the submenus for **Window > Toolbars** or **Window > Inspectors** or **Window > Panels** or **Window > Xtras** to show or hide any of the individual onscreen elements.

In addition to hiding panels, FreeHand lets you *Zip*, or close up, the panels. This helps if you are working on a small monitor.

To use the Zip feature (Mac):

1. Click the *left* Zip box in the upper-right corner of the panel ❷❻. This collapses the panel to show only the tabs.
2. Click the left box again to expand the panel.
3. Click the *right* Zip box in the upper-right corner of the panel ❷❼. This collapses the panel completely so that only the title bar remains visible.
4. Click the right box again to open the panel.

❷❻ *(Mac) Click the left* **Zip box** *of a panel to collapse or expand the panel but leave the tabs showing.*

❷❼ *(Mac) Click the right* **Zip box** *of a panel to completely collapse or expand the panel.*

❷❽ *(Win) Click the* **Minimize button** *of a panel to collapse the panel.*

㉙ *(Win) Click the* **Maximize button** *of a panel to expand the panel.*

panel tab

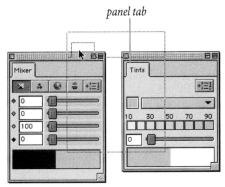

㉚ *Drag a* **tabbed panel** *by the tab to separate or join the panels.*

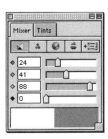

㉛ *After dragging the tab from one panel to the other, you have one merged panel with both tabs.*

To use the Zip feature (Win):

1. Click the Minimize box in the upper-left corner of the panel **㉘**. This collapses the panel.

2. Click the Maximize box in the upper-right corner of the panel **㉙**. This expands the panel.

In addition to changing the document views, you can also change how onscreen elements are moved and displayed. This is especially important if you do not have a large monitor.

To join tabbed panels:

1. Select the tab of a panel and drag the tab onto another panel.

2. Release the tab when the panel merges with the other panels **㉛**.

To separate tabbed panels:

1. Select the tab of a panel and drag the tab out from the rest of the panels **㉚**.

2. Release the tab when the panel separates from the rest of the panels.

Tabbed Panels

Tabbed panels are stacked together so that only one panel is visible at a time. FreeHand also lets you dock panels. Docked panels allow you to see both panels at once. Docked panels also open, close, and move together.

To work with docked panels:

1. Hold the Control/Ctrl key as you move one panel next to another.

2. A gray bar appears between them indicating that the panels are docked ☜.

3. To release the dock, click the gray bar.

TIP (Mac) Docked panels zip and unzip as a group when the *left* box is used to leave the panel tabs visible. Using the *right* box controls the panels individually.

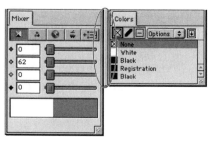

☜ The **docking bar** *(circled) indicates that the panels are docked.*

LAYERS AND LAYERING

❶ *Although it may not be obvious, one object is in front of the other.*

❷ *When two objects overlap, it is obvious which object is in front of the other.*

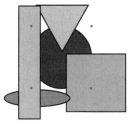

❸ *If you want to move an object to the foreground…*

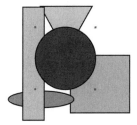

❹ *…select it and use the* **Bring To Front** **command**.

A s soon as you put more than one path on your page, you have already started working in layers. Since you can easily create hundreds of objects in a document, you need to manage the layers and layering of your objects.

In this chapter you will learn how to

Understand the differences between layering objects and the layers in the Layers panel.

Move objects within a layer.

Move objects between layers.

Create, rename, remove, reorder, display, hide, and lock layers.

Lock objects.

Set layers as printing or nonprinting.

Change the color assigned to paths for layers.

Objects are layered in the same order they were created. If you create a red circle and then a blue square, the circle is behind the square. Though you may not see this when the objects are side by side, it is apparent when they overlap ❶–❷. Once objects are in a certain order, you can move them to different positions on the layer.

To move objects to the front or back of a layer:

1. Click an object in your artwork.

2. Choose **Modify > Arrange > Bring To Front** ❸–❹ to move the object to the front of the objects in its layer.

3. Choose **Modify > Arrange > Send To Back** to move the object to the back of its layer.

TIP If you choose Bring To Front or Send To Back on a single object of a group, the object moves to the front or back of the group rather than the layer (*see Chapter 5, "Points and Paths," for working with groups*).

Sometimes you want to move an object in the middle of a layer. To do that, you use a different set of commands.

To move objects within a layer:

1. Select an object in your artwork.

2. Choose **Modify > Arrange > Move Forward** to move the object forward in its layer. This moves the object in front of only the first object it was behind.

3. If necessary, choose Move Forward to move the object again. Repeat until the object is in the correct position in the layer ❺–❻.

4. Choose **Modify > Arrange > Move Backward** to move an object backward.

5. Choose Move Backward again to move the object again. Repeat until the object is in the correct position in the layer.

Since it may be tedious to choose Move Backward or Move Forward over and over, FreeHand offers two other ways to move objects within their layer.

To move objects using Paste In Front or Paste Behind:

1. Select the object that you want to move and choose **Edit > Cut** ❼.

2. Choose the object that you want in front of the original object.

3. Choose **Edit > Paste Behind**. The original object is pasted behind the object you chose ❽.

   Choose **Edit > Paste In Front** to paste the original object in front of the object you chose.

TIP Locked objects cannot be moved within their layer.

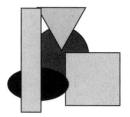

❺ *In this illustration, the circle needs to be in front of the triangle and square.*

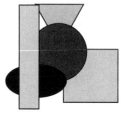

❻ *The same illustration after the* **Bring Forward command** *was applied twice to the circle.*

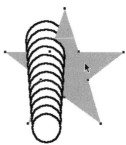

❼ *To move an object using* **Paste Behind,** *select the object you want to move and then choose Cut.*

❽ *After you select the place, in this case the fifth circle, choose* **Paste Behind** *to place the cut object where you want it.*

Move Objects within a Layer; Paste in Front or Behind

☉ *The* **Layers panel** *shows the three default layers: Foreground, Guides, and Background.*

You may find that moving objects within their layers is not enough. In that case, you will need to use FreeHand's Layers panel.

To view the Layers panel:

1. If you do not see the Layers panel on your screen, choose **Window > Panels > Layers**.

2. If you have not changed the default layers for your document, you should see three layers: Foreground, Guides, and Background **☉**.

Once you have created a new layer, you may want to rename it so that it reflects the items on that layer.

To rename a layer:

1. In the Layers panel, double-click the name of the layer you want to rename.

2. Type the new name of the layer.

3. Press Return or Enter, or click the Layers panel with the mouse.

To duplicate a layer:

1. Click the name of the layer you want to duplicate.

2. Open the Options pop-up menu in the Layers panel **⑩**.

3. Choose Duplicate. The layer and all of the objects on it will be duplicated.

TIP The Guides layer cannot be renamed or duplicated.

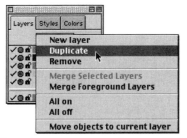

⑩ *The* **Options pop-up menu** *lets you add, delete, duplicate, or hide or show the layers.*

To remove a layer:

1. Click the name of the layer you want to remove.

2. Open the Options pop-up menu. Choose Remove. The layer and the objects on it will be removed.

TIP You cannot delete the Guides layer or the very last drawing layer of a document.

TIP An alert box warns you if you try to remove a layer that has objects on it.

View Layers Panel; Rename, Duplicate, and Remove Layers

The Layers panel lists layers from foreground to background. So the layer at the top of the list is in front of all the other layers. The ones that follow are stacked deeper and deeper in the background. Layers do not have to remain in the order in which you created them. You use the Layers panel to reorder layers.

To reorder layers:

1. In the Layers panel, select the name of the layer you want to reorder **⓫**.

2. Drag the name of the layer to the spot on the list that represents where you would like the layer to be.

3. Release the mouse button. The name of the layer disappears from where it was and reappears in its new position in the Layers panel. All objects on the layer are repositioned in the document **⓬**.

TIP If you want guides to appear in front of your artwork, drag the Guides layer above the layer that contains the artwork.

When you are working, the objects you create go on the active layer, the one that has the pen icon on the Layers panel. You may want to move artwork from one layer to another.

To move objects between layers:

1. Select the artwork you want to move to a new layer. The layer to which it belongs is highlighted **⓭**.

2. Click the name of the layer that is the destination for the artwork. The artwork moves to that new layer **⓮**.

TIP To convert a path into a guide, move the guide onto the Guides layer.

TIP You cannot move artwork onto a locked layer.

⓫ In this illustration, the objects for the referee need to be behind the player.

⓬ The result of dragging the Referee layer below the Player layer.

⓭ In this illustration, the wall needs to be moved from the Goal layer. The artwork has been selected.

⓮ *The same illustration after clicking the name of the Wall and Glass layer to finish moving the artwork from the Goal layer to the Wall and Glass layer.*

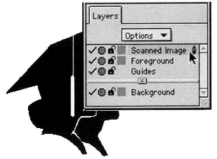

⓯ *To make a **nonprinting layer**, drag the name of the layer below the horizontal line.*

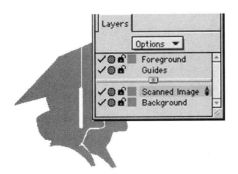

⓰ *Objects on nonprinting layers are dimmed in their display.*

A horizontal line divides the Layers panel. Objects on layers above the line appear normal onscreen and print. Objects on layers below the line appear dimmed onscreen and do not print. As you work, you may find that you want to move layers from the printing to nonprinting areas of the list.

To create a nonprinting layer:

1. Select the name of the layer you want to make nonprinting **⓯**.

2. Drag the name of the layer below the dividing line in the Layers panel.

3. Release the mouse button. The layer moves below the line, and any objects on the layer are dimmed and do not print **⓰**

TIP Use nonprinting layers to hold images that have been placed for tracing (*see page 45*).

To create a printing layer:

1. Select the name of the layer you want to make a printing layer.

2. Drag the name of the layer above the dividing line in the Layers panel.

3. Release the mouse button. The layer moves above the dividing line, and any objects on the layer will print.

TIP Objects on the Guides layer do not ever print, regardless of where the Guides layer is, either above or below the line.

Change Display of a Layer

You can also use the Layers panel to change the preview for the objects on each layer **17**. This is especially helpful if you work with very complicated illustrations and need to select just certain elements.

To change the display of a layer:

1. Click the checkmark to the left of the layer name to make the checkmark disappear and make the layer invisible.

2. If there is no checkmark, click the blank space to make the layer visible.

TIP Use the *All on* or *All off* commands in the Options pop-up menu to quickly show or hide all layers.

3. Click the solid gray dot to the left of the layer name. This changes the gray dot into a circle with an *X* in it and puts the layer in Keyline mode.

TIP Hold the Option/Ctrl key as you click the keyline/preview dots to switch them all at once to the changed state. This also works for the lock icons and for the display checks.

TIP You can drag the mouse up or down a column to switch the visibility checks, the preview icons or the lock icons to the state opposite the first icon clicked.

4. If there is a circle with an *X* to the left of the layer name, click the circle. This puts the layer into the Preview mode.

TIP (*See pages 13–14 for information about the Keyline and Preview modes.*)

The circle with the X indicates that this layer is in Keyline mode.

The solid gray dot indicates that this layer is in Preview mode.

No checkmark indicates that this layer is invisible.

17 *Use the Layers panels to control how artwork appears onscreen.*

The closed padlock indicates that this is a locked layer.

⓲ *Clicking an open padlock changes it to closed position and locks the layer. Clicking a closed padlock unlocks the layer.*

There may be times when you want to see the objects on a layer, but you do not want to be able to select those objects. In this case, you need to lock the layer.

To lock a layer:

1. Look at the padlock to the left of the layer name. If the padlock is in the open position, it means the layer is unlocked.

2. Click the padlock **⓲** to change the padlock to the closed position and lock all objects on the layer.

3. If the padlock is already in the closed position, click it to change the padlock to the open position and unlock all objects on the layer.

TIP Objects on locked layers cannot be selected, modified, or moved.

There may be times when you want to lock a single object on a layer. This is different from locking a layer.

To lock an object on a layer:

1. Select the object or objects you want to lock.

2. Choose **Modify > Lock**.

To unlock an object on a layer:

1. Select the object you want to unlock.

2. Choose **Modify > Unlock**.

TIP Locked objects can be selected and their fills and strokes modified.

TIP Locked objects cannot be moved, resized, transformed, or deleted.

TIP Locked text objects can have their text attributes changed or the text edited.

TIP Locked objects can be copied, but they cannot be cut.

When you select an object, the points and path outlines for that object are displayed in a color (*see Chapter 5, "Points and Paths"*). You can change that display color by using the Layers panel.

To change the display color of a layer:

1. Drag a color from the Color List or Color Mixer (*see Chapter 8, "Working in Color"*). A small swatch of that color appears.

2. Drag that swatch onto the name or color box of the layer you want to change **19**.

3. The colored square next to the name changes. All selected objects on that layer have their paths displayed in that color.

19 *To change the* **path display color** *of a layer, drag a color swatch onto the color box of that layer.*

CREATION TOOLS

❶ *The* **Rectangle tool** *selected in the Toolbox*

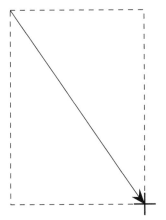

❷ *To* **draw a rectangle**, *drag the cursor along the diagonal line between two corners.*

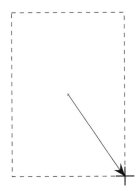

❸ *Hold the Option/Alt key to* **draw a rectangle from the center point** *outward.*

One of the best ways to learn a vector drawing program is to start by creating basic shapes. Rather than create these shapes from scratch, use FreeHand's wealth of tools to make all sorts of different objects.

In this chapter you will learn how to

Create rectangles, squares, rounded-corner rectangles, ellipses, circles, polygons, stars, and lines.

Use the Freehand, Variable stroke, and Calligraphic pen tools.

Know when to use the Pen and Bézigon. (*These two tools are covered in detail in Chapter 6.*)

Use the Spiral and Arc tools.

Use the Trace tool to convert scanned artwork.

One of the most basic objects to create is a rectangle. This includes regular rectangles, squares, and rounded-corner rectangles.

To draw a rectangle:

1. With a document open, click the Rectangle tool in the Toolbox **❶**.

2. Position the plus sign cursor (+) where you want one corner of the rectangle and press to start the rectangle.

3. Drag diagonally to the opposite corner **❷**.

4. Release the mouse button when you are satisfied with the size of the rectangle.

TIP Once you draw the rectangle, you can still change its dimensions (*see pages 59, 71, 76, and 78*).

TIP Hold the Option/Alt key to draw a rectangle outward from the center point **❸**.

You may think of a square as different from a rectangle, but FreeHand does not make the distinction. The rectangle tool creates squares.

To draw a square:

1. Follow the steps to start creating a rectangle.

2. As you drag, hold Shift key. This forces, or *constrains*, your rectangle into a square even if you do not follow the proper diagonal ❹.

TIP Whenever you hold a modifier, such as the Shift key, always release the mouse button first, then the modifier second.

TIP Hold both the Option/Alt and the Shift keys to draw a square outward from the center point.

Another type of rectangle has curved or rounded corners. The amount of the curve depends on the corner radius ❺.

To set the corner radius for a rectangle:

1. Double-click the Rectangle tool in the Toolbox to open the Rectangle Tool dialog box ❻.

2. In the Corner radius field, type the amount or drag the slider to set the number for the corner radius.

3. Click OK and draw your rectangle.

TIP You can change the corner radius for a rectangle at any time using the Object Inspector.

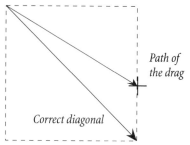

Path of the drag

Correct diagonal

❹ **Draw a square** *by holding the Shift key while you drag with the Rectangle tool.*

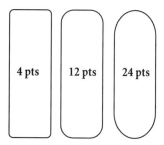

4 pts 12 pts 24 pts

❺ *Different* **Corner radius settings** *change the shape of rounded-corner rectangles.*

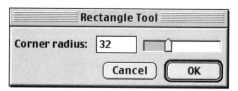

Rectangle Tool

Corner radius: 32

Cancel   OK

❻ *The* **Rectangle Tool dialog box** *lets you set the amount of the Corner radius.*

Draw a Square; Set the Corner Radius

❼ *The* **Ellipse tool** *selected in the Toolbox.*

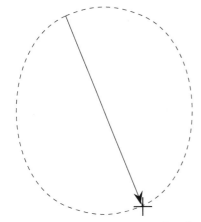

❽ *To* **draw an ellipse,** *drag the cursor along the diagonal line between two sides.*

❾ *The* **Line tool** *selected in the Toolbox.*

❿ *A* **straight line** *drawn with the Line tool.*

Another type of object you can create is the ellipse. The Ellipse tool also creates circles.

To draw an ellipse or circle:

1. Click the Ellipse tool in the Toolbox **❼**.
2. Position the cursor where you want one "corner" of the ellipse; press and drag to the opposite "corner" **❽**.

TIP Hold Shift key as you drag to create a circle.

TIP Hold the Option/Alt key to draw an ellipse from the center outward.

TIP Hold the Option/Alt and Shift keys to draw a circle outward from the center point.

FreeHand is definitely the program for anyone who has said they cannot even draw a straight line. The Line tool makes it easy!

To draw a straight line:

1. Click the Line tool in the Toolbox **❾**.
2. Position the cursor where you want the line to start.
3. Press and drag along the direction the line should follow.
4. Release the mouse button where you want the line to end **❿**.

TIP If you press the Shift key as you use the Line tool, your lines will be constrained to 45° or 90° increments of the Constrain Angle (*see page 77*).

Draw an Ellipse or Circle; Draw a Straight Line

In addition to rectangles, ellipses, and lines, you can draw other shapes with the Polygon tool ⑪. There are two types of objects you can create with the Polygon tool. The first is polygons.

To draw a polygon:

1. Double-click the Polygon tool in the Toolbox ⑫. The Polygon dialog box appears ⑬.

2. Enter the number of sides for your polygon by typing the number in the field or by dragging the slider.

3. Click OK. This returns you to the work page.

4. Position the cursor where you want the center of your shape and drag outward ⑭.

5. As you drag, you will see the shape that defines your polygon. Move the mouse to rotate the polygon to the position you want.

TIP If you do not like the orientation of the finished polygon, you can use the Rotation tool to change it (*see pages 70, 75, and 78*).

TIP To draw a rectangle that you can rotate as you draw, use the Polygon tool set for 4 sides.

6. Release the mouse button when you are satisfied with the size and position of the polygon.

TIP If you let go of the mouse button too soon, you can still change the dimensions of the polygon (*see pages 59, 71, and 76*).

⑪ *Objects drawn with the Polygon tool.*

⑫ *The **Polygon tool** in the Toolbox.*

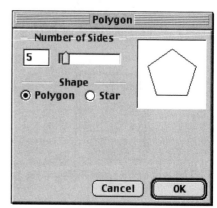

⑬ *The **Polygon tool** dialog box.*

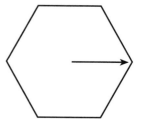

⑭ *A six-sided polygon drawn by dragging along the indicated line.*

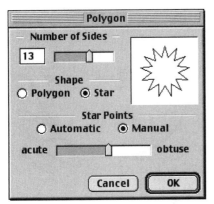

⓯ Star choices *in the Polygon dialog box.*

Stars are the second type of object that you can draw with the Polygon tool.

To draw a star:

1. Double-click the Polygon tool in the Toolbox.

2. Click the radio button for the Star shape. The Star settings appear ⓯.

3. Enter the number of points you want for your star in the number of sides fields.

4. If you want your star to have its segments automatically aligned, choose Automatic ⓰.

   or

   If you want to shape the star yourself, choose Manual and then adjust the slider from acute to obtuse. The preview window shows how your changes affect the star ⓱–⓲.

TIP When you change the settings in the Polygon dialog box, those settings remain in effect until you reset the the dialog box.

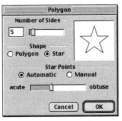

⓰ Automatic settings *for a five-pointed star.*

⓱ Acute settings *for a five-pointed star.*

⓲ Obtuse settings *for a five-pointed star.*

The Freehand tool has three different tool modes: Freehand, Variable stroke, and Calligraphic pen. Each of these modes creates a different look **⓴**.

The Freehand mode is useful for tracing over scanned images. The Variable stroke resembles a brushstroke. The Calligraphic pen resembles the stroke of a calligraphy pen.

Both Variable stroke and Calligraphic pen are especially effective if you are working with a pressure-sensitive drawing tablet and pen instead of a mouse. These tablets allow you to vary the width of the stroke, depending on how much or how little pressure you exert.

To set the Freehand tool mode:

1. Double-click on the Freehand tool in the Toolbox **⓴** to open the Freehand Tool dialog box **㉑**.

2. Click the Freehand radio button.

3. Set Precision to a high value to have your path follow any minor variables as you drag.

   or

   Choose a low value to smooth out any minor variables as you drag.

4. Click OK, which returns you to your work page.

   TIP If you drag too quickly, your stroke may not fill in correctly. Check the box for Draw dotted line. This creates a dotted line that follows your path. FreeHand then fills in that line with the actual path.

⓳ *Freehand tool modes:* **Freehand** *(top),* **Variable stroke** *(middle), and* **Calligraphic pen** *(bottom).*

⓴ *The* **Freehand tool** *in the Toolbox.*

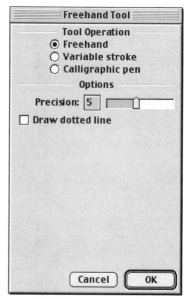

㉑ *The* **Freehand Tool** *dialog box.*

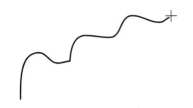

22 *The* **Freehand tool** *creates a line that follows the path you dragged.*

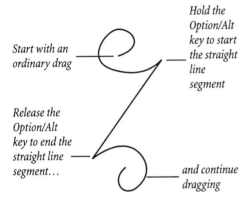

Start with an ordinary drag

Hold the Option/Alt key to start the straight line segment

Release the Option/Alt key to end the straight line segment...

and continue dragging

23 *Hold the Option/Alt key to create straight lines with the Freehand tool.*

Once you have set the Freehand tool, the settings remain until you change them.

To draw with the Freehand tool:

1. Drag the plus sign (+) cursor along the path you want to create.

2. Release the mouse button when you have completed your line **22**.

3. To join the ends of your path as a closed path, bring the line back to its origin and watch for a little square to appear next to the cursor. Once it appears, you can release the mouse button and FreeHand closes the path.

TIP As you draw, you can erase part of the path created with any of the Freehand modes by holding down the Command/Ctrl key and dragging backward over the path.

TIP If you want part of the path you are drawing with the Freehand tool to be straight, press the Option/Alt key as you drag. Release the Option/Alt key (but not the mouse button) to continue the path **23**.

Draw with the Freehand Tool

To set the Variable stroke mode:

1. Double-click the Freehand tool in the Toolbox. Choose Variable stroke in the dialog box **24**.

2. In the Min field, enter the size for the thinnest part of your brush stroke (any size from 1 to 72 points).

3. Set the precision you want using the slider or by typing a value into the field.

4. In the Max field, enter the size for the thickest part of your brush stroke (any size from 1 to 72 points).

5. Choose Auto remove overlap (slow) to eliminate any parts of the path that overlap. This makes it easier to reshape the path and avoid printing problems.

6. Click OK to return to your work page.

To draw with the Variable stroke tool:

1. If you have chosen the Variable stroke tool in the Freehand Tool dialog box, you should see its icon in the Toolbox **25**.

2. Drag to create the path.

3. If you have a pressure-sensitive tablet, any changes in the pressure you exert will change the thickness of your stroke **26**.

TIP The objects created by the Variable stroke and Calligraphic pen tools are closed paths. This means that rather than use the stroke settings to change the color of the object, you change the color of the fill.

TIP If you do not have a tablet, you can still vary your stroke for either the Variable stroke tool or the Calligraphic pen tool by holding these modifier keys:

To increase the thickness, press the right arrow or the number 2 key.

To decrease the thickness, press the left arrow or the number 1 key.

TIP If you draw with a mouse rather than a pressure-sensitive tablet, FreeHand uses the Min setting as the default width of the stroke.

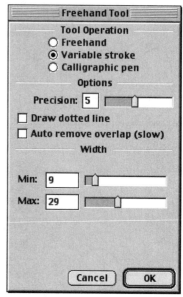

24 The **Variable stroke** options.

25 The **Variable stroke icon** in the Toolbox.

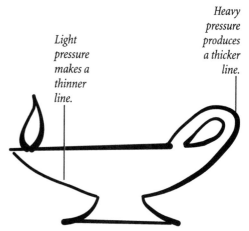

Light pressure makes a thinner line.

Heavy pressure produces a thicker line.

26 Changing the pressure while drawing with the Variable stroke tool (and a pressure-sensitive tablet) changes the thickness of the line created.

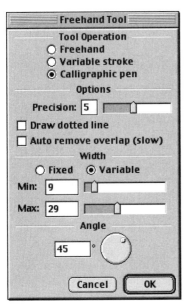

㉗ *The* **Calligraphic pen** *options.*

㉘ *The* **Calligraphic pen icon** *in the Toolbox.*

0°   45°   90°

㉙ *Changing the angle for the Calligraphic pen changes the shape of the curves.*

To set the Calligraphic pen mode:

1. Double-click the Freehand tool in the Toolbox. Choose Calligraphic pen in the Freehand Tool dialog box **㉗**.
2. Click the Variable button under the Width option if you want the thickness of the lines to change.
3. In the Min field, enter the size for the thinnest part of your brush stroke (any size from 1 to 72 points).
4. In the Max field, enter the size for the thickest part of your brush stroke (any size from 1 to 72 points).
5. Click the Fixed button to keep the width of the lines constant.
6. Under the Angle options, type the degree of the angle or rotate the wheel to set the angle your stroke uses for its calligraphic lines.
7. Click OK to return to your work page.

To draw with the Calligraphic pen tool:

1. If you have chosen the Calligraphic pen tool in the dialog box, you should see its icon in the Toolbox **㉘**.
2. Drag to create the path.

TIP As you change the direction of the path the angle determines the shape of the path **㉙**. This is similar to how a real calligraphic pen can create both thick lines and thin lines, depending on how you angle the pen tip as you draw.

The other two creation tools in the Toolbox are the Bézigon and the Pen tools. Both allow you much greater control over the shape of the path, especially when they are compared to the Freehand tool ㉚. Because these two tools are not as simple to use as the other creation tools, they are covered separately in Chapter 6.

FreeHand provides you with two more creation tools: the Spiral tool and the Arc tool.

To set the Spiral tool mode:

1. To open the Xtra Tools panel, choose **Window > Toolbars > Xtras Tools**.

TIP The Spiral tool is also found in the Toolbox.

2. Double-click the Spiral tool in the Xtra Tools Toolbar ㉛ to open the Spiral dialog box ㉜.

3. Choose between the nonexpanding and expanding Spiral type. Expanding-radius spirals open up as they move farther out from the center; nonexpanding spirals have a constant radius and look evenly spaced.

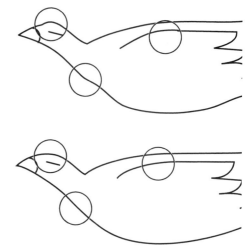

㉚ *Compare the same object drawn with the* **Freehand tool** *(top) and the* **Pen tool** *(bottom). Notice the uneven areas (circled) in the Freehand tool. The Pen tool makes it easier to draw smooth paths.*

㉛ *The* **Spiral tool** *in the Xtras Tools Toolbar.*

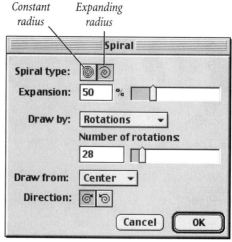

㉜ *The* **Spiral dialog box.**

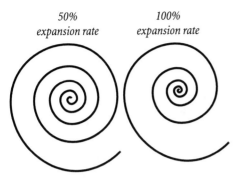

50% *100%*
expansion rate *expansion rate*

③③ *A comparison of two spirals drawn with different expansion rates.*

4. If you have chosen an expanding spiral, the Spiral dialog box shows an Expansion field. This controls how fast your spiral expands **③③**. The higher the number, the greater the expansion rate. Enter an amount by typing in the field or by dragging the slider.

5. Use the Draw by pop-up menu to choose between drawing by Rotations or Increments. Drawing by Rotations lets you specify the number of rotations in your spiral. Drawing by Increments lets you specify the amount of space between the curls in nonexpanding spirals or the starting radius for expanding spirals.

6. Use the Draw from pop-up menu to choose the point that the Spiral will start from: Center, Edge, or Corner **③④**.

7. Click one of the Direction icons to choose either a counterclockwise or a clockwise spiral.

8. Click OK to implement all your settings.

9. Drag to create the spiral.

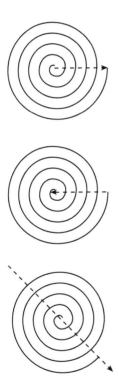

③④ *Changing the point that the spiral is drawn from: the* **Center** *(top), the* **Edge** *(middle), and the* **Corner** *(bottom). The dashed lines show the length and direction of the drags.*

Spiral Tool

To choose settings for the Arc tool:

1. Choose **Window > Toolbars > Xtra Tools** to open the Xtra Tools panel.

2. Double-click the Arc tool in the Xtra Tools panel ⓧ to open the Arc dialog box ⓧ.

3. Choose Create open arc if you want a simple arc. Deselect this option if you want your arc to form a wedge shape ⓧ.

4. Choose Create flipped arc to reflect the arc from one direction to another ⓧ.

5. Choose Create concave arc to create an arc that curves inside a corner ⓧ.

6. Click OK to return to the work page.

To draw with the Arc tool:

1. With the Arc tool selected, drag to create the arc on the page.

2. Release the mouse button when you are satisfied with the arc.

While you can use the Arc dialog box to set the various attributes of the arc, you can also hold the modifier keys to change the arc as you drag.

TIP Hold the Command/Ctrl key after you start the drag to close or open the arc ⓧ.

TIP Hold the Option/Alt key after you start the drag to flip the arc horizontally or vertically ⓧ.

TIP Hold the Control key (Mac) to switch between either concave or convex settings ⓧ.

TIP Hold the Shift key as you drag to constrain the arc to quarter circles.

ⓧ *The* **Arc tool** *selected in the Xtra Tools panel.*

ⓧ *The* **Arc dialog box** *allows you to choose from open, flipped, or concave arc settings.*

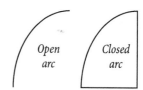

ⓧ *Notice the difference between an* **open arc** *and a* **closed arc**.

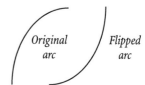

ⓧ **Flipping an arc** *transforms it to its mirror image.*

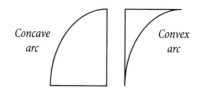

ⓧ *Closed arcs can be either a* **convex arc** *or* **concave arc**.

40 *An* **imported image** *appears on the work page with four anchor points.*

41 *It is easier to work with an imported image when it is on a layer that lightens the artwork.*

Sometimes you have a piece of scanned artwork that you want to convert into FreeHand paths. You may want to be able to scale that piece of artwork up or down without worrying about resolution, apply spot colors to certain parts of it, or make a rough sketch more precise. In these situations, you can use the Trace tool.

Before you use the Trace tool you need to import the scanned artwork into your FreeHand document.

To import artwork for tracing:

1. With your document open, choose **File** > **Import**.

2. Use the navigational tools to find the PICT, TIFF, or EPS file that you would like to trace.

3. After you choose the file you want to import, your cursor changes to a corner symbol.

4. Click with the corner symbol to place the image and its anchor points on the page **40**.

TIP Though you can trace art on any layer, most people put imported images on layers below the horizontal line of the Layers panel. This lightens the image so it is easier to work with **41** and ensures that it does not print (*see page 29*).

TIP Lock the layer with the imported image so that you do not inadvertently select it.

TIP For best results using the Trace tool, turn on the High-Resolution TIFF display (*see page 253*).

Import Artwork for Tracing

Once you have the imported image, you can use FreeHand's Trace tool to convert the image into vector objects.

To trace an image:

1. Double-click the Trace tool in the Toolbox **42** to open the Trace Tool dialog box **43**.

2. Use the pop-up menus to choose the number of colors, the resolution, what layers to trace, the type of tracing you want, and how detailed your tracing will be.

3. Click OK to apply those settings.

4. Use the Trace tool to drag a marquee around the part of the image you want to trace **44**.

5. Release the mouse button to finish tracing the artwork.

TIP When tracing photographic images, tracing creates many objects. Choose **Modify > Group** to join the objects into an easily selected group.

42 The **Trace tool** in the Toolbox.

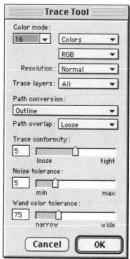

43 The **Trace Tool dialog box.**

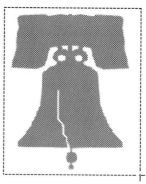

44 **Drag a marquee** with the Trace tool to trace an imported image.

Trace Tool

POINTS AND PATHS 5

Every object in FreeHand actually consists of an arrangement of points connected along a path. Understanding how points and paths work is crucial to understanding FreeHand.

① *The* **anchor points of a path** *show up as dark squares when the entire path is selected.*

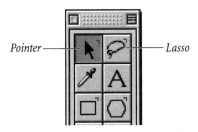

② *The* **Pointer and Lasso tools** *in the Toolbox.*

Pointer — Lasso

③ *A* **point on a path** *is displayed as a hollow dot when that single point is selected.*

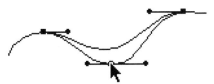

④ *One way to change the shape of a path is to drag a point on that path.*

In this chapter you will learn how to

Select single points, multiple points, an entire object, or multiple objects.

Group and ungroup paths.

Follow the rules for effective placement of points.

Understand the difference between the types of points: corner, curve, and connector.

Convert points from one type to another.

Add and delete points on a path.

Understand the difference between open and closed paths.

Convert closed paths into open ones, and vice versa.

Change the positions and dimensions of points and paths.

To select points by clicking:

1. Draw a wavy line with the Freehand tool (*see page 39*). As soon as you release the mouse button, the path appears with dark squares that show the anchor points that define the path **①**.

2. Click the Pointer tool in the Toolbox **②**.

3. Select the point by placing the tip of the arrow on one of the points. Click. The point turns into a hollow dot with two levers **③**.

4. To change the shape of the path, drag the point you have selected **④**.

5. Hold the Shift key to select more points.

Select Points

Another way to select points is by using the Pointer or Lasso tool to drag an area around the points you want to select.

To select points with a marquee:

1. Place the Pointer tool outside the point or points you want to select.

2. Press and drag to create a rectangle that surrounds the points you want selected **❺**. The area inside the rectangle is the *marquee*.

   or

   Place the Lasso tool outside the point or points you want to select. Press and drag to create a shape that surrounds the points you want selected **❻**.

3. Release the mouse button to select all points inside the area **❼**.

   TIP To select points in more than one area, create your first selection marquee as usual. Then press the Shift key and create your next selection marquee.

   TIP Hold the Command/Ctrl key to temporarily switch from another tool to the Pointer tool.

   TIP Click elsewhere on the work page to deselect points.

The basics of points

Once you start working with points, you will discover that there are levers, or handles, that extend out of points **❽**. These are called point handles or Bézier (pronounced Bay-zee-ay) handles, named after the French mathematician Pierre Bézier. Point handles are nonprinting lines that control the direction along which any path curves. Changing the direction of the point handles changes the shape of the path **❾**.

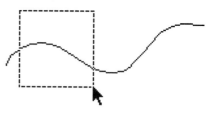

❺ Dragging a marquee *with the Pointer tool.*

❻ Dragging a selection area *with the Lasso tool.*

❼ *The points that were within the area created by the selection tool will be selected.*

❽ *An object with its point handles visible.*

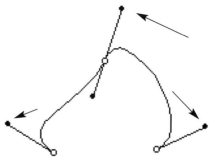

❾ *The results of moving the point handles in the directions indicated.*

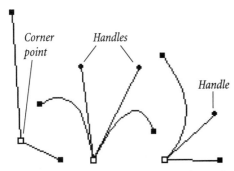

⑩ Corner points *are indicated by square dots and can have no handles (left), two handles (middle), or one handle (right).*

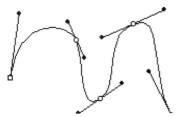

⑪ Curve points *are indicated by round dots and always have two point handles that govern the shape of the curve.*

⑫ Connector points *are indicated by triangular dots and always have point handles.*

⑬ *Rotating one handle of a curve point also moves the handle on the other side.*

Three different types of points make up FreeHand objects: corner points, curve points, and connector points. In order to have a complete understanding of FreeHand, it is vital to understand how these points work.

Corner points

Corner points are anchor points that allow paths to have an abrupt change in direction. Depending on how they were created, there are three different types of corner points: points with no handles, points with two handles, and points with one handle ⑩.

Curve points

Curve points are anchor points that make a smooth, curved transition along the direction of the path. The length of the point handles governs the shape of the curve ⑪.

Connector points

The purpose of connector points is to constrain the transition between segments so that they cannot be moved out of a special alignment ⑫. Connector points can have one or two point handles. When a connector point occurs between a straight-line segment and a curved segment, there is only one point handle, which runs along the same direction as the straight line. When a connector point is between two curved segments, there are two point handles which are constrained by the position of the points on either side of the connector point.

TIP FreeHand provides two types of handles on the levers that come out of the points. The illustrations in this book show the small handles. You can work with the large handles by switching the Preferences settings (*see page 248*).

TIP If you rotate the point handle on one side of the point, the handle on the opposite side also moves. It is this "lever" action that makes the curve transition smooth ⑬.

Basics of Points

The one-third rule

In general, you need only two curve points to create a curve on a path. If your curve is too steep, however, you will find that the point handles start to break the one-third rule. This rule states that the point handles for any segment should not extend more than one-third of the length of that segment ⑭

What happens if you break the one-third rule? Well, no one will come to arrest you, but you will find it difficult to edit your curves with long point handles that pivot all over the place.

Once you create an object's points, you may find that you want to eliminate them.

To delete a point from a path:

1. Select the point you want to delete.
2. Press the Delete key. The point is deleted and the path reshapes ⑮–⑯.

Adding a point to a path is a little more sophisticated. You must use either the Pen or the Bézigon tool.

To add a point to a path:

1. With the path selected, click either the Pen or the Bézigon tool in the Toolbox. (*See Chapter 6, "Pen and Bézigon."*)
2. Move the plus sign (+) cursor over the path where you want the new point and click ⑰.
3. A point appears where you clicked.

TIP If you click too far away from the path, you will create a new point that is not part of the path.

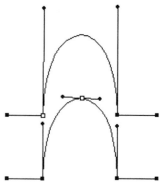

⑭ The **one-third rule** *says to limit the length of the point handles for any segment to no more than one-third of the length of that segment.*

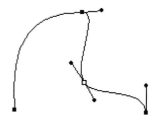

⑮ *To delete a point from a path, select the point and* **press the Delete key**.

⑯ *When you delete a point, you reshape the path.*

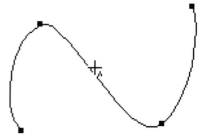

⑰ *To* **add a point to a path,** *click with the Pen or the Bézigon tool on the path.*

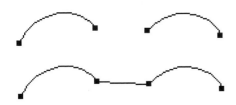

⑱ *The top paths were selected and the* **Join** *command was applied. This created a new line segment connecting the points.*

⑲ *The top path was selected and the* **Split** *command was applied, creating the bottom two paths. (Paths were moved to show the separation.)*

⑳ *You can* **manually drag a point handle** *back into its anchor point.*

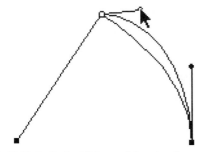

㉑ *Hold the Option/Alt key and then drag from a point to* **manually extend point handles** *from that point.*

To connect points:

1. Choose two open paths.

2. Choose **Modify > Join**. FreeHand creates a path between the two closest endpoints of the paths **⑱**. If the two points are on top of each other, FreeHand merges them into one point.

To split a point:

1. Choose a single point on a path.

2. Choose **Modify > Split**. FreeHand splits the point into two points on top of each other **⑲**.

TIP There is no indication that the points separate; select the points and then move one manually to see the split.

You can use the Pointer tool to manually retract or extend handles from a point.

To retract handles manually:

1. On a wavy line, select a point so that its handles are visible.

2. Place the Pointer tool on the dot at the end of the handle.

3. Drag the handle into the anchor point **⑳**.

To extend a single handle manually:

1. Use the Pointer tool to select the point from which you want to extend the handles.

2. Hold the Option/Alt key and then drag out from the point. The handle extends out from the point **㉑**.

You can also extend two handles at once from the points at either end of a segment.

To extend two handles manually:

1. Use the Pointer tool to select the line segment between two points.

2. Hold the Option/Alt key and then drag the line segment. A handle extends out from each of the points on either side of the segment **㉒**.

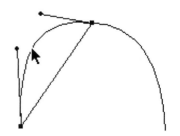

㉒ *Hold the Option/Alt key and then drag a line segment to* **manually extend point handles** *from both ends of the segment.*

The best way to learn about points is to convert them from one type to another. FreeHand makes this easy.

To manipulate points using the Object Inspector:

1. Use the Freehand tool to create a wavy line with at least three anchor points.

2. Use the Pointer tool to select one of the anchor points on the inside of the path.

3. Choose **Window > Inspector > Object**. Under Point type, you will see the Curve Point icon selected **㉓**.

4. Under Point type, click the Corner Point icon **㉔**. The anchor point changes from a circle to a square. Use the Pointer tool to drag one of the handles. Because it is now a corner point, you can change the angle of each handle **㉕**

5. To convert this point to a connector point, click the Connector Point icon in the Object Inspector **㉖**. The white square changes to a triangle. The two point handles that extend from a connector point cannot be moved from side to side but they can be lengthened **㉗**.

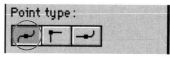

㉓ *The* **Curve Point icon** *in the Object Inspector.*

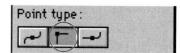

㉔ *The* **Corner Point icon** *in the Object Inspector.*

㉕ *Corner point handles can be manipulated individually.*

㉖ *The* **Connector Point icon** *in the Object Inspector.*

㉗ *Connector point handles maintain their relative positioning.*

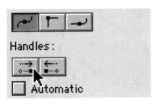

㉘ *Click the* **Handles icons** *to retract point handles.*

㉙ *Retracting a point handle.*

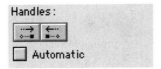

㉚ *Click the* **Automatic box** *to restore point handles to a curve or connector point.*

When you convert a curve point to a corner point, the handles do not change automatically. To create a corner point with straight lines extending from it instead of curved ones, you need to retract both of the handles into the point.

To retract point handles using the Object Inspector:

1. Select a corner point with two point handles that extend out from it.

2. Click one of the Handles icons in the Object Inspector **㉘**. One of the point handles on the corner point will retract **㉙**.

3. Click the other Handles icon to retract the other handle.

   If the points on either side are curve points, your line segment will not be straight. To make it straight, you need to retract the point handles for those curve points as well.

You can use the Object Inspector to extend retracted handles from a point.

To extend handles using the Object Inspector:

1. Click the point from which you want to extend the point handles.

2. If it is a corner point, convert it to either a curve point or a connector point.

3. Click the Automatic box under the Handles icons **㉚**. If the point is a curve point, two handles will appear. If the point is a connector point, one or two handles will appear, depending on the shape of the path.

There are two types of paths: open and closed. Open paths have endpoints. A piece of string is an example of an open path. Closed paths have no endpoints. A rubber band is an example of a closed path **③①**.

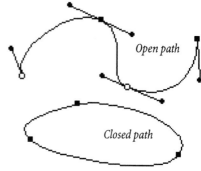

Open path

Closed path

To close a previously drawn path:

If you have already created an open path and decide you want to close it, use the Pointer tool to drag one of the endpoints onto the other. As soon as the points touch, the path closes **③②**.

③① *An open path (top) has endpoints. A closed path (bottom) has no endpoints.*

> **TIP** If Snap to Point is turned on, you see a small square next to the cursor when you are close enough to release the mouse button.

You can determine if a path is open or closed by looking at the Object Inspector.

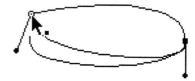

To determine if a path is open or closed:

1. Select the path with the Pointer or Lasso tool.
2. Choose **Windows > Inspectors > Object** to open the Object Inspector where you can see whether the Closed box is checked or not **③③**.

③② *To close a previously drawn path, drag one of the endpoints over the other.*

To open or close a path using the Object Inspector:

1. To close an open path, click the Closed box. The path closes by adding a segment between the two endpoints **③④**.
2. To open a closed path, click the Closed box. The path opens by deleting the segment between the two endpoints.

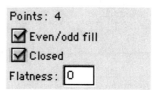

③③ *A checkmark next to Closed in the Object Inspector indicates a closed path.*

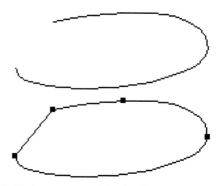

③④ *Closing an open path (top) adds a segment between the two endpoints (bottom).*

Close a Path; Determine if a Path is Open or Closed

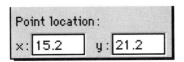

35 *The **x** and **y** coordinates of a point* are listed in the Object Inspector.

36 *The **x** and **y** coordinates of the lower-left anchor point of a grouped object** are listed in the Object Inspector.*

Though it is easy to manually move a point or reshape an object, you may want to do it numerically.

To move a point or a grouped object numerically:

1. Click the point or grouped object. Click the Object Inspector.

2. If you have chosen a point, the *x* and *y* coordinates for your Point location are shown at the bottom of the panel **35**.

3. If you have chosen a grouped object, the *x* and *y* coordinates for the lower-left group anchor point are shown in the panel **36**.

4. Double-click the *x* and *y* fields and enter the coordinates for the destination of the point or grouped object.

TIP The *x* coordinates start in the lower left of the page and increase as you move horizontally to the right. The *y* coordinates start in the lower left of the page and increase as you move up.

5. Press the Return or Enter key to set the new coordinates.

TIP To move an object numerically without grouping it, use the Move distance settings in the Transform palette (*see page 75*).

Move a Point or Object Numerically

In order to protect the shape of an object, or to make it easier to select objects, you can group the points on the path or the multiple objects.

To group paths:

1. Select the path or objects you want to group.
2. Choose **Modify > Group**. Instead of individual points, four group anchor points designate the corners of the path or paths **37**.

37 *A grouped object displays* **four anchor points** *at the corners when selected.*

To work with grouped objects:

1. To select a grouped object, click the Pointer tool on the object.
2. To resize a grouped object, drag on one of the four group anchor points that surround the object **38**. The four-headed arrow appears as the object is changed.
3. To resize the object without distorting its shape, hold the Shift key as you drag one of the group anchor points.

38 *Drag one of the group anchor points to resize a grouped object. (The anchor points disappear as the four-headed arrow resizes the object.)*

When an object is grouped, there are some special steps to select the points.

To select individual points in a group:

1. With the object selected, hold the Option/Alt key and click the Pointer tool on the object. The individual points of the grouped object appear **39**.
2. Continue to hold the Option/Alt key and click the point you want to select.
3. To select additional points, hold the Shift key and click those points.

TIP Rectangles and ellipses are grouped when you draw them.

TIP To ungroup a rectangle or ellipse so you can select the individual points, choose **Modify > Alter Path > Reverse Direction**.

39 *Hold the Option/Alt key to* **select individual points** *of a grouped object.*

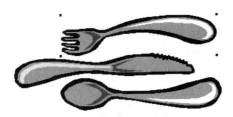

40 *To nest objects, group each of the individual objects. The four anchor points around the fork indicate that the object has been grouped.*

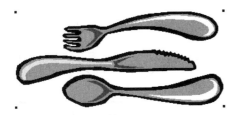

41 *Select all the individual groups and group them together. The four anchor points around all the objects indicate that they are all part of one group.*

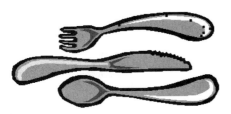

42 *To select an individual object or point in a nested group, hold the Option/Alt key as you click on the group. The individual anchor points appear.*

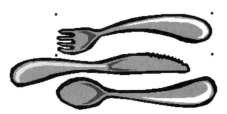

43 *To select the next level of the nest, press the tilde (~) key. Continue to press the tilde key until you see the group anchor points for the final level of the nest.*

When you are working with grouped objects, you may want to create various levels of groups to make it easier to select certain objects. This is called *nesting*.

To nest objects:

1. Select and group the first object **40**. After the object is grouped, deselect it.

2. Select the next object and group it. After that object is grouped, deselect it. Group any additional objects.

3. Select all the groups and group them **41**.

TIP There is a limit of eight levels for nested objects.

TIP Numerous nesting levels can cause problems when it comes to printing your file. Ungroup the objects if your file does not print.

Once you have taken the time to nest groups, you have the payoff of being able to easily select the individual groups within the nested group.

To work with nested groups:

1. Press the Option/Alt key to select an individual object or point in a nested group **42**.

2. Press the tilde (~) key to select the next level of the nest **43**.

3. Continue to press the tilde key until you have selected all the levels you want.

To ungroup an object:

1. Select the grouped object.

2. Choose **Modify > Ungroup**. This ungroups the object and displays the individual anchor points.

TIP If you have nested objects in a group, you have to ungroup them for each level of the nest.

To select and move an object:

1. Position the Pointer tool on the path of an object you want to move.

2. Press and hold; a four-headed arrow appears.

3. Pause a moment then drag to see a preview as you move the object **44**.

    or

    Drag immediately if you do not need to see the object as you move it. Instead you see a bounding box which shows only the size of the object **45**.

TIP If you do not see the preview when you drag multiple objects, change the Preferences setting for Redraw (*see page 253*).

To delete an object:

1. Choose the object so that all its anchor points are visible or its four group anchor points are visible.

2. Press the Delete key or choose **Edit > Clear** to delete the object.

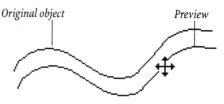

44 *A line dragged with a* **preview.**

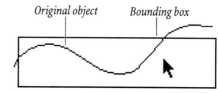

45 *A line dragged with a* **bounding box.**

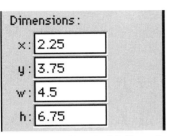

Dimensions:

x: 2.25
y: 3.75
w: 4.5
h: 6.75

46 **The width (w) and height (h) dimensions** *let you change the dimensions of a grouped object.*

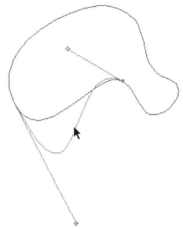

47 *Hold down the Option/Alt key to keep the anchor points in place while you modify the segment between them.*

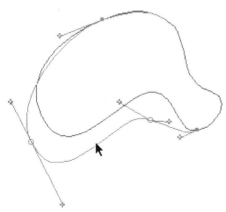

48 *Drag the segment without holding down the Option/Alt key to move the anchor points along with it.*

To change the size of a grouped object numerically:

1. Select the grouped object.
2. Choose the Object Inspector.
3. In the middle of the palette find the width (w) and height (h) listed under the Dimensions **46**.
4. Double-click the fields and enter the new dimensions for the grouped object.
5. Press Return or Enter to set the new coordinates.

TIP The *x* and *y* coordinates and width and height are in the same unit of measurement as the document. (*To change the unit of measurement for your document, see page 6.*)

To modify a path using Bend-O-Matic

1. Select the path you want to modify.
2. Press the Option/Alt key and click the Pointer tool on a segment of the path to subselect it.
3. Press the Option/Alt key as you drag the segment. The anchor points remain in place as the segment between them is distorted. The Bézier handles are adjusted as the curve changes **47**.

TIP Subselecting the segment and dragging it without holding the Option/Alt key moves the two anchor points at the ends of the segment **48**.

You may find that you want to select objects positioned behind others. Rather than move your mouse to a new position, you can use a modifier key to select behind objects.

(Mac) To select behind objects:

1. Position the cursor over the area where you want to select an object.
2. Hold down Control+Option keys.
3. Click as many times as necessary to select through to the object behind the others **49**.

(Win) To select behind objects:

1. Position the cursor over the area where you want to select an object.
2. Hold down Control+Alt keys.
3. Right-mouse click as many times as necessary to select through to the object behind the others **50**.

49 *(Mac) To select an individual object behind another object, hold the Control-Option keys and click until the object is selected.*

50 *(Win) To select an individual object behind another object, hold the Control-Alt keys and right-mouse click until the object is selected.*

PEN AND BEZIGON 6

A s mentioned previously, the Pen and the Bézigon tools allow you to draw much more precisely than the Freehand tool. However, learning to use these two tools is not as easy as working with the Freehand tool.

In this chapter you will learn how to

Understand the differences between the Pen and Bézigon tools.

Create different types of points and paths with each tool.

Add points to existing paths.

❶ *The **Pen tool** in the Toolbox.*

❷ *The **Bézigon tool** in the Toolbox.*

The difference between the Pen and Bézigon tools

Both the Pen ❶ and the Bézigon ❷ tools allow you to draw much more precisely than the Freehand tool. So what is the difference between the two tools? At first glance, there is very little difference. In fact, once a path has been created, there is no way to tell which tool created it.

The main difference is that the Pen tool allows you to manipulate handles as you place points. The Bézigon tool allows you to quickly click to place points, but all the point handles are set automatically. After you place points with the Bézigon tool, you must then go back to adjust the point handles. This makes the Bézigon tool easier to learn but makes the Pen tool faster when truly mastered.

Difference between Pen and Bézigon

To draw an object with straight sides:

1. Choose either the Pen or the Bézigon tool from the Toolbox.

2. Position the cursor where the path should start and click. A corner point appears as a white square ❸.

3. Position the cursor for the next point of the object and click. A line extends from the first point to the second point.

4. Continue clicking until you have created all the sides of your object ❹.

5. Create a closed path by clicking the first point again.

6. Once you finish a path, press Tab to deselect the path and start a new one.

TIP Hold the Shift key to constrain your lines to 45° increments relative to the constrain angle. The constrain angle is set in the Constrain dialog box that opens when you choose Modify > Constrain from the menu bar ❺.

The Pen and Bézigon tools both help you draw smooth curves. A smooth curve makes the transition from one direction to another with no abrupt changes, like the curve created by a roller-coaster ❻. With the Bézigon tool, holding the Option/Alt key places curve points.

To draw a smooth curved path with the Bézigon:

1. Choose the Bézigon tool and place your first curve point holding down the Option/Alt key.

2. Start with the left point and click each spot where the anchor points need to be.

3. Continue holding the Option/Alt key and clicking until you have completed laying down the points.

4. Use the Pointer tool to adjust the point handles so the curve is the proper shape.

❸ *Clicking with either the Pen or the Bézigon creates a* **corner point** *shown as a hollow square.*

❹ *Straight lines extend between each of the corner points.*

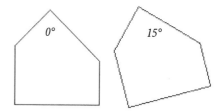

❺ *Compare an object drawn with the* **Constrain angle** *at 0° and the same object drawn with the constrain angle set to 15°.*

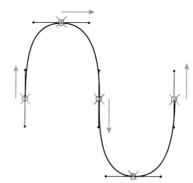

❻ *A* **smooth curved path** *with its point handles visible. The gray arrows show how the path is dragged with the Pen. The* **X**s *show where you would click with the Bézigon while holding down the Option/Alt key.*

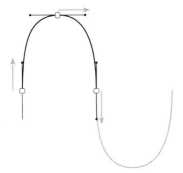

7 *To draw a smooth curved path with the Pen tool, drag to place curve points at each spot where the path changes direction. (The gray line indicates the intended paths.)*

8 *To start the* **bumpy curved path**, *click with the Bézigon tool to create a corner point.*

9 *To continue the bumpy curved path, Option/Alt-click with the Bézigon tool to create a curve point.*

10 *To continue the bumpy curved path, click with the Bézigon tool. This creates a corner point.*

To draw a smooth curved path with the Pen:

1. Choose the Pen tool.

2. Click the first point and drag up (do not release the mouse until you have created a point handle that extends about a third of the way up the curve you want to create) **7**.

3. Continue click-dragging to place curve points at each spot where the path changes direction.

4. Press the Tab key to deselect the path when you have finished creating the path.

TIP You can modify a path by changing both the lengths of the point handles and their directions. Do not limit yourself to changing just one or the other.

Life is not all smooth, and neither are most curved paths. So, there will be times you will need to create a bumpy curved path. Think of a bumpy curve as the path a bouncing ball would take. The abrupt change is where the ball hits the ground and then bounces back up.

To draw a bumpy curved path with the Bézigon:

1. Click with the Bézigon tool to create the first corner point **8**.

2. Hold the Option/Alt key as you click to create the curve point **9**.

3. Click to create the next corner point **10**. Notice that there are point handles from the corner points. This is because FreeHand automatically extends handles out from corner points that are connected to curve points.

4. Hold the Option/Alt key as you click to create the second curve point.

5. Click with the Bézigon tool to create the final point, a corner point.

6. Manually adjust the point handles until the curved path is the shape you want.

To draw a bumpy curved path with the Pen:

1. Hold the Option/Alt key as you drag with the Pen tool to create a corner point with a handle **⑪**.

2. Drag to create the second point, a curve point.

3. Drag down at the third point. Two point handles extend out from the sides of the point. Do not release the mouse button.

4. When the point handle in the back has extended out enough, press the Option key. This allows you to rotate the front point handle so that it aligns properly **⑫**. You may then release the mouse button.

5. Drag to create the next point, a curve point.

6. Drag to create the final point. Again two handles extend out. When the handle in the back has extended out enough, release the mouse button.

7. Press the Option/Alt key and click on the final point. This retracts the point handle in the front.

⑪ *To start the* **bumpy curved path**, *press the Option/Alt key and drag with the Pen tool. This creates a corner point with a handle.*

⑫ *To create a corner point with two handles, drag down. When the handle extends backward enough, hold the Option/Alt key and then drag in the direction of the second arrow.*

Imagine you are riding in a car, and there is suddenly a bump in the road. That is the shape of a straight-to-bumpy path.

To draw a straight-to-bumpy path with the Bézigon tool:

1. The first point is a corner point, so click with the Bézigon tool where the first point should be.

2. The next point is a corner point, so click with the Bézigon tool. To constrain the line as you click, hold the Shift key **⑬**.

3. Option/Alt-click with the Bézigon tool where the top of the bump should be.

4. Click with the Bézigon tool to create the next two corner points **⑭**.

5. Manually adjust the point handles to the shape you want.

⑬ *To start the straight-to-bumpy path, click with the Bézigon tool to create two corner points.*

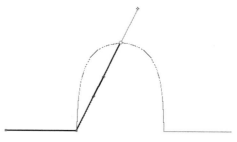

⑭ *Option/Alt-click for the top of the bump and then click with the Bézigon tool at the last two positions to create two corner points.*

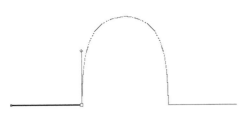

⓯ *To* **add a handle to a corner point,** *hold the Option/Alt key and then drag on the point.*

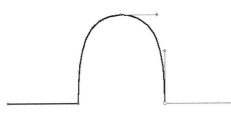

⓰ *To convert a curve point into a corner point with only one handle, press the Option/Alt key and click the point again. This retracts the forward handle coming out of the point, leaving just the one shown.*

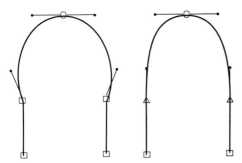

⓱ *The difference between using* **corner points as the transition** *between segments (left) and using* **connector points** *(right).*

To draw a straight-to-bumpy path with the Pen:

1. Click with the Pen tool to place the first corner point.

2. Click to create the next corner point. To add a handle to this point, hold the Option/Alt key and then drag with the Pen tool **⓯**.

3. Drag with the Pen tool to put the curve point at the top of the bump.

4. Drag with the Pen tool to create a curve point with two handles. Release the mouse button when you are satisfied with the length of the handle extending into the curve.

5. Hold the Option/Alt key and click the point you created in Step 4. This converts the point into a corner point and retracts the second handle **⓰**.

6. Click to place the last corner point.

TIP Press the Shift key as you drag out the handles *after* the anchor point is placed to constrain your point handles. If Shift is pressed *before* the point is placed, the position of the point itself is constrained. You can do both, if you like.

You can use connector points to create a smooth transition between a straight-line segment and a curved segment. Connector points are indicated by a triangle **⓱**.

To create connector points using the Bézigon:

With the Bézigon tool, press the Control key and click (Mac) or hold the Alt key and click with the right mouse button (Win). The handle will be created and aligned automatically when you create the segment that follows.

To create connector points using the Pen:

With the Pen tool, hold the Control key and click to create a connector point (Mac) or hold the Alt key and click with the right mouse button (Win).

You may finish creating a path and later realize you want to add more segments to it. You then add points to the end of the path. (This only works with open paths. Closed paths have no endpoints.)

To add points to the end of a path:

1. Select the path you want to extend.

2. Select one of the path's endpoints.

3. Click or drag with the Pen or the Bézigon tool at the spot where you want the next point to occur **⓲**. FreeHand fills in the line segment. Continue adding segments as needed.

TIP Other path operations, such as joining two open paths together, splitting paths, and cutting paths, are covered in Chapter 16, "Path Operations."

⓲ *To continue a path, select one of the endpoints. Then click or drag with the Pen or Bézigon tool where you would like to add the next point, indicated by "x".*

MOVE AND TRANSFORM

Once you have created an object, most likely you will need to change it at some other time. Even moving an object is considered changing it. In fact, it is by moving and transforming objects that you can convert simple shapes into dramatic and sophisticated effects.

In this chapter, you will learn how to

Understand the settings on the Info Toolbar.

Cut, copy and paste objects.

Move objects.

Copy objects as you move.

Move, scale, rotate, skew, and reflect objects both by eye.

Work with the Transform panel to modify paths.

Use the Clone command.

Use the technique called Power Duplicating.

Use the transformation handles.

Use the Freeform tool to modify objects.

As discussed in Chapter 5, you can move an object by simply selecting it and dragging it anywhere on your page. If you would like to know the details about the position of the object you are dragging, you can see that information in the Info Toolbar.

To read the Info Toolbar:

Choose **Window > Toolbars > Info** to show the Info Toolbar ❶.

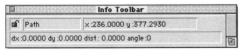

❶ *The* **Info Toolbar** *in the rectangle shape.*

Info Toolbar

The Info Toolbar readings

The Info Toolbar readings change depending on the position of your cursor, the tool chosen, or the action taken ❷–❺. The following are the various categories seen on the Info Toolbar.

x (Position field) position of the cursor along the horizontal axis

y (Position field) position of the cursor along the vertical axis

dx horizontal distance an object is moved

dy vertical distance an object is moved

dist total distance along any angle an object is moved

angle angle along which any object is moved, created, or transformed

x (Info field) horizontal location of the centerpoint around which any object is being created or transformed

y (Info field) vertical location of the center point that any object is being created or transformed around.

xscale horizontal scale or skew of an object expressed as a ratio to an object's original size (e.g., 1.00 = 100%)

yscale vertical scale or skew of an object expressed as a ratio to an object's original size (e.g., 1.00 = 100%)

width width of a rectangle or ellipse

height height of a rectangle or ellipse

radius size of a radius of a polygon

sides number of sides of a polygon

open padlock (Mac) **grey padlock** (Win) indicates the object is not locked

closed padlock (Mac) **red padlock** (Win) indicates the object is locked

TIP The Info Toolbar does not allow you to enter numbers directly into it.

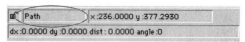

❷ *The **Object field** (circled) shows the type of object or the number of objects selected.*

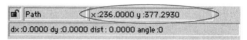

❸ *The **Position field** (circled) shows the x and y coordinates of the cursor position.*

❹ *The **Info field** (circled) shows various attributes of objects as they are created or manipulated.*

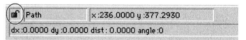

❺ *The **Lock field** (circled) shows if a selected object is locked or not.*

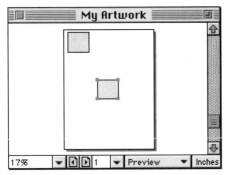

⑥ *An object that is cut or copied from one position (upper left) will be* **pasted in the center of the window.**

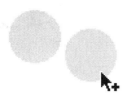

⑦ **To copy and object by dragging,** *hold the Option/Alt key as you move the object. The plus sign (+) next to the arrow indicates you are creating a copy.*

⑧ *Release the mouse to create the duplicate of the object moved.*

⑨ *Choose* **Edit > Duplicate** *as many times as necessary to create additional copies of the object.*

To cut, copy, or paste objects:

Once you have selected an object, you can choose **Edit > Cut** or **Edit > Copy**. You can then choose **Edit > Paste** to paste the object onto the same page, a different page, or a different document. The object is pasted in the center of the window **⑥**.

To move and copy an object:

1. Select the object you want to copy.

2. Drag to move the object to a new position. Press the Option/Alt key as you drag. The plus sign (+) next to the arrow **⑦** indicates that you are creating a copy of the object.

3. When the object is in the correct position, release the mouse button first and then the Option/Alt key. A copy of the original object is created at the point where you released the mouse **⑧**.

4. Choose **Edit > Duplicate** to continue to make copies of the original object, each positioned the same distance away from the previous copy **⑨**.

The transformation tools allow you to modify simple objects into more sophisticated shapes. Rotation allows you to change the orientation of an object.

To rotate an object by eye:

1. Select the object you want to rotate and click the Rotating tool in the Toolbox **10**.

2. Move your cursor to the work page. Your cursor turns into a star.

3. Position the star on the spot around which you would like the object to rotate **11**. This is the transformation point.

4. Press on the point you have chosen. Do not release the mouse button. A line extends out from the transformation point. This is the rotation axis **12**.

TIP The transformation point for the rotation tool and the other tools does not have to be a point on the object. You can transform an object around a point anywhere on the page or the work area.

5. Still pressing, drag the cursor away from the transformation point. Then move the rotation axis. The object rotates as you move the rotation axis **13**.

TIP Hold down the Shift key to constrain the rotation to 45° increments.

6. Release the mouse button when you are satisfied with the position of the rotated object. Your object is rotated into position.

TIP The farther you drag your cursor away from the transformation point during rotation or reflection, the easier it is to control the transformation.

10 *To rotate an object by eye, click the* **Rotating tool** *in the Toolbox.*

11 *Position the* **Rotating tool cursor** *on the pivot point you want the object to rotate around.*

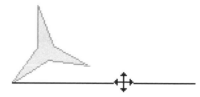

12 *Press with the Rotating tool to reveal the rotation axis — the line that the object will be rotated around.*

13 *The rotation axis and the preview show the position to which the object will be rotated.*

⓮ *To scale an object by eye, click the* **Scaling tool** *in the Toolbox.*

⓯ *Position the* **Scaling tool cursor** *on the point you want the object to scale from.*

⓰ *Drag with the Scaling tool to scale the object up or down.*

Scaling allows you to change the size and proportions of an object.

To scale an object by eye:

1. Choose the object you want to scale and click the Scaling tool in the Toolbox **⓮**.

2. Move your cursor to the work page. Your cursor turns into a star **⓯**.

3. Position the star on the spot from which you would like the object to scale. This is the transformation point.

4. Press down on the point you have chosen. Do not release the mouse button.

5. Drag the cursor away from the transformation point. An outline of the object changes to show how the object is being scaled **⓰**.

TIP Press the Shift key if you want to constrain the scale to a proportional change.

6. Release the mouse button when you are satisfied with the size of the scaled object. Your object scales into position.

Scale by Eye

Reflection allows you to create a mirror image of an object. This is very helpful when making shadows.

To reflect an object by eye:

1. Choose the object you want to reflect and click the Reflecting tool in the Toolbox **17**.

2. Move your cursor to the work page. Your cursor turns into a star.

3. Position the star on the point around which you want the object to reflect **18**. This is the transformation point.

4. Press on the point you have chosen. Do not release the mouse button. A line extends out from the star. This line is the reflection axis. (Think of the reflection axis as the mirror in which your object is being reflected.)

5. Drag the cursor away from the transformation point. The outline of the object changes its position and shape as you move the cursor **19**.

TIP Hold the Shift key to constrain your reflection to 45° increments.

6. Release the mouse button when you are satisfied with the position of the reflected object. Your object is reflected into position.

17 *To reflect an object by eye, click the* **Reflecting tool** *in the Toolbox.*

18 *Position the* **Reflecting tool cursor** *on the point you want the object to reflect around.*

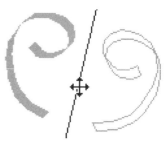

19 *Drag with the Reflecting tool to create a mirror image of the object.*

⑳ *To skew an object by eye, click the* **Skewing tool** *in the Toolbox.*

㉑ *Position the* **Skewing tool cursor** *on the point you want the object to be skewed from.*

㉒ *Press with the* **Skewing tool** *to create a sheared or skewed image of the object.*

Skewing (sometimes called shearing) is a way of distorting an object along an axis. This type of distortion is very common when making shadows.

To skew an object by eye:

1. Choose the object you want to skew and click the Skewing tool in the Toolbox **⑳**.

2. Move your cursor to the work page. Your cursor turns into a star.

3. Position the star on the point around which you want the object to skew **㉑**. This is the transformation point.

4. Press down on the point you have chosen. Do not release the mouse button.

5. Drag the cursor away from the transformation point. The outline of the object changes its shape as you move the cursor **㉒**.

TIP Hold the Shift key to constrain the skew. Drag in a general horizontal direction to constrain the skew exactly horizontal. Drag in a general vertical direction to constrain the skew exactly vertical.

6. Release the mouse button when you are satisfied with the position of the skewed object. Your object skews into position.

Skew by Eye

Just as you can make a copy of an object as you move it, you can also make a copy of an object as you transform it.

To copy and transform an object:

1. Hold the Option/Alt keys as you begin the transformation of the object. A plus sign (+) appears next to the star cursor.

2. Release the mouse button first and then the Option/Alt key to create a copy of the original object transformed to the position you chose ❷❸.

   If you do not see the plus sign (+), check that the Object Preference for Option/Alt dragging to create copies is selected (*see page 249*).

3. Choose **Edit > Duplicate** ❷❹ to create additional transformed copies.

❷❸ *The plus sign indicates that a copy of the object is being made as part of the transformation.*

❷❹ *Choosing* **Edit > Duplicate** *creates additional transformed copies of the object.*

FreeHand offers a technique called *Power Duplicating* that allows you to store up to five transformations. You can then apply all the transformations as you make copies.

To use the transformation tools for Power Duplicating:

1. Choose the object you want to transform.

2. Choose **Edit > Clone**. This creates a copy of the object on top of the original.

3. Move the clone or use any of the transformation tools to modify it.

4. Apply any of the other transformations.

5. Each of the transformations is now stored.

6. Choose **Edit > Duplicate**. The object is copied and modified according to the stored transformations.

7. Choose **Edit > Duplicate** as many times as needed. Each command creates a new object transformed according to the stored transformation settings ❷❺.

❷❺ **Power Duplicating** *allows you to store transformations and then apply them again and again to copies. In this case, the object is both rotated and scaled.*

Copy and Transform; Power Duplicating

❷❻ *The* **Move settings** *in the Transform panel.*

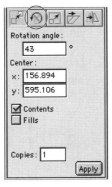

❷❼ *The* **Rotation settings** *of the Transform panel.*

❷❽ *The top whale was rotated to the bottom two positions. The bottom left rotated the contents with the object. The horizontal lines in the bottom right show that the contents did not rotate.*

So far, you have done your transformations by eye. If you have a steady hand and a keen eye on the Info Toolbar, you can be pretty precise. To work even more precisely, you need to use the Transform panel.

To view the Transform panel:

Choose **Window > Panels > Transform** or double-click any of the transformation tools in the Toolbox. The Transform panel appears.

To move using the Transform panel:

1. Choose the object you want to move. Click the Move icon in the Transform panel **❷❻**.

2. Enter the distance amounts you want to move the object in the *x* and *y* fields.

3. Check the Contents or the Fills settings to have any contents or fills moved along with the path.

4. Click the Apply (Mac) or Move (Win) button or press Return or Enter to apply the move.

To rotate using the Transform panel:

1. Choose the object you want to rotate. Click the Rotation icon in the Transform panel **❷❼**.

2. Enter the number of degrees you want to rotate the object in the Rotation angle field.

3. To change the point of transformation from the center, enter the coordinates you want in the *x* and *y* fields. (To find the coordinates for a certain point, position your cursor over that point and look at the *x* and *y* listings in the Info Toolbar.)

4. Check the Contents and/or the Fills settings to have any contents or fills rotated along with the path **❷❽**.

5. Click the Apply (Mac) or Rotate (Win) button or press Return or Enter to apply the rotation.

To scale using the Transform panel:

1. Choose the object you want to scale. Click on the Scale icon in the Transform panel **㉙**.

2. Enter the percent you want to change the object.

3. For a proportional scale, keep the Uniform box checked. To scale the object nonproportionally, deselect the Uniform box. Enter values in the *x* (horizontal) and *y* (vertical) (Mac) or **h** (horizontal) and **v** (vertical) (Win) fields that open.

4. To change the point of transformation from the center, enter the coordinates in the *x* and *y* fields.

5. Check the Contents, Fills, or Lines settings to have any contents, fills, or strokes scaled along with the path **㉚**.

6. Click the Apply (Mac) or Scale (Win) button or press Return or Enter to apply the scale.

㉙ *The* **Scale settings** *of the Transform panel.*

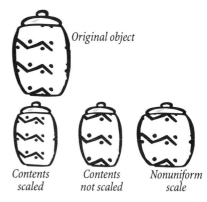

Original object

Contents scaled *Contents not scaled* *Nonuniform scale*

㉚ *Various ways to scale an object and its contents.*

To skew using the Transform panel:

1. Choose the object you want to skew. Click the Skew icon in the Transform panel **㉛**.

2. Enter the horizontal angle amount of the skew in the **h** field. Enter the vertical amount of the skew in the the **v** field.

3. To change the point of transformation from the center, enter the coordinates you want in the *x* and *y* fields.

4. Check either the Contents or Fills settings to have any contents or fills skewed along with the path.

5. Click the Apply (Mac) or Skew (Win) button, or press Return or Enter to apply the skew.

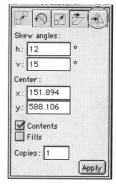

㉛ *The* **Skew settings** *of the Transform panel.*

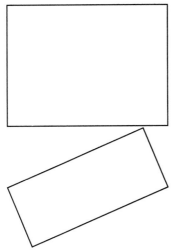

32 *The* **Reflection settings** *of the Transform panel.*

33 *Use the* **Constrain dialog box** *to change the horizontal axis along which objects are drawn.*

34 *The top rectangle was drawn with a Constrain axis of 0°. The bottom rectangle had a Constrain axis of 23°.*

To reflect using the Transform panel:

1. Choose the object you want to reflect. Click the Reflection icon in the Transform panel **32**.

2. Enter the angle amount that you want the object to reflect around in the Reflect axis field.

3. To change the point of transformation from the center, enter the coordinates you want in the *x* and *y* fields.

4. Check the Contents and/or Fills settings to have them reflected along with the path.

5. Click the Apply (Mac) or Reflect (Win) button or press Return or Enter to apply the reflection.

As you draw, move, or transform objects, the objects are positioned along an invisible line called the Constrain axis. The default setting of this axis is 0°. This means that your objects line up in an ordinary horizontal fashion. However, by changing the Constrain axis, you can make all your objects automatically align along any angle you choose.

To change the Constrain axis:

1. Choose **Modify > Constrain**. The Constrain dialog box appears **33**.

2. Enter the angle you want for the Constrain axis by typing the amount in the Angle field or by rotating the wheel. Click OK. All objects will be drawn along the angle you have just set **34**.

TIP Changing the Constrain axis only affects those objects created from that point on. It does not affect previously created objects.

At times it may be cumbersome to stop working on artwork to choose the scale or rotation tools. The Transformation handles let you modify objects directly on the page.

To use the Transformation handles:

1. With the Selection tool, double-click the selected object. A rectangular box with eight Transformation handles appears **35**.

2. Move the cursor near any one of the handles. The curved arrow Rotation icon appears **36**. This indicates that you can drag to rotate the object.

3. Move the cursor directly onto one of the handles. The double-headed arrow Scale icon appears **37**. This indicates that you can drag to scale the object.

4. Place the cursor between the handles to activate the Skew icon so you can drag to skew the object **38**.

5. Drag the Transformation point icon away from the center of the object. This changes the point around which the transformation occurs **39**.

6. Putting the cursor inside the box changes it to the Move icon so you can drag the box to a new position on the page.

7. Double-click again to get rid of the Transformation handles.

TIP Hold the Option/Alt key as you drag with the Transformation handles to copy the object as it is transformed.

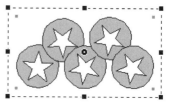

35 *The* **Transformation handles** *around a grouped object.*

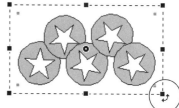

36 *The* **Rotation icon** *(circled) lets you use the Transformation handles to rotate an object.*

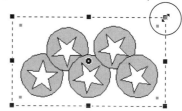

37 *The* **Scale icon** *(circled) lets you use the Transformation handles to scale an object.*

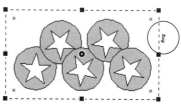

38 *The* **Skew tool** *(circled) lets you skew the object around the Transformation point.*

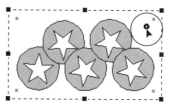

39 *Drag the* **Transformation point icon** *(circled) to change the location around which the transformation occurs.*

Transformation Handles

⓵ *The Freeform tool in the Toolbox set for the* **Push/Pull tool.**

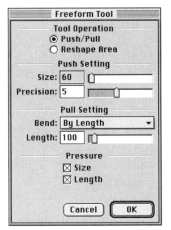

⓵ *The* **Push/Pull settings** *of the Freeform tool dialog box.*

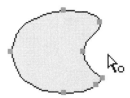

⓶ *The* **Push icon** *indicates that the Freeform tool bends and changes the shape of the segment.*

⓷ *The* **Pull icon** *indicates that the Freeform tool adds a segment where the path is pulled.*

Once you have created an object, you may find it difficult to work with the Bézier handles to reshape the path. The Freeform tool allows you to change the shape of an object without worrying about adding or modifying points. There are two modes to the Freeform tool: Push/Pull tool and Reshape Area tool.

The Push/Pull tool allows you to pull to add new segments to a path or push to distort the shape of the segment.

To use the Push/Pull Freeform tool:

1. Double-click the Freeform tool in the Toolbox **⓵**. The Freeform Tool dialog box appears **⓵**.

2. Set the Tool Operation to Push/Pull.

3. Use the slider or click in the Size field to set the size of tool. This controls how large an area is pushed by the tool **⓶**.

4. Use the slider or click in the Precision field to set the precision amount — the greater the amount, the more sensitive the tool is to minor movements of the mouse.

5. Use the Pull Setting pop-up menu to specify how the tool works. Choose Bend By Length to pull anywhere along a path. Choose Bend Between Points to restrict the pull to only between existing anchor points.

6. Use the slider or click in the Length field to set how much the Pull will alter the path **⓷**.

7. If you have a pressure-sensitive tablet, check the Size and/or Length boxes to set how the pressure on the tablet affects the tool.

TIP If you do not have a pressure-sensitive tablet, press the **1**, **[**, or left arrow keys as you drag to decrease the size of the Freeform tool effect.

TIP Press the **2**, **]**, or right arrow keys as you drag to increase the size of the Freeform tool effect.

Like the Push/Pull tool, the Reshape Area tool allows you to add new segments to a path and to distort the path in a variety of ways controlled by the settings in the Freeform Tool dialog box.

To use the Reshape Area Freeform tool:

1. Double-click the Freeform tool in the Toolbox ❹❹. The Freeform Tool dialog box appears.

2. Set the Tool Operation to Reshape Area ❹❺.

3. Use the slider or click in the Size field to set the size of the Reshape Area tool.

4. Use the slider or click in the Strength field to set how long the tool will work during a drag — the greater the amount the longer the tool distorts the path ❹❻–❹❼.

5. Use the slider or click in the Precision field to set the precision amount — the greater the amount, the more sensitive the tool is to minor movements of the mouse.

6. If you have a pressure-sensitive tablet, check the Size or Length boxes to set how the pressure on the tablet affects the tool.

❹❹ *The **Reshape Area tool** in the Toolbox.*

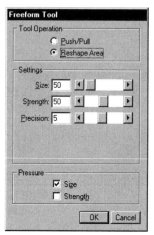

❹❺ *The **Reshape Area settings** of the Freeform Tool dialog box.*

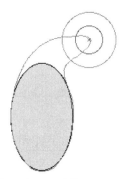

❹❻ *The **Reshape Area** tool distorts a path into a new shape.*

❹❼ *The results of using the Reshape Area tool on the top of an ellipse.*

O ne of the most versatile parts of FreeHand is the way it works with color. Not only can you choose what color modes to work in, but you can add, remove, and swap colors at any time.

In this chapter you will learn how to

Define colors in the Color Mixer.

Use the Color List to add, rename, convert, duplicate, or remove colors.

Use the Eyedropper tool to copy colors.

Create tints of colors.

Work with color-matching libraries.

Create custom color libraries.

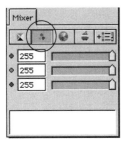

❶ *Click the* **CMYK icon** *(circled) to display the Color Mixer in CMYK mode.*

You define new colors in the Color Mixer panel.

Color Mixer in CMYK mode

The CMYK mode defines the color according to the four process colors used by most commercial printers—cyan, magenta, yellow, and black. This is the most common and best-known color system used by graphic artists ❶.

Color Mixer in RGB mode

❷ *Click the* **RGB icon** *(circled) to display the Color Mixer in RGB mode.*

The RGB mode defines the color according to red, green, and blue components. This is primarily a video color system and is the system used by your own monitor. Many people who design for multimedia and the World Wide Web use RGB to define colors ❷.

Color Mixer in HLS mode

❸ *Click the* **HLS icon** *(circled) to display the Color Mixer in HLS mode.*

Defines the color according to hue, lightness, and saturation components. This system lets you pick different colors with similar values. For example, pastel colors have similar lightness and saturation but different hues ❸.

Color Mixer

Color Mixer in Windows mode (Win)

The Windows button ❹ opens the Windows colors ❺ where you can pick from the colors installed in the Windows operating system.

Color Mixer in Apple mode (Mac)

The Apple button ❻ opens the Macintosh color picker ❼ where you can pick colors according to a number of different models installed in the Mac OS.

You can use not only the CMYK and RGB models of color definition, but HLS and HSV as well. In addition, you can choose from the 60 preset colors on the Crayon picker or the 216 Web colors that the HTML picker can be set for ❽.

❹ *In the Windows color mixer, there is a* **Windows button** *(circled).*

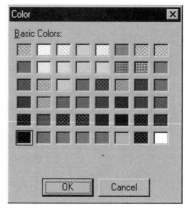

❺ *Clicking the Windows button displays the* **Windows Basic Colors choices**.

❻ *In the Macintosh Color Mixer there is an* **Apple button** *(circled).*

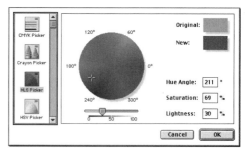

❼ *Clicking the Apple button displays the* **Macintosh color picker** *and all the options it offers.*

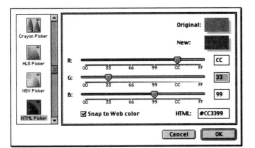

❽ *The* **HTML Picker** *lets you select from the 216 "Web safe" colors or to choose colors between them.*

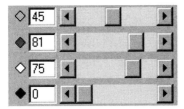

❾ *The* **sliders** *let you change the CMYK values of a color.*

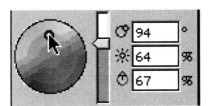

❿ *In the* **HLS mode**, *click on the color wheel to define the hue and saturation. Use the slider to adjust the lightness.*

Which color system to use

If you are defining a color for use in a four-color printing process, the CMYK color system will most likely be the best choice because you will know exactly the percentages of ink that make up each color. Otherwise, choose the most appropriate color-mixer mode to match the way you intend to print or display your finished artwork.

To define a CMYK color:

1. Choose **Window > Panels > Color Mixer**.
2. Click the CMYK icon.
3. Click the cyan, magenta, yellow, or black fields and enter values for the color.

   or

   Drag the cyan, magenta, yellow, or black sliders to enter values for the color ❾.

To define an RGB color:

1. Choose **Window > Panels > Color Mixer**.
2. Click the RGB icon.
3. Click the red, green, or blue fields and enter values for the color.

   or

   Drag the red, green, or blue sliders to enter values for the color.

To define an HLS color:

1. Choose **Window > Panels > Color Mixer**.
2. Click the HLS icon.
3. Find the hue and saturation you want on the color wheel and click it ❿.
4. Use the vertical slider to adjust the lightness.

Define a Color

Once you have defined a color in the Color Mixer, you need to store that color so you can define other colors. To do that, you use the Color List.

To add a color to the Color List:

1. Open the Color List, by choosing **Window > Panels > Color List**.

TIP You can also open the Color List by double-clicking the bottom area of the Color Mixer.

2. Define the values for the color using any of the color modes.

3. Click the Add to Color List button ⑪ in the Color Mixer. The Add to Color List dialog box appears ⑫.

TIP The Add to Color List button works even if the Color List is hidden behind the tab of the Color Mixer.

TIP Hold the Command/Ctrl key to bypass the Add to Color List dialog box.

4. Name the color and set the color as process or spot.

5. Click OK. The color is added to the Color List.

TIP You can also drag the color swatch ⑬ from the Color Mixer onto the Color List drop box ⑭ or onto the list of color names itself.

To rename a color:

1. Double-click the name of the color in the Colors panel. This highlights the name, indicating that it is selected ⑮.

2. Type the new name for the color.

3. Press Return to complete the process of renaming the color.

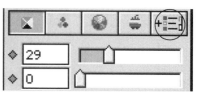

⑪ *Click the* **Add to Color List** *button (circled) to add a color from the Mixer to the Color List.*

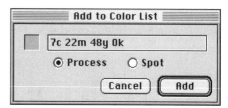

⑫ *The* **Add to Color List** *dialog box allows you to rename the color and set it as process or spot.*

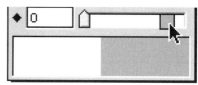

⑬ *You can also* **drag colors from the Color Mixer** *to the Color List.*

⑭ *You can drag a color swatch from the Color Mixer and drop it on the Color List* **drop box** *(circled).*

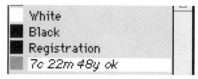

⑮ *To rename a color in the Color List, double-click the name of the color, type the new name, and press Return or Enter.*

Add a Color; Rename a Color

⑯ *The Color List displays* **process colors in italics,** **spot colors in roman**.

⑰ *To convert spot and process colors, use the* **Options pop-up menu** *in the Color List.*

⑱ *You can drag colors from one position to another in the Color List.*

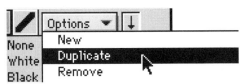

⑲ *Choose* **Duplicate** *from the Options pop-up menu to make a copy of the selected color.*

By default, all colors you define in the Mixer are process colors, which means they will be separated onto CMYK color plates. You can change any color from process to spot color, which is separated onto its own plate. On the Color List, process colors appear in italic type, spot colors in roman.

To convert process to spot color:

1. Choose the color you want to convert from the Color List **⑯**.

2. Open the Options pop-up menu **⑰** and choose Make spot.

To convert spot to process color:

1. Choose the color you want to convert from the Color List.

2. Open the Options pop-up menu and choose Make process.

When you add colors to the Color List, they appear in the order that they were added. You may want to move the colors in the Color List to different positions.

To change the order of the colors on the list:

1. Select the color you want to move.

2. Drag it to the new position and then release the mouse button **⑱**.

If you want to make slight changes to a color, it may be easier to duplicate the color and then make the changes than to start afresh.

To duplicate colors:

1. Click the name of the color you want to duplicate.

2. Choose Duplicate from the Options pop-up menu **⑲**. The duplicate color appears on the Color List with the name "Copy of [Color Name]."

You can remove colors you are no longer using from the Color List.

To remove colors:

1. Click the name of the color you want to remove. The name highlights.
2. If you want to remove a group of adjacent colors, click the top name, hold the Shift key, and click the bottom name. All the names highlight.
3. Choose Remove from the Options pop-up menu ⓴. All the highlighted colors are deleted.

⓴ *Choose* **Remove** *from the Options pop-up menu to remove all selected colors from the Color List.*

When you make changes to a color on the Color List, all the instances of that color in the document are changed as well.

To replace colors:

1. Click the name of the color you want to replace. The name highlights.
2. Choose Replace from the Options pop-up menu. The Replace Color dialog box appears ㉑.
3. Choose a replacement color from the current Color List or one of the Color Libraries (*see page 89*).
4. Click OK, and the original color is replaced by the new one throughout your document.

㉑ *The* **Replace Color dialog box** *lets you substitute one color in the Color List for another.*

You can also add the colors in your objects to the color list.

To drag colors from a drawing to the color list:

1. Choose the Eyedropper tool from the Toolbox ㉒.
2. Click the tool on an area of color and drag a swatch to the color list. Release the mouse to add the color to the list.

TIP You can also use the Eyedropper tool to move colors directly from one object to another.

㉒ *The* **Eyedropper tool** *lets you drag colors from objects to the Color List or to other objects.*

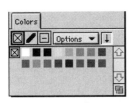

23 *The Color List displays the swatches only after choosing* **Hide names**.

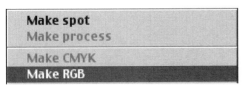

24 *The Options pop-up menu allows you to change from CMYK model for print to the RGB model for video colors.*

25 *Converting a color from RGB (left) to CMYK (right) can change the appearance of the color.*

26 *Colors defined in the RGB or HLS mode display a small* **tricolored icon** *in the list.*

If you have many colors in the Color List, you may find it difficult to scroll through a long list of color names. FreeHand lets you hide the names of the colors in the Color List so that the panel takes up less space onscreen.

To hide the color names:

1. Choose Hide names from the Options pop-up menu in the Color List to display the Color List as swatches only **23**.

2. Choose Show names to display the Color List as names and swatches.

FreeHand also lets you switch a color between the CMYK and RGB modes. This can be helpful if you are converting print artwork which is defined in the CMYK mode to video or Web artwork which is defined in the RGB mode.

To change the color mode:

1. Select the color you want to change.

2. Choose Make RGB from the Options pop-up menu to change the color from CMYK to RGB **24**.

   or

   Choose Make CMYK to change the color from RGB to CMYK.

   TIP RGB colors may look different when converted to the CMYK mode **25**.

   TIP Colors defined using either the RGB or HLS mode have a small tricolored icon to the right of their names **26**.

Hide Color Names; Change Color Mode

If you have defined a color, you can use that color as the basis for a tint. This is handy if you are working with spot colors and want to apply tints of those colors.

To make a tint of a color:

1. Open the Tints panel by choosing **Window > Panels > Tints**.

2. Use the pop-up menu in the Tints panel to choose the color from the Color List.

3. Choose the tint amount by adjusting the slider, typing in a percentage, or clicking one of the tint swatches in the Tints panel **②**.

4. Click the Add to Color List icon in the Tints panel. The Add to Color List dialog box appears **②**.

TIP Hold the Command/Ctrl key to bypass the Add to Color List dialog box.

5. The name of the tint is shown as a percentage of the color's name. You can rename the color by typing in the field.

6. Click the Add button to add the tint to the Color List.

TIP If you change a base color from process to spot (and vice versa), any tints defined from that base color also change from process to spot.

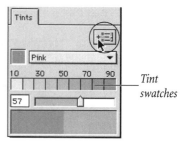

② *The Add to Color List button (circled) in the* **Tints panel** *stores tints in the Color List.*

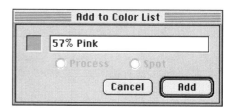

② *The Add to Color List dialog box for a tint.*

So far you have been adding colors to the Colors panel one at a time. Though this is fine for one or two colors, it could be laborious if you need to add many colors. FreeHand has other ways of adding colors to the Color List.

To add colors from copied objects:

If you have created an object with a named color in one FreeHand file and you copy and paste that object into another file, its color automatically goes on the Color List.

Crayon
DIC COLOR GUIDE
FOCOLTONE
Greys
MUNSELL® Book of Color
MUNSELL® High Chroma Colors
PANTONE ProSim EURO®
PANTONE® Coated
PANTONE® HEXACHROME Coated
PANTONE® HEXACHROME Uncoated
PANTONE® Process
PANTONE® Process Euro
PANTONE® ProSim
PANTONE® Uncoated
PANTONE© Metallics Unvarnished
PANTONE© Metallics Varnished
PANTONE© Pastels Coated
PANTONE© Pastels Uncoated
TOYO COLOR FINDER
TRUMATCH 4-Color Selector
Web Safe Color Library

㉙ *The Options pop-up menu of the Colors panel lists the* **FreeHand color libraries***.*

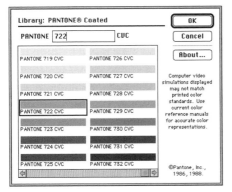

㉚ *In the* **Library dialog box***, type in the name or code number of the color or click on the color you want to add to your Color List.*

To add colors from imported EPS files:

If you import an EPS file that uses named colors, those named colors will be added to the Color List. *(For more information about importing images, see pages 206–207.)*

Color-matching system libraries

FreeHand supplies you with various color libraries **㉙** that are used by many commercial printers, artists, and designers. Some of these color libraries are process color, some spot. They are customarily used with printed swatches that allow you to pick a name from the library and compare it to a specific printed color.

The color-matching systems that ship with FreeHand include Pantone (both process and spot), Trumatch (process), Toyo (spot), DIC (spot), Focoltone (process), and web-safe colors. If you need more information on which color-matching system to use, consult with the print shop that will be printing your work.

FreeHand also supplies two libraries of colors called Crayon and Greys. Neither the Crayon nor the Greys library is part of any standard color-matching system. They are included to give you an easy way to import a range of colors.

To add colors from color-matching system libraries:

1. Choose the name of the color-matching system from the Options pop-up menu.

2. In the Library dialog box, type in the name or code number of the color or click the color you want to add to your Color List **㉚**.

3. Click OK to add the color to the Color List.

TIP If you want to add more than one color, press the Shift key and drag the mouse across the colors.

Once you have created your own list of colors, you can export those colors as your own custom color library.

To export a custom color library:

1. Choose Export from the Options pop-up menu **31**.

2. The Export Colors dialog box appears. Hold down the Shift key to select a continuous range of colors from the Colors panel **32**. Click OK.

3. In the Create color library dialog box, enter the Library name and the File name **33**. The Colors per column and Colors per row fields control how the library will be displayed.

4. Choose Save to place your custom color library in the Color folder located in the FreeHand application folder. Choose Save as to specify a different folder or disk.

TIP To delete custom color libraries from the Options pop-up menu, remove them from the Color folder in the FreeHand application folder.

TIP To have a set of colors appear in all new documents, add those colors to the FreeHand Defaults file. (*To create a new defaults file, see page 256.*)

TIP The FreeHand Xtras commands give you additional ways of working with colors. (*See Chapter 17, "Xtras."*)

31 *To create your own* **custom color library**, *choose Export from the Options pop-up menu.*

32 *Use the Shift key in the* **Export Colors dialog box** *to select the colors to be exported.*

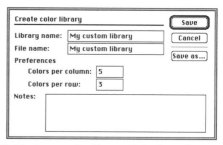

33 *The* **Create color library dialog box** *allows you to group your own colors into a custom library.*

O nce you have created the outline of a path, it is an empty shell waiting to be filled. Adding a fill to an object can change it from ordinary to exciting. FreeHand offers a wealth of choices for fills ranging from a simple basic color fill to sophisticated gradients to special effects using transparency and magnification lenses.

In this chapter, you will learn how to

Choose the fills from the Fill Inspector.

Apply and modify the fill choices: Basic, Gradient, Lens, Tiled, Custom, Textured, Pattern, and PostScript fills.

Use None as a fill.

Use the Overprint option.

In order to apply any of the different types of fills, you need to display the Fill Inspector.

To display the Fill Inspector:

1. Choose **Window > Inspectors > Fill**.

2. The Fill Inspector appears.

Open paths may or may not display the fill settings. The display is controlled by the Preferences. *(See Chapter 22, "Customizing FreeHand.")*

The most common fill is the Basic fill. This is the equivalent of filling the object with a solid color.

To apply a Basic fill using the Fill Inspector:

1. Select the object.

2. With the Fill Inspector displayed, choose Basic from the Fill pop-up menu **❶**.

❶ *Use the* **Fill Inspector pop-up menu** *to display the various fill choices.*

Once you apply a Basic fill, you can change the fill color using the Color List, the Fill Inspector, or by dragging directly onto the object. Use whichever method is most convenient.

To change a fill color using the Color List:

1. Select the object.

2. Make sure that Basic is chosen in the Fill Inspector.

3. Click the Fill drop box in the Color List to make sure it has a black line around it. This indicates that the next step will change the fill color.

4. Click the name of the color you want in the Color List. **❷**.

   or

   Drag a color swatch from the Color Mixer onto the Fill drop box in the Color List **❸**.

   TIP The box next to the Fill drop box controls the stroke color. *(See Chapter 10, "Strokes.")*

To change a fill color using the Fill Inspector:

1. Select the object.

2. Make sure that Basic is chosen in the Fill Inspector.

3. Open the Colors pop-up menu in the Fill Inspector to display the colors currently in the Color List **❹**.

4. Choose one of the colors from the pop-up menu.

   TIP You can also drag a color swatch from the Color Mixer or the Color List directly onto the drop box in the Fill Inspector **❺**.

   TIP If no object is selected, any changes you make to the Fill Inspector or Color List are applied to the next object you create.

Fill drop box selected

❷ *Click the name of the color in the* **Color List** *to apply that color to the fill of the selected object.*

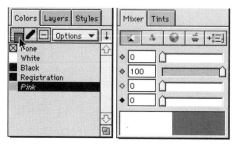

❸ **Colors may be dragged** *from the Color Mixer onto the Fill drop box.*

❹ *Press on the* **Colors pop-up menu** *in the Fill Inspector to change a Basic fill color.*

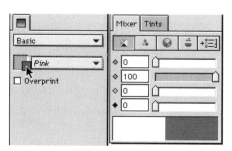

❺ **Colors may be dragged** *from the Color Mixer onto the drop box of the Fill Inspector palette.*

Change Fill Color

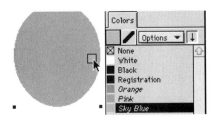

❻ Colors may be dragged *from the Color List directly onto an object.*

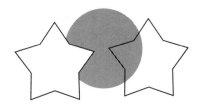

❼ *Selecting a* **fill of None** *lets you see through an object, as seen in the star on the right.*

❽ *The Fill drop box with a fill of None applied.*

To change a fill color by dragging:

Drag a color swatch from the Color Mixer or the Color List directly onto the object **❻**.

TIP You do not have to select an object to drag a color swatch onto it.

TIP Hold the Shift key as you drag the color swatch onto the object to make sure that only the fill color changes.

In addition to the colors, there is another item in the Color List called *None*. While not a color *per se*, the None fill is very important. When you apply the None fill to an object, the fill of the object becomes transparent **❼**.

To change a fill to None:

1. Choose the object you want to become transparent.

2. Make sure the Fill drop box is selected in the Colors panel.

3. Click None in the Color List. An *X* appears in the Fill drop box, indicating that there is no fill **❽**.

TIP Objects with no fill color are invisible unless they have a stroke applied. *(See Chapter 10, "Strokes.")*

Gradient fills start with one color and change into others. The two types of Gradients are linear and radial. In a linear gradient, the colors change along a line that can be angled in any direction. A radial gradient is circular.

To create a linear gradient fill:

1. With the object selected, choose Gradient from the pop-up menu in the Fill Inspector. The settings for the Gradient fills appear ❾.

2. Use one of the Color pop-up menus to choose the color for one end of the linear gradient. (You can also drag colors from the Color List into the Fill drop box in the Colors panel.)

3. Use the other Color pop-up menu to choose the color for the other end of the gradient.

4. Click the Linear icon in the Fill Inspector.

5. Use the Angle field or rotate the wheel to set the angle for the fill.

6. Choose Linear or Logarithmic from the Taper pop-up menu. A linear taper changes in uniform increments from one color to another. A logarithmic taper changes more drastically from one color to another ❿.

Changing the direction of the gradient fills creates the illusion of light reflecting off different surfaces. This creates a 3D effect ⓫.

To create a 3D effect using linear gradients:

1. Create a circle. Fill it with a linear gradient from black to white along a 180° angle with a Linear taper.

2. Create a smaller circle and place it inside the larger one.

3. Fill the smaller circle with a linear gradient from black to white along a 0° angle with a Logarithmic taper.

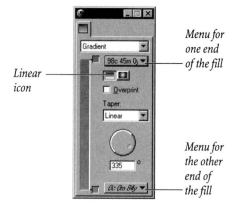

Linear icon

Menu for one end of the fill

Menu for the other end of the fill

❾ *The* **linear gradient settings** *in the Fill Inspector.*

❿ *The difference between a* **Linear fill** *(left) and a* **Logarithmic fill** *(right), both set to 90° angles.*

⓫ **Different angles** *of linear gradients create 3D effects.*

(side margin) Linear Gradient; 3D Effect

⓬ *Hold the Control key as you* **drag a color swatch to apply a linear gradient** *to an object.*

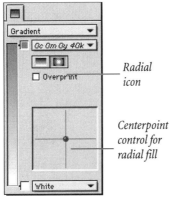

Radial icon

Centerpoint control for radial fill

⓭ *The* **radial gradient settings** *in the Fill Inspector.*

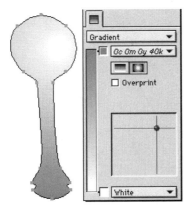

⓮ *Move the* **centerpoint control** *to change the position of the inside color of the Radial gradient.*

FreeHand also lets you apply a linear gradient by dragging a color without using the Fill Inspector and without selecting the object.

To apply a linear gradient by dragging a color:

1. Press the Control key and then drag a color swatch onto an object that has one color already applied as a Basic fill.

2. A linear gradient fills the object with the color of the swatch applied as the second color **⓬**.

TIP Where you drop the swatch determines the angle of the fill.

In a radial gradient, the color starts at a center point and moves outward in a circle. A radial gradient is like a sun radiating colors outward.

To create a radial gradient:

1. With the object selected, choose Gradient from the pop-up menu in the Fill Inspector. The settings for the gradient fills appear **⓭**.

2. Click the Radial icon in the Fill Inspector.

3. Choose the color for the outside of the radial fill by changing the top color.

4. Choose the color for the inside of the radial fill by changing the bottom color.

5. Drag the centerpoint control to change the position of the inside color **⓮**.

Like the linear gradient, the radial gradient can create 3D effects. The key to creating this effect is changing the center of the radial gradient.

To create a 3D effect using radial gradients:

1. Create a circle and fill it with a radial gradient from black outside to white inside.

2. Position the gradient centerpoint in the middle of the object.

3. Create a smaller circle and place it inside the larger one. Fill this circle with a radial gradient from black to white.

4. Position the center of the fill in the upper-left quadrant of the object. The button takes on a 3D appearance **⑮**.

⑮ *Different centers of radial gradients create 3D effects.*

To apply a radial gradient by dragging a color:

1. Press the Option/Alt key and then drag a color swatch onto the object.

2. A radial gradient is applied to the object **⑯**.

TIP The color of the swatch is applied as the inside color of the radial gradient.

TIP Where you drop the swatch determines the center of the radial gradient.

⑯ *Hold the Option/Alt key as you drag a color swatch to apply a radial gradient to an object.*

Gradient fills can contain more than one color.

To add colors to gradient fills:

1. Drag a color swatch onto the gray area between the top and the bottom colors **⑰**. You can drag swatches from the Color List, the Color Mixer, or the color boxes in the Fill Inspector.

2. Drag as many colors as you want.

3. To delete a color, drag the color box off the gray area. (You can not delete the top or bottom color boxes of a gradient fill.)

TIP Alter the spacing between the colors for more dramatic effects.

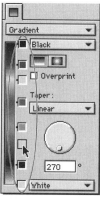

⑰ *To add colors to a gradient, drag a color swatch onto the circled area next to the **gradient ramp**.*

Transparency mode menu

⓲ *The* **Transparency controls** *of the Fill Inspector.*

One of the most dramatic features in FreeHand is the set of lens fills. These allow you to create transparency effects and use one object to magnify others.

To create a transparent lens fill:

1. With the object selected, choose Lens from the pop-up menu in the Fill Inspector.

2. Choose Transparency from the mode pop-up menu ⓲.

3. Choose a color from the color pop-up menu.

4. Use the Opacity slider or the field to set the amount of transparency for the lens ⓳.

5. Click Objects Only to have the effects of the lens seen only on objects, not the page ⓴.

6. Click Snapshot to freeze the lens effect within the object. The object may then be moved to another spot without changing the image within the lens ㉑.

⓳ *Changing the* **Opacity setting** *changes the amount of transparency in a lens.*

⓴ *The* **Objects only** *setting makes the lens work only on objects, not the page area.*

㉑ *The* **Snapshot setting** *freezes the image in the lens so you can move it.*

Transparent Lens Fill

The magnify lens lets one object act as a magnifying glass on whatever objects it covers.

To create a magnify lens fill:

1. With the object selected, choose Lens from the pop-up menu in the Fill Inspector.

2. Choose Magnify from the mode pop-up menu.

3. Use the Magnification slider or the field to set the amount of magnification for the lens **22**.

TIP Magnification can be set from 1 (actual size) to 20 times bigger in whole numbers.

4. The object appears inside the lens as if it were scaled larger **23**.

22 *The* **Magnify controls** *of the Fill Inspector.*

There may be times when you want the lens object to be applied on an area that it is not located over. This is especially helpful for callouts of technical drawings or insets of maps. To accomplish this, use the centerpoint control.

To use the centerpoint control:

1. Position the magnify lens where you want it in your image—do not worry yet about what shows in the lens.

2. Check the Centerpoint box in the Fill Inspector. A centerpoint control appears.

TIP If the centerpoint is not visible, check to see if the object is a group. If so, ungroup it.

3. Drag the centerpoint control to the center of the area you want to be visible within the lens **24**.

23 *A* **Magnify lens** *shows a closer view of an object.*

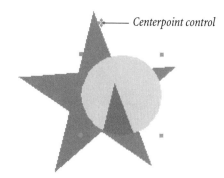

Centerpoint control

24 *Drag the* **centerpoint control** *to focus a lens over a certain area of the artwork.*

⑳ *The **Invert lens** reverses the colors of the objects the lens passes over.*

㉖ *The **Lighten lens** lightens the colors of the objects the lens passes over.*

㉗ *The **Darken lens** darkens the colors of the objects the lens passes over.*

㉘ *The **Monochrome lens** changes the hue of the colors of the objects the lens passes over.*

To use the Invert lens fill:

Choose Invert from the mode pop-up menu to have the lens object invert the colors in the objects it passes over **㉕**. This means that the black objects turn white, the red objects turn green, the yellow objects turn blue, and so on.

To use the Lighten lens fill:

Choose Lighten from the mode pop-up menu to have the lens object lighten the colors in the objects it passes over **㉖**. This is similar to adding white to the colors. Use the slider to increase or decrease the effect.

To use the Darken lens fill:

Choose Darken from the mode pop-up menu to have the lens object darken the colors in the objects it passes over **㉗**. This is similar to adding black to the colors. Use the slider to increase or decrease the effect.

To use the Monochrome lens fill:

Choose Monochrome from the mode pop-up menu to have the lens object convert all the colors in the objects it passes over to a shade of the monochrome object **㉘**.

Working with spot colors

All of the lens effects convert spot colors to process. When you apply the lens effect, an alert box appears with the message that spot colors viewed through a Lens fill are converted to process colors. This means that if you work with spot colors you most likely will not want to apply any of the lens effects. To turn off the warning, check the Don't Show Again box.

You have to create the next kind of fill—called a Tiled fill—by yourself. A more common term for a Tiled fill is pattern.

To create and apply a Tiled fill:

1. Create the artwork you would like to repeat and copy it **29**.
2. Select the object you want to fill with the Tiled fill.
3. Choose Tiled from the Fill Inspector pop-up menu.
4. Click Paste in. The artwork you copied appears in the Tiled preview box **30**. The selected object displays the Tiled fill **31**.

TIP To make the background of the Tiled fill transparent, leave the artwork on an empty area or on a rectangle with no fill.

TIP To give the Tiled fill a white or colored background, place the artwork on a rectangle filled with white or the color. Select the artwork and the rectangle to paste into the Tiled fill box.

TIP The more complex the tiled artwork, the longer it takes for your screen to redraw and for the artwork to print.

TIP Tiled fills cannot contain objects that have Lens fills or Tiled fills applied to them.

TIP Tiled fills cannot contain bitmapped graphics.

29 To create a **Tiled fill**, select and copy the artwork that you would like to turn into a pattern.

30 Click Paste in to transfer the copied artwork into the **Tiled fill settings box**.

31 The object selected displays the Tiled fill.

Tiled Fill

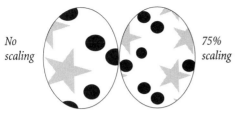

No scaling   *75% scaling*

❷ *The effects of scaling a Tiled fill object.*

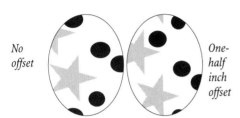

No offset   *One-half inch offset*

❸ *The effects of offsetting a Tiled fill object.*

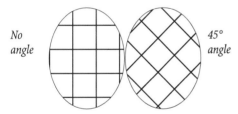

No angle   *45° angle*

❹ *The effects of changing the angle of a Tiled fill object.*

To adjust a Tiled fill:

1. With the Fill Inspector displayed, select the Tiled fill object.

2. To change the size of the Tiled fill **❷**, use the Scale % *x* and *y* fields. To scale the fill uniformly, use the same amounts for both the *x* and *y* fields.

3. To move a Tiled fill within the object **❸**, enter positive or negative values in the Offset *x* and *y* fields.

TIP Positive *x* values in the Offset field move the fill to the right. Negative *x* values in the Offset field move the fill to the left. Positive *y* values in the Offset field move the fill up. Negative *y* values in the Offset field move the fill down.

4. To angle a Tiled fill within the object **❹**, move the angle wheel or enter the exact angle in the Angle field.

Adjust a Tiled Fill

Custom and Textured fills are premade patterns that simulate the look of various textures. After you choose a Custom or Textured fill, you can still make changes to the texture.

To apply a Custom or Textured fill:

1. Select an object and choose Custom or Textured from the pop-up menu in the Fill Inspector .

2. Choose one of the Custom or Textured fills from the second pop-up menu that appears.

3. If applicable, change the color and make any other changes you want to the settings of the fill.

4. Instead of seeing a preview of the fill in the object, you see a series of Cs that fill the object 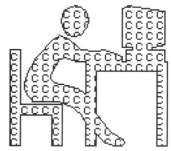. You can only see the fill by printing the artwork .

TIP To see a printout of the Custom and Textured fills, refer to Appendix C.

TIP Custom and Textured fills cannot be scaled with an object and do not print to non-PostScript printers.

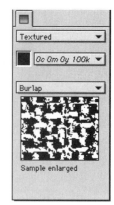

35 *The settings for the* **Custom and Textured fills.**

36 *The* **onscreen representation** *of a Custom or Textured fill.*

37 *The* **print output** *of a Custom or Textured fill displays the proper image.*

③ The **Pattern fill settings** *in the Fill Inspector palette.*

③ *An object filled with a Pattern fill displays and prints that pattern.*

Pattern fills are bitmapped patterns that can be edited pixel by pixel.

To apply a Pattern fill:

1. Select an object and choose Pattern from the Fill Inspector pop-up menu.

2. Use the slider bar to choose one of the Pattern fills from the series of small boxes **③**.

3. Use the large preview box on the left to edit the pattern by clicking on each of the pixels. The large preview box on the right shows what your pattern will look like when applied to the object.

4. Use the Clear button to delete all the dark pixels from the large preview boxes to editing a pattern again.

5. Use the Invert button to change the black pixels into white and vice versa.

TIP Objects behind Pattern fills are not visible through the white spaces of the fills.

6. Use the color drop box to apply any color to the dark pixels of a pattern.

TIP Colors are applied to the solid-color portion of the fill. White areas remain white.

7. The Pattern fills appear the same way onscreen as they will print **③**.

TIP To see printouts of all the Pattern fills, refer to Appendix C.

TIP Pattern fills cannot be transformed with an object.

TIP Pattern fills are designed for use on low-resolution printers, not high-resolution imagesetters and film recorders.

Pattern Fill

To apply a PostScript fill:

When you choose a PostScript fill from the Fill Inspector pop-up menu, you see a large box with the word "fill" in it **40**. The purpose of this box is to allow you to type in specific PostScript code to create a pattern. Learning and working with PostScript code is much too advanced to cover here. If you are interested in working with PostScript in FreeHand, consult *Real World FreeHand* by Olav Martin Kvern (Peachpit Press).

40 *The* **PostScript fill settings** *in the Fill Inspector palette.*

To use the Overprint feature:

If you set an object to Overprint, that object will not knock out any colors below **41**. Instead it will mix the colors. You cannot see overprinting on your screen. Any objects that have an overprint applied will be displayed with a pattern of white *O*s on top **42**. You do not see overprinting in the output of most color printers. You need to make separations of your colors to see where the colors will overprint.

TIP To hide the *O*s in an overprinting object, you can change the Preferences settings (*see page 253*).

TIP If you do not understand overprinting, talk to the print shop that will be printing your artwork before you set anything to overprint.

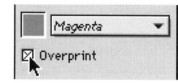

41 *Setting a Basic fill to* **Overprint**.

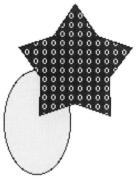

42 *How an overprinting object appears onscreen.*

J ust as fills occupy the inside of objects, strokes surround the outside of objects. In some page layout programs they would be called frames. While there are not as many choices for strokes as there are for fills, there are still quite a few types of effects you can create using strokes—and some effects using strokes can seem like fills.

In this chapter you will learn to

Set the color of a stroke.

Set the width of a stroke.

Set the cap of a stroke.

Set the join of a stroke.

Set the miter limit of the joints.

Apply a dash pattern to a stroke.

Use the Dash Editor.

Apply arrowheads to a stroke.

Use the Arrowhead Editor.

Set Custom, Pattern, and PostScript effects to a stroke.

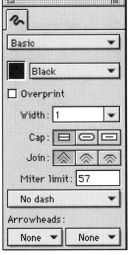

❶ *The **Basic** choices of the **Stroke Inspector**.*

All the strokes in FreeHand are chosen through the Stroke Inspector.

To apply a Basic stroke:

1. Select the object to which you want to apply the stroke.

2. Choose **Window > Inspector > Stroke** to open the Stroke Inspector.

3. Choose Basic from the pop-up menu **❶**.

Once you have applied a Basic stroke, you can change the color. There are five different methods to change the color of a stroke.

Stroke drop box

To change the color of a stroke using the Color List:

1. Select the object using either the Pointer tool or the Lasso tool.

2. Click the Stroke drop box in the Color List ❷.

3. Click the name of the color you wish to change the stroke to in the Color List.

or

Drag a color swatch from the Color List or the Color Mixer onto the Stroke color drop box.

❷ *The highlighted **Stroke drop box** indicates that the box is selected so that any changes in the Color List will apply to the stroke.*

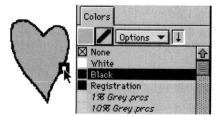

To change the color of a stroke by dragging:

Hold down the Command (Mac) or Ctrl+Shift (Win) keys and drag a color swatch from the Color List or Color Mixer onto the object. The cursor will change to a box, indicating that only the stroke will be affected ❸.

❸ *Hold the **Command (Mac)** or **Ctrl+Shift (Win)** keys while dragging a **color swatch** onto an object to change its stroke color.*

To change the color of a stroke using the Stroke Inspector:

Use the Colors pop-up menu in the Stroke Inspector. Choose from the list of colors ❹.

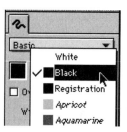

To change the color of a stroke using the Eyedropper tool:

1. Select the Eyedropper tool from the Toolbox.

2. Click on a color somewhere in the document and drag it onto the path you want to modify.

3. Hold down the Command (Mac) or Ctrl+Shift (Win) keys. The cursor turns into a box indicating that only the stroke will be affected.

4. Release the mouse button to change the stroke color before releasing the Command (Mac) or Ctrl+Shift (Win) keys.

❹ *Open the **Colors** pop-up menu in the **Stroke Inspector** to choose a stroke color.*

Change the Color of a Stroke

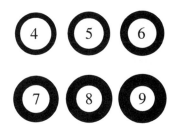

⑤ *Changing the **Width** value changes the thickness of the stroke. These circles were drawn to the same size but have stroke widths ranging from 4 through 9 points.*

⑥ *The three different **Cap** choices: **Butt** (top), **Round** (middle), and **Square** (bottom). The difference between the Butt and Square is that the Square extends out beyond the anchor points.*

Once you have applied a stroke, you can change the *width* ⑤, or how thick that stroke appears.

To change the width of a stroke:

1. Select the object you want to change.

2. Open the Stroke Inspector. It should show that the Basic stroke is applied.

3. In the Width field, type the value (in the unit of measure chosen for the document) for the thickness for your stroke.

   or

   Choose a value in points from the pop-up menu next to the field.

4. Press Return or Enter or click anywhere on the Stroke Inspector to implement a value you have typed into the field.

TIP You can specify stroke widths in any units using letter codes. *(See page 6.)*

TIP The width of a stroke is applied to both the inside and outside of the path.

TIP You can change the width of a stroke using the keystrokes listed in Appendix B.

The Cap of the stroke is the end of the stroke. Changing the Cap of a stroked object affects only open paths because they are the only ones with end points.

To apply a cap to a stroke:

1. Select an open path. In order to see the effects of changing the cap, choose a thick width, such as 24 points ⑥.

   The default cap is the Butt cap. This cap means that the stroke stops exactly on the endpoint of the path.

2. Click the Round cap icon to make the stroke extend past the endpoints in a curved shape.

3. Click the Square cap icon to make the stroke extend past the endpoints in a square shape.

Next you will choose how the joints of the stroke will be treated. This is called the *join*.

To change the join of a stroke:

1. Select a path with at least one corner point or connector point. In order to see the effects of changing the join, choose a thick width.

2. In the Stroke Inspector, click the Miter icon ❼ to control the *V* where the line segments intersect. The sharper the angle, the longer the strokes extend.

3. Click the Round join icon ❽ to form a curve between the two line segments.

4. Click the Bevel join icon ❽ to cut the stroke in a line between the segments.

TIP The Round join with the Round cap creates a look similar to a marker pen. (*See the middle example in* ❼.)

The next choice you have is the miter limit. Changing the miter limit of a stroked object prevents joins with very steep angles from becoming too spikey.

To change the miter limit:

1. Select a path with a miter join. In order to see the effects of changing the miter limit, choose a rather thick width such as 24 points and create two line segments with a very acute angle between them. If the miter limit is high, it should look like a spike ❽.

2. In the Stroke Inspector, lower the miter limit to 1 or 2 and notice how you have eliminated the spike between the two segments ❽.

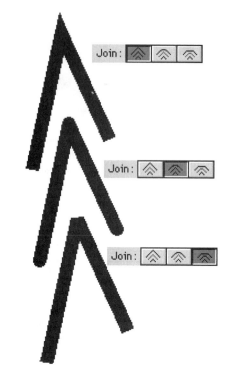

❼ *The three* **Join** *choices:* **Miter** *(top),* **Round** *(middle), and* **Bevel** *(bottom).*

❽ *A* **miter limit** *of 7 (left) allows a spike between line segments. A low miter limit (right) cuts the spike off into a Bevel join.*

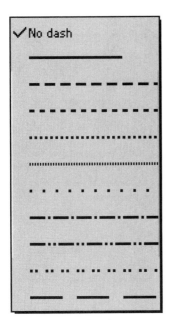

*The default pop-up list of **Dash** patterns.*

Now you'll choose the dash pattern of the stroke. Both open and closed paths, with any kinds of points, can have dash patterns applied to them.

To apply a dash pattern:

1. Select a path. In order to see the effects of changing the dash, choose a rather thick width such as 24 points. Choose a Butt cap.

2. In the Stroke Inspector, use the Dash pop-up menu to choose from the default list of premade dash patterns ❾.

TIP The spaces between the dashes of a stroke are transparent, not white. If you lay your dashed stroke over another object, you will see through the spaces to that other object.

You may want to create your own dash patterns for strokes. You do that by using the Dash Editor dialog box.

To edit a dash pattern:

1. With the Stroke Inspector displayed, hold down the Option/Alt key as you click to select one of the dash patterns from the Basic stroke settings. The Dash Editor dialog box appears ❿.

2. Set the length of the visible portion of the dash by entering a number in the On field.

3. Set the length of the space between the dashes by entering a number in the Off field.

4. You can enter up to four different sets of On and Off values.

5. When you have finished entering the pattern, click OK. The dash pattern you created is added to the bottom of the dash list. You do not eliminate the original pattern when you add your own.

❿ *The **Dash Editor** dialog box lets you enter your own dash patterns. Choose up to four sets of On and Off patterns.*

With just a little experience you can create very sophisticated effects using dashes.

To create a multicolored dash:

1. Create a line with the Basic stroke you want. Use a fairly thick stroke, such as 12 points, with no dash.

2. Choose **Edit > Clone**. This makes a copy of that line on top of your original line.

3. Choose a smaller width and add a contrasting color for the clone. Choose a dash pattern that creates large spaces in the cloned line. You now have a dashed line with two colors **⑪**.

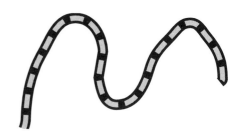

⑪ *To create multicolored dashed lines, use two or more stacked lines. This effect uses a bottom, solid black line and a top dashed line stroked with a lighter color and with a smaller stroke width.*

The last choice for Basic strokes is arrowheads. You can see arrowheads only on open paths. A closed path to which arrowheads have been applied shows them only when the path is opened.

To apply arrowheads:

1. Select a path with a Basic stroke set for a thick width.

TIP Arrowheads take their size from the point size of the stroke.

2. Display the Stroke Inspector with its two Arrowheads pop-up menus **⑫**. The left menu controls arrowheads for the start of the path, the right menu for the end of the path.

3. Using the appropriate menu, choose an arrowhead you like.

To create new arrowheads:

1. Open either Arrowheads pop-up menu and choose New. The Arrowhead Editor dialog box appears **⑬**.

2. Use any of the Arrowhead Editor tools to draw the arrowhead.

3. When you are satisfied with the results of your work, click New. The arrowhead you created appears as a new item at the end of both arrowhead menus.

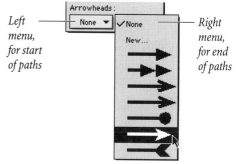

⑫ *The **Arrowheads** pop-up menu lets you add arrowheads to open paths made with Basic strokes.*

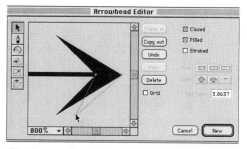

⑬ *The **Arrowhead Editor** dialog box lets you modify the program's arrowheads or create your own custom arrowheads.*

Multicolored Dash; Arrowheads

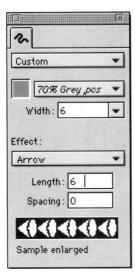

⑭ *Choose **Custom** from the **Stroke** icon section of the **Stroke Inspector** palette to see the settings for the Custom strokes.*

To edit arrowheads:

1. Hold down the Option/Alt key as you select one of the arrowheads from the pop-up menu.

2. In the Arrowhead Editor that appears, modify the arrowhead.

3. Click New to complete your edit.

TIP Use the Paste in and Copy out buttons to transfer arrowheads between the Arrowhead Editor and the work page. This allows you to use all the FreeHand tools to create arrowheads.

Just as there are Custom fills, FreeHand provides Custom stroke patterns.

TIP Custom strokes do not display onscreen. To see all the default Custom strokes, see Appendix C.

To apply a custom stroke pattern:

1. Choose Custom from the Stroke pop-up menu of the Stroke Inspector **⑭**.

2. Choose a stroke effect from the Effect pop-up menu.

3. Choose the color and width for your stroke.

4. Set the Length field to control the size of the repeating element in the stroke.

5. Set the Spacing field to control the space between each repeating element.

TIP The Length and Spacing fields are in the unit of measurement for the document, but you can override this by specifying another unit.

TIP You can also use the blend on a path (*see Chapter 11, "Blends"*) to create similar effects.

Pattern strokes are bitmapped patterns that can be edited pixel by pixel.

TIP To see all the default Pattern strokes, see Appendix C.

To apply a pattern stroke:

1. Select the object and choose Pattern from the Stroke Inspector.

2. Use the slider bar at the bottom of the palette to choose one of the Pattern strokes **⑮**.

3. Use the preview box to edit the pattern by clicking each pixel you want to turn on or off.

4. Use the Clear button to clear all the pixels from the preview boxes.

5. Use the Invert button to change the black pixels into white pixels and vice versa.

6. Use the color drop box to apply a color to the dark pixels.

TIP Pattern strokes are designed for use on low-resolution printers (including non-PostScript devices).

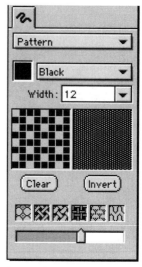

⑮ *The **Pattern** stroke settings in the **Stroke Inspector** palette.*

PostScript strokes

When you choose a PostScript stroke from the Stroke Inspector pop-up menu, you will see a large box with the word *stroke* in it **⑯**. This box is where you can type in a specific PostScript code to create a pattern. Learning and working with PostScript code is much too advanced to cover here. If you are interested in working with PostScript in FreeHand, consult *Real World FreeHand* by Olav Martin Kvern (Peachpit Press).

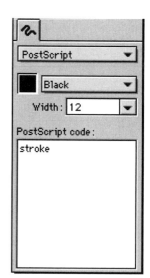

⑯ *The **PostScript** stroke settings in the **Stroke Inspector**.*

BLENDS

B lends are one of the most sophisticated features of FreeHand. With blends, you can create subtle shadings and contours, dramatic changes of shape, 3D looks, special stroke effects, and many other looks.

In this chapter, you will learn how to

Understand the difference between blends and gradients.

Use blends for more than just color changes.

Create blends.

Set the number of steps in a blend.

Modify existing blends.

Align blends to paths.

Follow the rules of working with blends.

View blends optimally onscreen.

Make sure blends print correctly.

❶ *A blend with* **hundreds of steps** *(left) and the same blend with only a* **few steps** *(right).*

❷ *Two shapes with* **a linear gradient fill** *(left) and* **radial gradient fill** *(right).*

❸ *The same shapes with* **blends.**

Blends create the effect of one object turning into another. When you see an object that seems to change into another object, what you are actually seeing is hundreds of intermediate steps in which the object has been reshaped ever so slightly ❶.

If all you want to do is make an object change from one color to another, then all you need is a linear gradient fill or radial gradient fill ❷. (*For more information on gradient fills, see Chapter 9, "Fills."*) But if you would like the object to transform into another shape during the color change, then you need to use blends ❸.

113

While there are thousands of different effects you can create with blends, they all start with the same basic blend command.

To create a simple blend:

1. Start with a simple shape such as an oval or a rectangle. Fill this object with a dark color.

2. Create a second shape such as a star or a triangle. Fill this object with a lighter color or white.

3. Create a third shape. Fill this object with a dark color **❹**.

4. Select all three objects.

5. Choose **Modify > Combine > Blend**. The three objects blend together **❺**

TIP Blends are always created in straight lines between the objects. To make a blend follow a curve, see the section later in this chapter on aligning blends to a path.

TIP You can use blends to create intermediate steps where both the stroke width and the stroke shape change **❻**.

❹ *To create a* **simple blend,** *select two or more objects.*

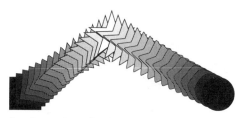

❺ *After applying the* **Blend command,** *the objects are blended with intermediate steps.*

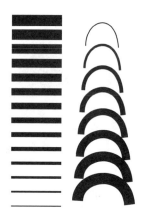

❻ *Using blends to* **change the width and shape of stroked objects.**

❼ An **automatic blend** *between two objects with no points selected.*

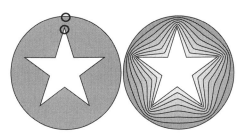

❽ A **custom blend** *between two objects created by selecting two points (circled).*

❾ A **custom blend** *created by selecting two different points (circled).*

You may find your blends do not look as smooth as you would like or that the objects do not change in the manner you expect. This is because FreeHand automatically calculates the blend using the points from which it wants to blend **❼**. You can create a custom blend by forcing FreeHand to use specific points for the blend.

To create a custom blend:

1. Use the Pointer tool to select a point on the first of the objects from which you want the blend to begin.

2. Hold the Shift key to select a point on the second object.

3. Continue to select additional points on each of the objects in the blend.

4. Choose **Modify > Combine > Blend.** The intermediate steps of the blend are created by creating shapes between the selected points **❽–❾**.

TIP To make blends as smooth as possible, pick points on each object that are in equivalent positions.

TIP To select points on ellipses or rectangles, first change them to paths by selecting **Modify > Alter Path > Correct Direction** (or Reverse Direction or Remove Overlap).

Custom Blend

Blends are actually special groups. You may want to unblend your objects. This is as simple as ungrouping them.

To ungroup a blend:

1. With the blend selected, choose **Modify > Ungroup**.
2. The original objects of the blend are selected along with the intermediate steps.
3. The intermediate steps can then be selected as a group and deleted or modified **10**.

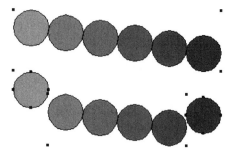

10 *The top blend was* **ungrouped** *to create the bottom objects: the original two objects and the intermediate steps, which are grouped.*

Once you have a blend, you may want to change the number of steps. You might want to make the blend as smooth as possible or modify it to show the intermediate steps.

To change the number of steps in a blend:

1. With the blend selected, open the Object Inspector **11**.
2. Enter the number of steps you want in the Number of steps field.
3. Press Return. The blend reforms with the new number of steps.

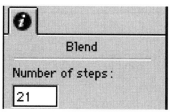

11 *In the* **Number of steps** *field, type the number of steps you want between the original objects in the blend.*

To change the number of blend steps in a document:

FreeHand calculates the number of steps in a blend from the Printer resolution in the Document Inspector (*see page 7*). Higher resolutions give you a greater number of steps. Changing the resolution changes the number of steps for new blends. Blends made before you changed the Printer resolution do not change. If you change the resolution of your document, you may need to change the number of steps in blends that were created previously.

TIP Use the Find & Replace Graphics dialog box to find all blends with a certain number of steps and change them to a different number of steps (*see pages 162 and 163*).

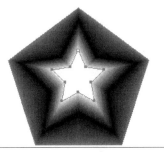

⑫ *To* **modify an object in a blend**, *hold the Option/Alt key and select one of the original objects in the blend.*

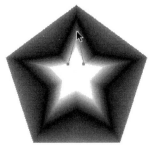

⑬ *Make whatever changes you want to the object.*

⑭ *The blend automatically redraws.*

Once you have created a blend, you can still make changes to any of the original objects of the blend. This is called Live Blends.

To modify a blend shape:

1. Hold the Option/Alt key and select one of the original objects of the blend **⑫**.
2. Make any changes to specific points on the object or move the object into a new position **⑬**.
3. The blend automatically redraws when you release the mouse button **⑭**.

To modify a blend color by dragging:

1. Drag one of the swatches from the Color List onto one of the original objects of the blend.
2. The blend automatically redraws when you release the mouse button.

To modify a blend color from the Color List:

1. Hold the Option/Alt key and select one of the original objects of the blend **⑫**.
2. Open the Color List.
3. Change the color of the stroke and or the fill by dragging color swatches to the drop boxes or by selecting the boxes and clicking on the color names.

Modify Shape; Modify Color

Once you have created a blend, you can then align the blend to a path. This feature allows you to create all sorts of effects, the most exciting of which is the ability to create your own custom stroke effects (*see pages 110–112*).

To align a blend to a path:

1. Create a blend and a path. Select both the blend and the path ⓯.

2. Choose **Modify > Combine > Join Blend to Path**.

3. The blend automatically aligns to the shape of the path ⓰.

4. To see the path, click Show path in the Object Inspector ⓱.

5. To change the orientation of the objects in the blend, click Rotate on path in the Inspector palette ⓲.

To release a blend from a path:

1. Select a blend that has been aligned to a path.

2. Choose **Modify > Split**.

3. The blend separates from the path ⓳.

TIP Blends that have been aligned on a path can still be modified using the principles of Live Blends (*see the previous page*).

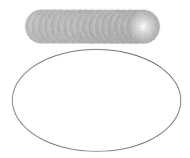

⓯ *To* **align a blend to a path**, *select the blend and the path to which you want to align it.*

⓰ *The results of aligning a blend to a path.*

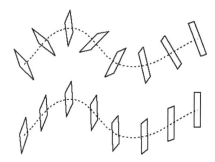

⓱ *The* **Show path and Rotate on path** *boxes control whether the path on which the blend is aligned is shown and whether the axes of the shapes rotate as they follow the path.*

⓲ *A blend with* **Rotate on path** *selected (top) and unselected (bottom).*

⓳ *The results of using the Split command to* **release a blend from a path.**

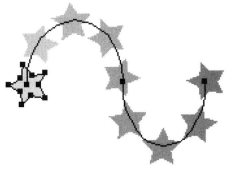

⓴ *Hold the Option/Alt key to* **select the original objects** *in a blend.*

To select objects blended along a path:

1. Hold down the Option/Alt key and select one of the original objects of the blend **⓴**.

2. Hold down the Option/Alt and Shift keys to select additional objects.

3. Hold down the Shift key to deselect any objects.

4. Make any changes to the selected objects.

To view blends:

Once you have a blend, you may find that you do not like the way it looks onscreen. This is a function of the screen display. If you want to see your blend with a smoother display, you can change the Preferences settings (*see page 253*).

You can also change the way blends appear on screen by choosing the Fast Preview and Fast Keyline modes (*see pages 13–14*).

The rules of blends

There are limitations to which objects can be used in a blend. The blend command does not work in the following instances:

- You cannot blend between paths that have different types of strokes or fill.

- Pattern fills do not blend; they switch abruptly from one to the other.

- Texture and custom fills must be identical at both ends of the blend.

- Blends between more than two objects follow the order in which the objects are layered.

- Blends between two spot colors must remain grouped in order to mix as spot colors.

- You cannot blend between objects that have lens fills.

- Blends cannot be made between radial and linear gradient fills.

If you are printing to a low-resolution device such as a laser printer, you may not be satisfied with the printout of the blend. That is because those printers cannot reproduce all the tones necessary to create a smooth blend.

If you are printing on a high-resolution device such as an imagesetter, your blend should print smoothly. However, sometimes blends produce an effect called *banding* **㉑**. The following may help you avoid banding when printing on PostScript devices. (*For more information on printing, see Chapter 21, "Printing."*)

To avoid banding in blends when printing:

- Print at high resolutions. For most work, this is a minimum of 2400 dpi.

- If you have banding, use a lower screen ruling. This is especially helpful when printing to laser printers.

- Avoid blends over 7 inches long. This is especially true if you are outputting to a PostScript Level 1 device. If you are outputting to a PostScript Level 2 device, you may not need to limit the length of your blends.

- Examine the difference between the percentages of each of the CMYK colors. If you are getting banding, try increasing the difference between the percentages.

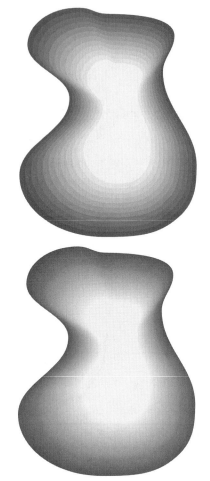

㉑ *A blend with* **banding** *(top). The same blend with* **more steps used to decrease the banding** *(bottom).*

BASIC TEXT 12

M ost people think of FreeHand as a program for creating graphics, but it also provides a wealth of page layout features for working with text.

In this chapter, you will learn how to

Create text blocks.

Use standard and auto-expanding text blocks.

Change the size of text blocks.

Use the link box.

Apply borders to text blocks.

Place text blocks precisely.

Import text.

Format character attributes.

Format paragraph attributes.

Use indents, tabs, text rulers, columns, and rows to create paragraph effects.

Turn on and control hyphenation.

Set tabs and align text.

Link text from one object or page to another.

Use the Copyfit controls.

FreeHand uses two basic types of text block. A standard text block is a fixed-size container. As you type, the block fills from the top and automatically wraps to the next line until it reaches the bottom. Any further typing is not displayed, but the link box at the lower-right corner gets filled in to indicate the overflow.

Auto-expanding text blocks never fill up. If the horizontal control is set to auto-expand, the line just keeps growing until you type either Return or Shift-Return. If only the vertical auto-expand feature is selected, your text block keeps getting taller to fit your text which wraps to stay within the fixed width of the block.

Standard and Auto-expanding Text Blocks

To create a standard text block:

1. Select the Text tool ❶ from the Toolbox and drag across your work page. How far you drag determines the size of the text block.

2. Release the mouse button to see the text block and the text ruler ❷.

3. Start typing. Your text fills the text block. You do not have to press Return at the end of a line. The text automatically wraps within the text block.

TIP If you do not see the text ruler, choose **View > Text Rulers**.

To create an auto-expanding text block:

1. Select the Text tool from the Toolbox and click anywhere on your page. You will see a blinking insertion point and a text ruler.

2. Start typing and you will see your text. Your text does not automatically wrap within the text block. If you want the text to shift to the next line, press Return or Shift-Return. If your text does wrap within the box, check your Preferences settings for auto-expansion of text blocks (*see page 249*).

Once you have created a text block, you may want to change its size. You use different techniques for doing this depending on how the auto-expansion feature is set.

To change the auto-expansion settings:

1. With the text block selected, click the Object Inspector.

2. Click to change the expansion icons. If the icon is light, the field is not set for auto-expansion ❸. If the icon is dark, the field is set for auto-expansion as new text is entered ❹.

3. When auto-expansion is off, you can drag to resize the text block or enter new measurements in the width and height fields.

❶ *The* **Text tool** *in the Toolbox.*

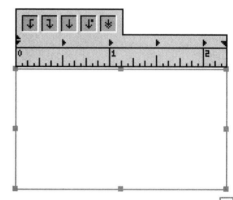

❷ *A* **text block** *with a* **text ruler.**

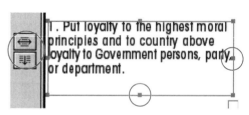

❸ *When the expansion icons are light (circled at left) or when the side handles are dark (circled), the field is* **unlocked and auto-expansion is off.**

❹ *When the expansion icons are dark (circled at left) or when the side handles are white (circled), the field is* **locked and auto-expansion is on.**

1. Put loyalty to the highest moral principles and to country above loyalty to Government persons, party, or department.

❺ *To manually* **change the size of a text block,** *drag one of the corner points of the block.*

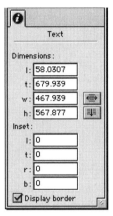

❻ *When a text block is selected, you can change its dimensions numerically in the Object Inspector.*

1. Put loyalty to the highest moral principles and to country above loyalty to Government persons, party, or department.

1. Put loyalty to the highest moral principles and to country above loyalty to Government persons, party, or

1. Put loyalty to the highest moral principles and to country above loyalty to Government persons, party, or

❼ *An* **open link box** *(top) indicates that all the text is visible in the text block. A* **circle in the link box** *(middle) indicates an overflow.* **Two arrows** *(bottom) show that the text is continued in another text block to which it is linked.*

To change the size of a standard text block:

Use the Selection tool and drag one of the corner points of the text block **❺**.

or

With the text block selected, click the Object Inspector. Under Dimensions, change the measurements in the **w** (width) or **h** (height) fields **❻**.

TIP Set the height of a text block for auto-expansion but keep auto-expansion turned off for the width to create a column of text.

TIP A shortcut for making text blocks with a fixed width but changeable height (Mac): Hold down the Control key as you drag horizontally to create the text block.

TIP A shortcut for making text blocks with a fixed height but changeable width (Mac): Hold down the Control key as you drag vertically to create the text block.

The little square at the bottom of the text block is called the Link box. The different states for the Link box convey important information about the text.

To recognize the status of the Link box:

• If the Link box is white, then all the text in the block is visible.

• If there is a black circle inside the Link box, it means there is more text than can fit inside the text block **❼**. This is called an overflow.

• If there are left and right arrows inside the Link box, it means the text block has been linked to another object (*see page 136*).

Another way to resize a text block is to shrink the block to fit the size of the text.

To automatically shrink a text block:

1. Select a text block that has extra space not filled by text.

2. Using the Selection tool, double-click the Link box of the block ❽. The text block automatically shrinks to fit the text.

TIP If there is no text in a text block, double-clicking the Link box deletes the text block.

Just as in a page layout program, FreeHand lets you stroke or frame the outside border of a text block.

To apply a border to a text block:

1. Select the text block that needs a border.

2. Click the Object Inspector.

3. Click the Display border box ❾. This allows you to see the border, but it does not create the line.

4. To apply a border, choose the Stroke Inspector.

5. Apply a stroke using any of the stroke styles. The border appears around the text block ❿.

Once you have given a text block a border, you will probably want to inset the text to add some white space between the text and the border.

To inset text:

1. Select the text block.

2. Choose the Object Inspector.

3. Under Inset ⓫, enter the amounts you would like to move the text in the *l* (left), *t* (top), *r* (right), and *b* (bottom) fields. Press Return or Enter to set the amounts and check to make sure you like the results ⓬.

TIP Negative values make the text lap over the borders of the block.

❽ *Double-clicking the Link box (circled) shrinks a text box with extra space (top) to the actual size of the text (bottom).*

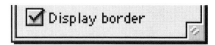

❾ *The **Display border box** of the Object Inspector controls if a stroke or border is visible around a text block.*

❿ *The Stroke Inspector applies the actual border to a text block. In this case a dashed line was applied to the text block.*

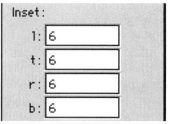

⓫ *The **Inset fields** set text away from the edges of a text block. The amount listed is in the unit of measurement for the document.*

```
┌─────────────────────────────┐
│ Amendment III               │
│ No Soldier shall, in time of peace │
│ be quartered in any house, without │
│ the consent of the Owner, nor in │
│ time of war, but in a manner to be │
│ prescribed by law.          │
└─────────────────────────────┘
```

12 *This text is set away from the border by 6 points to make the text more legible.*

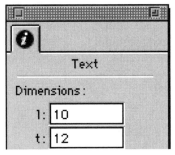

13 *The* **Dimensions fields** *let you move a text block to a specific position.*

CODE OF ETHICS

FOR GOVERNMENT SERVICE

Any person in Government service should:

1. Put loyalty to the highest moral principles and to country above loyalty to Government persons, party, or department.

CODE OF ETHICS
FOR GOVERNMENT SERVICE
Any person in Government service should:
1. Put loyalty to the highest moral principles and to country above loyalty to Government persons, party, or department.

14 *Text in the RTF format (top) imports with all its formatting and styling. The same text in the ASCII format (bottom) imports only the characters and takes its typeface from the default typeface for the document.*

You can move a text block by dragging, or you can move it numerically to a precise position.

To position a text block numerically:

1. Select the text block.
2. Choose the Object Inspector.
3. Under Dimensions, enter the coordinate you want for the left edge of the text block in the *l* field.
4. Under Dimensions, enter the coordinate you want for the top edge of the text block in the *t* field. Press Return or Enter **13**.

TIP Unless you have changed the zero point of the rulers, your page origin is at the bottom-left corner.

If you are working with long documents, you ought to import the text from a word processing program rather than typing it in FreeHand. To prepare text for exporting, in the word processor save your work in one of two formats **14**.

RTF Text (rich text format), which keeps the text formatting.

ASCII (pronounced As-kee), which keeps only the characters without any formatting.

To import text:

1. Choose **File > Import** and choose the text file you want to import. Your cursor changes into a corner symbol.
2. Position the corner symbol where you want your text to start.
3. If you want your text block to be a certain size on the page, drag the corner symbol to create a rectangle the size you want the text block to be.

   or

   If you just want the text on the page, click and watch as the text block is created and filled with text.

Position Numerically; Import Text

FreeHand gives you several places to change character attributes; two are the Text menu and the Text toolbar.

TIP You can also modify text by making selections from the Font, Size, Style, Effect, Align, Leading, and Convert Case submenus under the Text menu.

⓯ *The* **Text Toolbar.**

To change character attributes using the toolbar:

1. Select the text by dragging across it with a the Text tool. (If you format without selecting any text, any text you type afterwards will be styled accordingly.)

2. To change the font, size, type style, or leading choose those items from the Text toolbar **⓯** and make the changes.

⓰ *The* **Text Inspector** *has five subdivisions. From left to right: character, paragraph, spacing, rows and columns, and copyfitting.*

To change character attributes using the Inspector:

1. Select the text by dragging across it with a the Text tool. (If you format without selecting any text, any text you type afterwards will be styled accordingly.)

2. Select the Text Inspector **⓰** and change the font, type style, size, leading, kerning, baseline shift, or text effect.

TIP Type size is always measured in points, regardless of which unit of measurement has been selected for the document.

TIP The Text toolbar can be set to adhere to the edge of your screen or float as a panel. You can also change which items appear in the toolbar (*see page 254*).

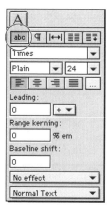

⓱ *Press the* **Character icon** *in the Text Inspector to see the various character attributes.*

Left   Centered   Right   Justified

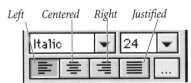

⓲ *The **four alignment icons**.*

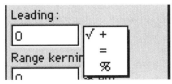

⓳ *The Leading pop-up menu.*

⓴ *A **Kerning** value of -10.5 has been applied to the letters **T** and **r** in the bottom word, decreasing the separation between the letters.*

㉑ *A Range kerning value of 15 has been applied to the letters **U**, **S**, and **A** in the bottom initials.*

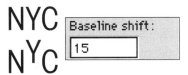

㉒ *A baseline shift of 15 has been applied to the letter **Y**, moving it higher than the other letters.*

To change character attributes:

1. Select the text you want to change by either selecting the entire text block or dragging to select a portion of the text within a block.

2. To change the typeface, use the font, style, and point size pop-up menus.
   or
   Drag across the field and type in the name or point size desired.

3. Click the character icon in the Text Inspector **⓱** and choose the alignment from the four Alignment icons **⓲**.

4. Press on the pop-up menu to choose one of the leading (line-spacing) options: +, = or % **⓳**. The + sign adds space between the lines in addition to the space used by the characters. The = sign sets an amount of space that does not change if the text size changes. The % sign adds an amount of space that is a percentage of the point size of the text.

5. If your insertion point is between two letters, enter a value in the Kerning field. Positive values increase the space between the letters. Negative values decrease the space **⓴**.

6. If you select more than two characters, you can enter a value in the Range kerning field and change the spacing between all the selected letters **㉑**.

7. Enter an amount in the Baseline shift field. Positive values raise the text above the normal baseline for the text. Negative values lower the text **㉒**.

TIP Drag the top or bottom middle handles of a text block to increase or decrease the leading of an entire text block.

TIP Drag the left or right middle handles to increase or decrease the Range kerning of an entire text block.

TIP Hold down the Option/Alt key as you drag the left or right middle handles of a text block to increase the Range kerning between words.

The Spacing subpanel contains controls for character scaling, spacing, and grouping.

To change the horizontal scaling of the typeface:

1. Select the text that you want to change, choose the Text Inspector, and then click the Spacing icon **㉓**.

2. Enter the amount you want to horizontally scale the text in the Horizontal scale field **㉔**.

TIP Hold down the Option/Alt key and drag a corner handle to change the horizontal scale of all the text in a text block.

TIP Extreme amounts of horizontal scaling are unacceptable to professional typographers. If you need condensed or expanded type, you should use a typeface that is designed that way.

The horizontal spacing values control the entire paragraph for which they are specified.

To change the horizontal spacing in a type block:

1. Select the paragraphs you want to change. If you want to change only one paragraph, it is enough to put the cursor anywhere within it.

2. Enter the percentage values you want for both word and letter spacing in the fields in the spacing subpanel.

These values affect not only the spacing between words and letters, but how words break at the end of a line **㉕**.

㉓ *Press the* **Spacing icon of the Text Inspector** *to see the Horizontal scale, Spacing, and Keep together controls.*

JULY 4
JULY 4

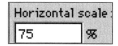

㉔ *A* **Horizontal scale** *value of 75% has been applied to the text, distorting the characters.*

1. Put loyalty to the highest moral principles and to country above

1. Put loyalty to the highest moral principles and to country

㉕ *Changing the values for Spacing % in the Text Inspector adds space between letters and words.*

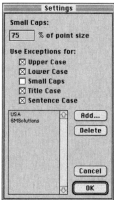

㉖ *The* **Settings** *dialog box.*

CODE OF ETHICS —— *Upper*
code of ethics —————— *Lower*
CODE OF ETHICS ——— *Small Caps*
Code Of Ethics ——— *Title*
Code of ethics———— *Sentence*

㉗ *Text changed using the Convert Case command.*

㉘ *Click the* **paragraph icon of the Text Inspector** *to see the various paragraph attributes.*

> Put loyalty to the highest moral principals and to country above loyalty to Government persons, party, or department.

㉙ *A* **First line indent** *of 8 points.*

> Put loyalty to the highest moral principals and to country above loyalty to Government persons, party, or department.

㉚ *A* **Left margin indent** *of 8 points.*

> Put loyalty to the highest moral principals and to country above loyalty to Government persons, party, or department.

㉛ **Left and Right margin indents** *of 8 points.*

> • Put loyalty to the highest moral principals and to country above loyalty to Government persons, party, or department.

㉜ **Left and Right margin indents** *of 8 points with a First line indent of −8 points to place the bullet in the margin.*

Once you have text on your page, you may want to convert the case from upper to lower, etc. FreeHand has several sophisticated Convert Case commands.

To use the Convert Case commands:

1. Choose **Text > Convert Case > Settings** to open the **Settings** dialog box **㉖**.

2. Set the percentage of point size for the Small Caps to whatever amount you want the text reduced for Small Caps.

3. Click Add to add entries to the Exceptions list. This allows you to set words that do not change even if a Convert Case command is applied.

4. Select the text to be converted and then choose **Text > Convert Case > Upper** (or **Lower/Small Caps/Title/Sentence**). The text is converted **㉗**.

TIP The Small Caps command changes the point size of the letters to approximate the look of a small caps font.

Once you have text inside a text block, you can format its paragraph attributes.

To change paragraph attributes:

1. Select the paragraph or paragraphs that you want to change. Choose the Text Inspector and then click the paragraph icon **㉘**.

2. To add space above or below the paragraph, enter the amount of space you want under Paragraph spacing in the Above or Below fields.

TIP The unit of measurement is the same as the document's unit of measurement. However, you can enter the amount in a different unit of measurement by adding the proper suffix (*see page 6*).

3. To change the margin indents, enter the values in the Left, Right, or First fields **㉙–㉜**.

FreeHand also lets you use the text ruler to set the margin indents **33**.

To change margin indents using the text ruler:

1. Double-click the text block you wish to modify.

2. If the text ruler is not visible, choose **View > Text Rulers**.

3. Click in the paragraph you want to change. The insertion point will be in the paragraph.

4. Drag the bottom part of the left indent triangle to the spot on the ruler where you want the left margin.

5. Drag the right indent triangle to the spot on the ruler where you want the right margin.

6. Drag the top part of the left indent triangle to the spot on the ruler where you want the first line of the paragraph.

To create hanging punctuation:

If you want your punctuation to *hang* outside the margins, click Hang punctuation in the paragraph attributes of the Text Inspector. This keeps paragraphs from looking ragged **34**.

TIP Ordinarily hanging punctuation is used only for display text such as headlines and book titles. However, it can be found in the body copy for advertising and other specialized text designs.

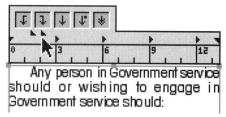

33 *Dragging the* **indent triangles** *of the text ruler allows you to change margin indents.*

"We hold these truths to be self-evident, that all men are created equal, that they are endowed by their Creator with certain unalienable Rights, that among these are Life, Liberty and the pursuit of Happiness."

"That to secure these rights, Governments are instituted among Men, deriving their just powers from the consent of the governed."

34 *An example of* **hanging punctuation.** *Notice how the quotation marks float outside the margins of the paragraph.*

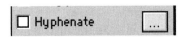

③⑤ *The* **Hyphenate box.**

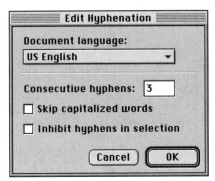

③⑥ *The* **Edit Hyphenation dialog box.**

Put loyalty to the highest moral principles and to country above loyalty to Government persons, party, or department. Uphold the Constitution, laws, and legal regulations of the Unit- ed States and of all governments therein and never be a party to their evasion. Give a full day's labor for a full day's pay; giving to the performance of his duties his earnest effort and best

③⑦ *An example of* **hyphenated text.**

To use automatic hyphenation:

1. Select the text to be hyphenated by selecting the entire text block or dragging to select specific paragraphs within the text block.

2. Choose the paragraph icon of the Text Inspector.

3. To turn hyphenation on, click so that an "x" appears in the Hyphenate box **③⑤**. To turn hyphenation off, click so that the "x" disappears.

To control the hyphenation:

1. To fine tune how the hyphenation occurs, click the Ellipse (...) button. The Edit Hyphenation dialog box appears **③⑥**.

2. If you have foreign language dictionaries installed, use the pop-up menu to choose the correct language.

3. To limit the number of consecutive lines that may end with hyphens, enter the number in the Consecutive hyphens field.

4. To prevent capitalized words from being hyphenated, click Skip capitalized words.

5. To prevent a specific word (such as a company name) from being hyphenated, select the text and click Inhibit hyphens in selection.

6. Click OK to see the how your selected text is being hyphenated **③⑦**.

Hyphenation

FreeHand also offers the ability to align text using five different types of tabs. Each one aligns the text in a specific way ㊳–㊷.

To align text by using tabs:

1. Begin typing the text you want to align.

2. As you type, press the Tab key to insert a tab character into the text.

3. The tabbed text automatically aligns at .5" intervals from the rest of the text. The default tab settings are at .5" intervals.

Congress	Majority	Minority
1899-1901	R-NY	D-TN
1901-1903	R-NY	D-TN
1903-1905	R-NY	D-MS

㊳ *Text set with* **Left alignment tabs.** *(Gray arrows mark where the tab characters were entered.)*

Congress	Majority	Minority
1899-1901	R-NY	D-TN
1901-1903	R-NY	D-TN
1903-1905	R-NY	D-MS

㊴ *Text set with* **Right alignment tabs.**

Congress	Majority	Minority
1899-1901	R-NY	D-TN
1901-1903	R-NY	D-TN
1903-1905	R-NY	D-MS

㊵ *Text set with* **Center alignment tabs.**

1899-1901	2.5M	4.2M
1901-1903	3.05M	1.75M
1903-1905	2.25M	12.3M

㊶ *Text set with* **Decimal alignment tabs** *(circled).*

Majority	Minority
Sereno E. Payne, R-NY	James D. Richardson, D-TN
Sereno E. Payne, R-NY	John Sharp Williams, D-MS

㊷ *Text set with* **Wrapping tabs.**

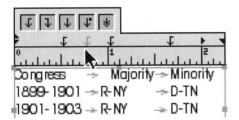

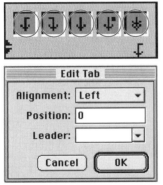

43 *To set a tab position, drag a **tab arrow** directly to the text ruler.*

44 *To open the **Edit Tab dialog box**, double-click the tab arrows on the text ruler (circled). This lets you set tabs numerically and add tab leaders.*

To set the tabs by dragging:

1. Select the paragraphs whose tabs you want to change.

2. If the text block does not have a text ruler visible, choose **View > Text Rulers**.

3. Drag the appropriate tab arrow from the top of the text ruler down to the area just above the numbers **43**.

4. Release the mouse button when the tab arrow is where you want it. The text realigns.

To set the tabs numerically:

1. Double-click any of the tab icons at the top of the ruler to open the Edit Tab dialog box **44**.

2. Choose the type of tab you want from the Alignment pop-up menu.

3. Enter a number in the Position field for where you want the tab located. This number is in relation to the left side of the text block.

TIP Use the Leader field or Leader pop-up menu to choose a repeating character that will automatically fill the space between the tabbed elements.

TIP To change the repeating characters of a tab leader, double-click the characters as they appear in the text and change their size, font, color, and so on.

To delete existing tabs:

To delete a tab from the text ruler, drag the tab arrow down off the ruler and then release.

To move a tab to a new position:

To move a tab to a new position, drag the tab arrow along the ruler to the position you want.

FreeHand gives you the ability to divide text blocks into columns and rows **45**.

To create columns and rows:

1. With the text block selected, choose the Text Inspector and then the Column-and-Row icon **46**.

2. Enter the number of columns you want in the Columns field.

3. To change the height of the columns, or the spacing between each column, enter those amounts in their fields.

4. Enter the number of rows you want in the Rows field.

5. To change the width of the rows, or the spacing between them, enter those amounts in their fields.

6. Click the Flow icon to direct the text flow down or across the columns and rows.

January 27	February 14–23
Senate convenes at 12:00	President's Day Recess
April 3–20	May 22–June 1
Spring Recess	Memorial Day Recess
June 26–July 6	August 1–31
Independence Day Recess	August Recess

45 *Special effect created with columns and rows.*

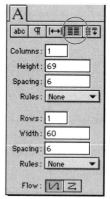

46 *Press the* **Column and Row icon** *of the Text Inspector to see the column and row controls.*

Create Columns and Rows

January 27 Senate convenes	February 14–23 President's Recess
April 3–20 Spring Recess	May 22–June 1 Memorial Recess

January 27 Senate convenes	February 14–23 President's Recess
April 3–20 Spring Recess	May 22–June 1 Memorial Recess

47 *The difference between* **Full rules** *(top) and* **Inset rules** *(bottom).*

FreeHand also lets you create rules that fit in the spaces between columns or rows **47**.

To add rules to columns and rows:

1. Select the text block to which you want to add rules. Choose the Text Inspector and then click the Column-and-Row icon.

2. Select a rule style from the Rules pop-up menu under Columns or Rows. Full width or Full height cross over the space between the columns or rows. Inset rules break in the spaces between the columns or rows.

3. With the text block still selected, choose the Stroke Inspector to change the appearance of the rules.

TIP If the rule is not visible, go to the Stroke Inspector and set the rule to Basic.

TIP Try to limit your use of rules in tables because they call attention to the grid rather than to the content of the table.

Add Rules to Columns and Rows

While it is very easy to create columns within a text block, you may want to have text flow from one text block to another. Or, you may want your text to flow onto an open path or into a closed path. You can link the text in these ways by using the Link box of the text block.

To link text between objects:

1. Select a text block you would like to link to another object.

2. Using the Selection tool, drag from the Link box of the text block. You will see a wavy line extend out.

3. Drag the wavy line onto the object to which you want to link your text **48**.

4. Release the mouse button. If you had an overflow of text, the text flows into the new object and you see arrows in the Link box **49**.

TIP If you did not have an overflow, you still see arrows in the Link box. This indicates that if you add text or decrease the size of the first text box, the text will appear inside the new object.

TIP You can link text within a page or across pages.

48 *To* **link text**, *drag from the Link box to the text block or object to which you want the text to link.*

49 **Text linked** *from a text block to an ellipse.*

⑤⓪ *Click the* **Adjust columns icon** *of the Text Inspector to see the copyfitting controls.*

> Give a full day's la-
> bor for a full day's
> pay.
>   Engage in no busi-
> ness with the govern-
> ment, inconsistent
> with the performance
> of his governmental
> duties.
>   Make no private
>
> promises of any kind
> binding upon the du-
> ties of office.
>   Never use any in-
> formation coming to
> him confidentially in
> the performance of
> governmental duties
> as a means for mak-
> ing private profit.

⑤① *Copyfitting by balancing the columns.*

> Give a full day's la-
> bor for a full day's
> pay.
>   Engage in no busi-
> ness with the govern-
> ment, inconsistent
> with the performance
> of his governmental
> duties.
>   Make no private
>
> promises of any kind
> binding upon the du-
> ties of office.
>   Never use any in-
> formation coming to
> him confidentially in
> the performance of
> governmental duties
> as a means for mak-
> ing private profit.

⑤② *Balancing the columns and modifying the leading to fill the text box.*

> Give a full day's
> labor for a full
> day's pay.
>   Engage in no
> business with the
> government, in-
> consistent with the
> performance of his
> governmental du-
> ties.
>   Make no private
>
> promises of any
> kind binding upon
> the duties of office.
>   Never use any
> information coming
> to him confidential-
> ly in the perfor-
> mance of govern-
> mental duties as a
> means for making
> private profit.

⑤③ *Copyfitting by changing the type size fills the text block and keeps leading proportional.*

Copyfitting is the technique used to change text so that it fits in the space provided. You may need to use the copyfit commands to balance your columns.

To copyfit text:

1. Select the text block you want to adjust. Choose the Text Inspector and then click the Adjust columns icon **④⑨**. The Copyfit subpanel opens.

2. To adjust the columns so there are an equal number of lines in each, check Balance.

3. To fill the text block by adjusting the leading, check Modify leading.

4. To adjust the columns by changing the point size of the text, enter values in the Mini and Maxi fields. Values below 100 will reduce the point size. Values above 100 will increase it.

5. To move the first line down from the top of a column, change the amount in the First line leading field.

6. The text reflows into equal columns **⑤①**-**⑤③**.

TIP Use the Paragraph spacing fields, rather than extra paragraph returns, to add space between paragraphs.

Copyfit Text

Sometimes it is important to keep selected words or lines together to make the text easier to read, even if spaces are created that violate the visual perfection of the design.

To keep words and lines together:

1. Choose the Text Inspector, and then click the Spacing icon ㉓.
2. To keep one word with another (such as a proper noun or a title), select the text and click Keep together: Selected words 54.
3. To keep paragraphs from breaking with fewer than a certain number of lines across columns, enter that number in Keep together: Lines 55.

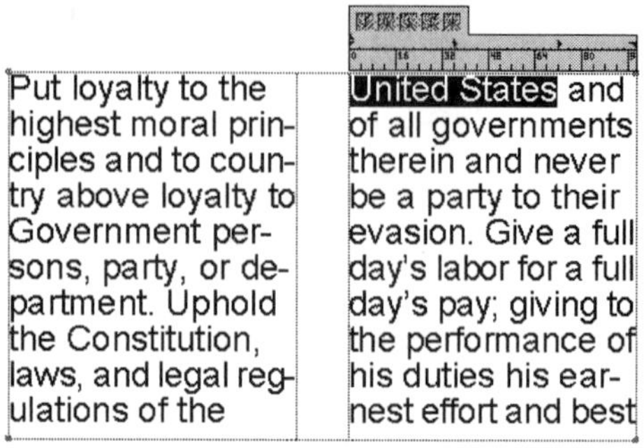
Put loyalty to the highest moral principles and to country above loyalty to Government persons, party, or department. Uphold the Constitution, laws, and legal regulations of the
United States and of all governments therein and never be a party to their evasion. Give a full day's labor for a full day's pay; giving to the performance of his duties his earnest effort and best

54 *An example of* **Keep together selected words**. *Although there is room for more text at the bottom of the left column, the words-together setting has forced the selected words to the top of the right column.*

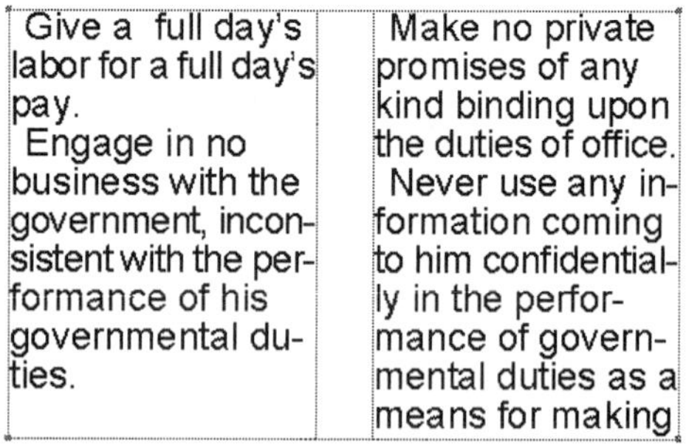
Give a full day's labor for a full day's pay.
Engage in no business with the government, inconsistent with the performance of his governmental duties.
Make no private promises of any kind binding upon the duties of office.
Never use any information coming to him confidentially in the performance of governmental duties as a means for making

55 **Keep together lines** *forces the column to break to keep the lines of the third paragraph together rather than use the available space at the bottom of the left column.*

W ith FreeHand, you can create looks for text that would be difficult, if not impossible, to create using an ordinary page layout program. This makes FreeHand an excellent choice for adding special effects to text.

In this chapter you will learn how to

Attach text to a path.

Adjust text on a path.

Apply the built-in special text effects.

Edit the built-in special text effects.

Add automatic rules to paragraphs.

Wrap text around graphics.

Create an inline graphic.

Convert text into artwork.

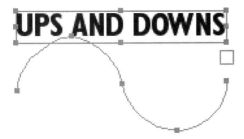

❶ Text and a path *selected.*

❷ *The results of applying the* **Attach To Path** *command.*

❸ Inserting a paragraph return *causes the text to attach to both sides of an ellipse.*

One of the most popular effects in graphic design is to align text to a path. The path can be open or closed, with curve or corner points. The text can even be linked to other paths or text blocks.

To attach text to a path:

1. Select both the text block and the path to which you want the text aligned ❶.

2. Choose **Text > Attach To Path**. The text aligns with the selected path ❷.

TIP If you are aligning text to a closed path, such as an oval, insert a paragraph return in the text to align the text to both the top and bottom of the path ❸.

TIP If the path is not long enough to display all the text, the overflow box fills.

TIP To remove text from a path, select the path and choose **Text > Detach From Path**.

To change the direction in which the text flows:

1. Hold the Option/Alt key and click with the Pointer tool to select just the path.

2. Choose **Modify > Alter Path > Reverse Direction**. The text flows in the opposite direction ❹.

To move the text along the path:

1. With the Pointer tool, click the path. A small white triangle appears.

2. Drag the triangle to move the text in either direction along the path ❺.

To change the text alignment:

1. Open the Object Inspector to show the Text on a path options ❻.

2. Use the Top and Bottom Text alignment pop-up menus to control where the text sits in relation to the path.

   Baseline puts the baseline of the characters on the path ❼.

   Ascent puts the ascenders, such as the tops of the letter *t* on the path ❼.

   Descent puts the descenders, such as the bottom of the letter *g*, sit on the path ❼.

TIP An alignment setting of None causes the text to disappear.

TIP The Top pop-up menu controls text before the paragraph return. The Bottom pop-up menu controls text after the paragraph return.

❹ *The* **Reverse Direction** *command causes the text (top) to change its direction (bottom).*

❺ *To move the text along the path,* **drag the white triangle** *next to the text on the path.*

❻ *The Object Inspector shows the* **Text on a path** *options.*

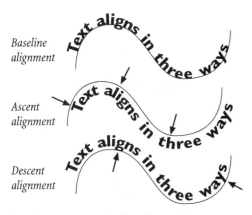

Baseline alignment

Ascent alignment

Descent alignment

➐ *The ways text can be aligned to a path.*

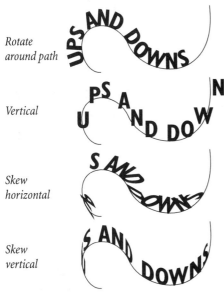

Rotate around path

Vertical

Skew horizontal

Skew vertical

➑ *The ways text can be oriented to a path.*

To change the orientation and rotation:

Use the Orientation pop-up menu to change how the text is oriented to the path.

- Rotate around path keeps the text in a perpendicular orientation as it moves around the path ➑.

- Vertical makes each character stand up straight no matter how the path curves ➑.

- Skew horizontal exaggerates the text's horizontal tilt up to a 90° rotation and distorts the characters' shapes as the text follows the path ➑.

- Skew vertical maintains a vertical rotation but distorts the characters' shapes as the text follows the path ➑.

To move text numerically:

Rather than move the text by dragging, you can move it by setting the precise amounts in the Left and Right Inset fields.

To display and print the path:

Check Show path to see the fill and stroke of the path. Then use the Fill and Stroke Inspectors to choose the color and style of the path.

TIP Select text on the path using the Text tool. Once it is highlighted, this text can be modified using any of the functions of the Type menu or the Type palette.

To apply any of the special text effects:

1. Select the text by highlighting it or by selecting the text block with the Pointer tool.

2. Click the Character icon of the Text Inspector.

3. Choose one of the special effects from the pop-up menu: Highlight, Inline, Shadow, Strikethrough, Underline, or Zoom ❾.

TIP You can turn the visual display of the text effects on or off by changing your Preferences settings (*see page 253*).

TIP Text effects may slow your screen redraw. Apply them after you have finished most of your work, or work in the Fast Keyline or Keyline modes.

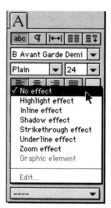

❾ *Use the* **Effects pop-up menu** *of the Text Inspector to apply the special text effects.*

Highlight creates a color or tint block around the text ❿. Strikethrough draws a line that runs across the text ⓫. Underline runs a line underneath the text ⓬. Highlight, Underline, and Strikethrough effects are actually just variations on the same effect so the settings work the same way for all three.

To edit the Highlight, Underline, and Strikethrough text effects:

1. Select the text that has the effect applied to it and choose Edit from the pop-up menu. The dialog box appears ⓭.

2. In the Position field, enter the distance from the baseline for the effect.

3. In the Stroke Width field, enter the value of the thickness for the effect.

4. To change the color of the effect, use the color pop-up menu.

5. To apply a dash pattern, choose a pattern from the Dash pop-up menu.

6. Overprinting is one way of compensating for slight misregistrations in the printing process. To allow the effect to overprint the original text, click Overprint.

We, the people of the United States, in order to form a more perfect Union

❿ *The* **Highlight** *effect on text.*

We, the ~~folks~~ people of the ~~Federated~~ United States, in order to form a more perfect ~~Club~~ Union...

⓫ *The* **Strikethrough** *effect on text.*

perfect Union, establish <u>justice</u>, ensure <u>domestic</u> tranquility, ...

⓬ *The* **Underline** *effect on text.*

Highlight; Strikethrough; Underline

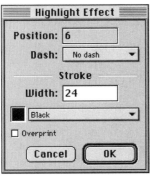

*The edit dialog boxes for **Highlight**, **Underline**, and **Strikethrough** effects all have the same settings.*

The Inline effect creates outlines of strokes and colors that surround the text ⓮.

To edit the Inline effect:

1. Select the text that has the Inline effect and choose Edit from the pop-up menu. The Inline Effect dialog box appears ⓯.

2. In the Count field, enter the number of sets of outlines you want to surround the text.

3. In the Stroke Width field, enter the width of the stroke.

4. To change the color of the stroke, choose from the color pop-up menu.

5. In the Background Width field, enter the width of the background color that will be between the stroke and the text.

6. To change the background color, choose from the color pop-up menu.

⓮ *The **Inline** effect on text.*

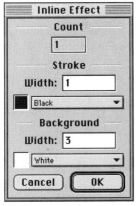

⓯ *The **Inline Effect** dialog box.*

143

The Shadow effect creates an automatic drop shadow behind the text **⑯**.

To use the Shadow effect:

Choose Shadow effect from the Effects pop-up menu of the Text Inspector. There is no dialog box for editing the Shadow effect. The values of the Shadow effect are fixed. The shadow is always 50% gray. Its position is always down and to the right of the original text.

⑯ *The Shadow effect on text.*

Zoom creates a 3D effect where the text has one look in the background and changes into another in the foreground **⑰**.

To edit the Zoom effect:

1. Select the text that has the Zoom effect applied to it and and choose Edit from the pop-up menu. The Zoom Effect dialog box appears **⑱**.

2. In the Zoom To field, enter the percentage that you want the foreground object to be.

TIP A value of 100% keeps the foreground the same size as the background. A value greater than 100% makes the foreground object larger than the background for a greater perspective effect.

3. In the *x* and *y* Offset fields, enter the distance you want to move the foreground object from the original text.

4. To change the color of the background object, use the From pop-up menu.

5. To change the color of the foreground object, use the To pop-up menu.

⑰ *The Zoom effect on text.*

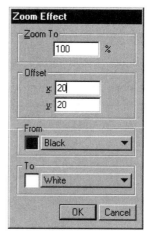

⑱ *The Zoom Effect dialog box.*

Senate Calendar:

January 27 Senate convenes
at 12:00 Noon ET/9:00 am PT

February 14 - 23 President's Day Recess

April 3 - 20 Spring Recess

⑲ **Paragraph rules** *that are aligned to the text.*

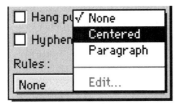

⑳ *The* **Paragraph Rules** *pop-up menu.*

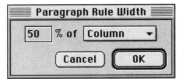

㉑ *The* **Paragraph Rule Width** *controls.*

Rather than use the Line tool, FreeHand lets you create automatic paragraph rules that will flow along with the text **⑲**.

To create paragraph rules:

1. Select the paragraphs where you want the rules.

2. Click the paragraph options of the Text Inspector and open the Rules pop-up menu **⑳**. Choose Centered or Paragraph to add the rules to the text.

   Choose Centered to have the rule centered on the last line or column. Choose Paragraph to have the rule follow the alignment for the paragraph.

3. Once you have applied rules, choose Edit to open the Paragraph Rule Width dialog box **㉑**. This is where you can change the width and position of the rule.

   TIP The above steps add rules to the text, but they do not display the rules. To see the rules onscreen and have them print, you need to perform the following two steps.

4. Make sure Display border is checked in the Object Inspector.

5. Select the text block as an object and then set the stroke. Your rules appear under the paragraphs that were selected.

FreeHand lets you position graphics so that the text automatically flows around the graphic. This is called text wrap.

To wrap text around a graphic element:

1. Select the graphic element you want the text to wrap around. Do not group.

2. Move the graphic so that it is in the proper position in relation to the text.

3. Make sure the graphic is in front of the text block.

4. With the graphic still selected, choose **Text > Run Around Selection**. This displays the Run Around Selection dialog box **㉒**.

5. Click the top right icon to display the Standoff distances fields. The Standoff is the space between the text and the edges of the graphic.

6. Enter the standoff amount for each side of the graphic.

7. Click OK when you are finished. The text automatically flows around the graphic **㉓**.

TIP To get more control over the wrap, draw an outline around the object. Do not give this outline a fill or a stroke. Give this object the text wrap. You can then manipulate the outline to create a more precise text wrap.

To change a text wrap:

1. Select an object with a text wrap.

2. Choose **Text > Run Around Selection**.

3. Change the amounts in the Standoff distances fields as necessary.

To undo a text wrap:

1. Select an object with a text wrap.

2. Choose **Text > Run Around Selection**.

3. Click the top left icon of the Run Around Selection dialog box.

TIP You can also open the Run Around Selection dialog box by clicking the icon on the Text toolbar **㉔**.

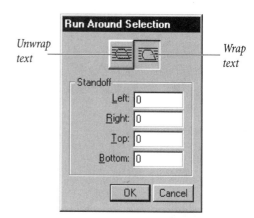

Unwrap text / *Wrap text*

㉒ *The **Run Around Selection** dialog box. Choosing the top right icon lets you enter the Standoff distances for the four sides of the object.*

We hold these truths to be self-evident, that all men are created equal, that they are endowed by their Creator with certain unalienable Rights, that among these are Life, Liberty and the pursuit of Happiness

㉓ *A **Text wrap** around a graphic element.*

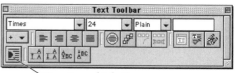

Run Around Selection

㉔ *The **Runaround Selection** icon in the Text toolbar.*

We hold these truths to be self-evident, that all men are created equal

㉕ *To create an* **inline graphic**, *select the graphic and choose Copy or Cut.*

We hold these truths to be self-evident, that all men are created equal

㉖ *The* **inline graphic** *as it appears within the text.*

You can also add inline graphics to text. This lets you create elements, such as ornate letters or logos, that are part of the text. So if the text reflows, the inline graphic flows along with the text.

To create an inline graphic:

1. Create the graphic you want to place inline. Examples of these graphics may be FreeHand objects, text on a path, text blocks, or placed TIFF or EPS images.

2. Use the Selection tool to select the graphic, and choose Copy or Cut from the Edit menu **㉕**.

3. Use the Text tool to place an insertion point in the text where you want the inline graphic.

4. Choose **Edit > Paste**. The inline graphic appears and flows along with the text **㉖**.

TIP To remove an inline graphic from text, use the Text tool to drag across the graphic as you would a text character. Choose **Edit > Cut** or **Edit > Clear**.

TIP To move the inline graphic up or down on the baseline, drag across the graphic as you would a text character. Change the Baseline shift.

TIP If you select an inline graphic, the Effects pop-up menu displays the words *Graphic Element*. Click Edit and use the Text Wrap dialog box to add more space around the inline graphic.

TIP If you select all the text in a text block, including the inline graphic, and then change the point size of the text, the inline graphic scales up or down along with the text.

Inline Graphic

So far, all the effects you have created with text have kept the text as text. This means that you can still edit the text. There may be times, however, when you will prefer to convert the text to paths that can be edited as artwork **27**.

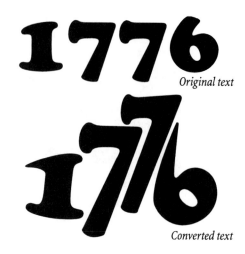

Original text

Converted text

27 *Text that has been **converted to paths** and manipulated as art.*

To convert text into paths:

1. Use the Selection tool to select the text block or the text on a path you want to convert.

2. Choose **Text > Convert To Paths**.

TIP If you convert text aligned to a path, the path disappears, leaving only the text.

3. To manipulate the individual paths of the characters, choose **Modify > Ungroup** or hold the Option/Alt key as you click each individual path.

TIP Text that has been converted to paths does not require fonts installed for it to print.

TIP You cannot change the font, spelling, or characters of text that has been converted to paths.

TIP Characters that have holes, such as the letters *A*, *O*, or *B*, are converted as a joined or composite path (*see page 170*).

TIP Text must be converted to paths in order to use the Paste Inside command to have the text act as a mask (*see page 171*).

TIP You must convert text to paths in order to apply most of the FreeHand and third-party Xtras that create special effects (*see page 198*).

Although you can certainly edit text manually, you will find it much easier to use the built-in text editing features. If you are familiar with a word processing program, you will find these features easy to understand.

In this chapter, you will learn how to

Use the Text Editor.

Recognize the invisible characters.

Insert special typographic and formatting commands.

Use the Spelling checker.

Use the Find Text feature to automate text editing.

The Text Editor lets you view and change text all in one place without the formatting.

To open the Text Editor:

1. Select the text block or path, or click with the Text tool inside the text.

2. Choose **Text > Editor** to open the Text Editor dialog box **❶**.

3. Click 12 Point Black to view the type in that point size and color.

4. To change any attributes of the text, highlight the text in the Text Editor and make whatever changes you want via the Text menu or the Text Inspector.

5. To see the text changes in the text block or path, click Apply. When you are satisfied with your changes, click OK.

TIP Hold the Option/Alt key as you click in a text block to open the Text Editor.

TIP Hold the Option/Alt key as you create a text block to open the Text Editor. You can then type your text directly into the Text Editor.

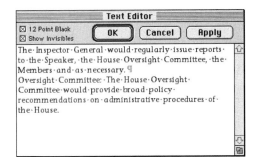

❶ *The* **Text Editor** *lets you work with text that might be difficult to read on the document page.*

Text Editor

FreeHand allows you to insert special typographic characters that improve the look of the text or control the flow of the text.

To use the special characters:

1. Place your insertion point where you would like the special character.

2. Choose **Text** > **Special Characters** and then choose one of the special characters from the drop-down list.

End of Column

Inserts an invisible character that forces the text to the next column or next text block ❷.

End of Line

Inserts an invisible character that forces the text to the next line ❸.

Non-Breaking Space

Inserts a space that does not break across lines. This can be used to keep titles with the names they modify, for example ❹.

Em Space

Inserts a space the width of the current type size ❺.

En Space

Inserts a space one-half the width of the current type size ❺.

Thin Space

Inserts a space that is fixed as 10% of an em in width ❺.

Em Dash

Inserts an em dash, that is the length of one em. Used to indicate an abrupt change in thought ❻.

En Dash

Inserts an en dash, that is the length of one-half em ❻. Used to indicate duration.

The Inspector General would regularly issue reports to the Speaker, the House Oversight Committee, the Members and as necessary. Oversight	Committee: The House Oversight Committee would provide broad policy recommendations on administrative procedures of the House.
The Inspector General would regularly issue reports to the Speaker, the House Oversight Committee, the Members and as necessary.	Oversight Committee: The House Oversight Committee would provide broad policy recommendations on administrative procedures of the House.

❷ *Text before (top) and after (bottom) inserting the* **End of Column** *character.*

to which the Laws of Nature and of Nature's God

to which the Laws of Nature and of Nature's God

❸ *Text before (top) and after (bottom) inserting the* **End of Line** *character.*

We congratulate Dr. DuPrât on her recent promotion

We congratulate Dr. DuPrât on her recent promotion

❹ *Text before (top) and after (bottom) inserting a* **Non-Breaking Space** *character.*

Space Regular

Space   Em

Space En

SpaceThin

❺ *Compare the spaces to see how the different types of* **spaces** *appear.*

Pop-up menu

Nothing—I meant nothing.

April–July

❻ *Compare how the different types of* **dashes** *appear: (top to bottom) hyphen, em dash, en dash.*

Discretionary Hyphen

Inserts a hyphen that is visible only if the word breaks across lines.

Rather than use the Special Characters menu, you can also insert the character directly into your text by typing keystrokes.

Typing with the Special Characters (Mac)

End of column Command-Shift-Enter

End of line Shift-Enter

Nonbreaking space Option-Spacebar

Em space Command-Shift-M

En space Command-Shift-N

Thin space Command-Shift-T

Em dash Option-Shift-Hyphen

En dash Option-Hyphen

Discretionary hyphen Command-Hyphen

Typing with the Special Characters (Win)

End of column Ctrl-Shift-Enter

End of line Shift-Enter

Nonbreaking space Ctrl-Shift-H

Em space Ctrl-Shift-M

En space Ctrl-Shift-N

Thin space Ctrl-Shift-T

Em dash Alt-1, 5, 1 (keypad + number lock on)

En dash Alt-1, 5, 0 (keypad + number lock on)

Discretionary hyphen Ctrl-Shift-_

Special Characters

Invisible characters such as the End-of-column character do not print and are not visible on your page. However, you can use the Text Editor to view these invisible characters.

To see the invisible characters:

1. Open the Text Editor and click the Show Invisibles box.

2. Invisible characters such as spaces, paragraph returns, end of column markers, and tabs show up in the text as gray symbols ❼.

You may want to make sure the text in your document is spelled correctly. To do so, you can use the spelling checker.

To use the spelling checker:

1. Use the Selection tool to select the text block or path.

    or

    Place your insertion point at the point in the text where you would like the spelling check to start.

2. Choose **Text > Spelling**. The Spelling dialog box appears ❽.

    TIP If no text blocks are selected, the spelling checker checks the entire document.

3. To start checking the spelling of your text, click Start. The spelling checker looks through the text and stops when it finds an error.

4. If the spelling checker finds a word it does not know, it displays the word in the top field. If possible, it shows alternates.

    TIP To see the section of text currently being checked by the spelling checker, click Show selection.

    TIP The spelling checker is not a grammar checker or a proofreader. It does not find typos such as *He was reel good,* since the word *reel* is a known word.

| 1998☐Senate·Calendar:⤶ |
| ¶ |
| ¶ |
| →January·27·Senate·convenes·at↵ |
| 12:00·Noon⸱·ET/9:00·am·PT¶ |
| ¶ |
| →February·1⼞–⼞23·President's·Day·Recess ¶ |
| April·3⼞–⼞20·Spring·Recess ¶ |
| May·22⼞–⼞June·1·Memorial·Day·Recess ¶ |
| June·26⼞–⼞July·6·Independence·Day·Recess ¶ |

❼ The **Invisibles** *in the Text Editor let you see the nonprinting characters for tabs, returns, special spaces, and so on.*

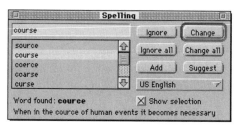

❽ The **Spelling checker** *looks for unknown words, capitalization mistakes, and duplicate words.*

❾ The **Change button** *changes the word to one of the suggested alternates.*

❿ The **Change all button** *changes all instances of the word.*

⓫ *The **Ignore** button skips the word.*

⓬ *The **Ignore all** button skips all instances of the word.*

⓭ *The **Add** button adds the word to the dictionary that FreeHand uses during a spelling check.*

⓮ *Click the **Suggest** button to see the list of suggested alternates.*

To use the Change button:

1. If the original word is incorrect, choose one of the alternates.
2. If none of the alternates are correct, type the correct word and then click Change ❾. The incorrect word is deleted and the correct word is inserted.

To use the Change all button:

If you suspect that other uses of the word are incorrect in the document, choose one of the alternates and then click Change all ❿.

To use the Ignore button:

If the original word is correct, click Ignore ⓫. The spelling checker skips over that instance of the word, but stops again if the word is elsewhere in the text chain.

To use the Ignore all button:

If all the instances of the original word are correct, click Ignore all ⓬. The spelling checker ignores all instances of that word until you quit that session of FreeHand.

To use the Add button:

If the original word is correct, click Add ⓭. This adds the word to the spelling dictionary and stops the spelling checker from identifying the word as misspelled in the future.

TIP To change how the spelling checker finds and adds words, change the spelling preferences (*see page 252*).

To use the Suggest button:

To see the list of suggested words, click Suggest ⓮.

TIP To check the spelling of just a portion of a lengthy text block, use the Text tool to select just that portion and then run the spelling checker.

Spelling Checker

If you are dealing with long amounts of text, you may need to use FreeHand's Find Text dialog box.

To use the Find Text dialog box:

1. Place your insertion point in the text block, or select the text block or path.

2. Choose **Edit > Find & Replace > Text** or click the Find Text icon on the Text toolbar ⓯ to open the Find Text dialog box ⓰.

3. In the Find field, type the text string you want to search for. In the Change to field, type the text string you want as a replacement.

4. To search for only the word listed, click the Whole word box. If you want to search for the text exactly as typed in uppercase and lowercase, click Match case.

5. Use the Special pop-up menus ⓱ to insert the codes for the special characters into the Find and Change to fields or type the codes into the fields.

6. Click the Find First button to find the first instance of the text string.

7. To change the text, click Change. Click the Find Next button to find the next instance of the text string.

8. To change all occurrences of the text string, click Change all.

TIP To see the text currently being searched by the Find Text dialog box, click Show selection.

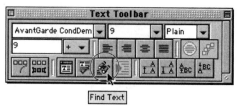

⓯ *The **Find Text icon** opens the Find Text dialog box so you can find and change text in a document.*

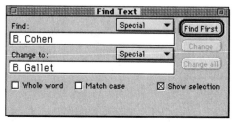

⓰ *The **Find Text dialog box** allows you to search and replace text strings or invisible characters.*

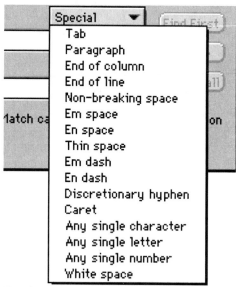

⓱ *The **Special pop-up menus** allow you to insert special characters into the Find and Change to fields.*

AUTOMATING FREEHAND

I f you are working on a simple document, it is rather easy to make changes by selecting objects one at a time. But if you are working on a complicated document, you will find you often need to make changes to many objects, and doing this object by object would be tedious and time consuming. Fortunately FreeHand has several features to help you make changes to complicated documents: Styles, Find & Replace Graphics, and Copy/Paste Attributes.

In this chapter, you will learn how to

Open the Styles palette.

Work with the two default styles.

Apply styles.

Define and edit styles.

Base one style on another.

Change the view for the Styles palette.

Create Parent and Child styles.

Duplicate styles.

Use the Find & Replace Graphics dialog box.

Copy and paste attributes.

Use symbols to create instances.

Create symbols.

Export and import symbols.

Working with styles

If you have worked in a word processing program or a page layout application, you may have used styles to automate text formatting. FreeHand has both text styles and object styles. So in addition to changing text, you can change the fills, strokes, colors, and other attributes of objects. Using styles, you can change the look of an entire document with just a few actions.

It does take a little preparation to work with styles. You may need to plan the color schemes for your artwork as well as the stroke weights, text formatting, and so on. However, if you have planned your styles well, changes that might have taken hours to fix can be finished in a matter of minutes.

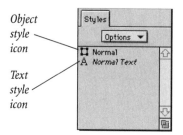

Object style icon

Text style icon

❶ *The Styles palette with the two default styles.*

In order to see the styles in your document, you open the Styles palette.

To view the default styles:

1. Choose **Window > Panels > Styles**.
2. If you have not added any styles to your document, you see the two default styles ❶.
3. The Normal style has an Object style icon next to it. This is the default style for objects.
4. The Normal Text style has a Text style icon next to it. This is the default style for text.

TIP All new documents have the same default Normal styles. You can change those styles by changing the FreeHand Defaults file (*see page 256*).

❷ **Selecting New from the Styles palette** *creates a new style based on the object currently selected.*

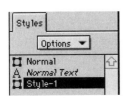

❸ *A new style is created with the name* **Style-1**.

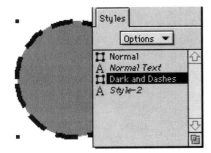

❹ *To apply a style to an object or text, select the object or text and then* **click the name of the style** *in the Styles palette.*

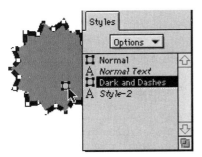

❺ *Styles can also be applied by* **dragging the icon for the style** *onto the object or text.*

The easiest way to define a style is by example. This means you can create the object or text and then use it as the reference to define the style.

To define a style by example:

1. Draw an object. In this case, draw a circle or type some text.

2. Choose the fill and the stroke or font attributes you want for your object or text.

3. With the object or text selected, open the Options pop-up menu of the Styles palette and choose New ❷.

4. A new style named *Style-1* appears ❸. This style contains all the attributes of the selected object.

Once you add a style, it is easy to change the name of the style.

To rename a style:

1. Double-click the name of the style in the Styles palette to highlight the name.

2. Type the new name of the style.

3. Press Return or Enter to apply the new name

Once you have defined a style, you can then use it to change the attributes of any objects or text.

To apply a style:

1. Select an object or text that you want to change.

2. Select the style in the Styles palette. The style attributes are automatically applied to the object or text ❹.

TIP Styles are applied to an entire paragraph of text. You can apply a text style to a paragraph by clicking anywhere in the paragraph and selecting the style.

TIP You can also apply styles by dragging the object style icon onto an object or paragraph ❺.

Define a Style; Rename a Style; Apply a Style

You can also define a style by selecting all its attributes in the various Inspector panels and then defining the style according to those attributes.

To define a style by attributes:

1. Press Tab to deselect all objects and text blocks.
2. Make sure that one of the object or text styles is selected in the Styles palette.
3. Use the various Inspectors panels to choose the object or text attributes you would like for your style.
4. When you are satisfied with the attributes, choose New from the Options pop-up menu of the Styles palette. The new Style appears with the name *Style-1*.

The real power of styles lies in their ability to make global changes in a document by redefining a style. For instance, if you change the definition of a fill color from solid to a gradient, all objects that have that style applied are filled with the gradient — even if they are not selected. The easiest way to redefine a style is by example.

To redefine a style:

1. Select an object.
2. Use the Inspector palette or Type menu to change the object's attributes.
3. When you are satisfied with the new attributes, choose Redefine from the Options pop-up menu of the Styles palette. The Redefine Style dialog box appears.
4. Click the name of the style you want to redefine and then click OK ❻.
5. All objects that have the style applied to them automatically update with the new attributes ❼–❽.

TIP If you copy an object or text with a style and paste it into a new document, the object or text styles appear automatically in the Styles palette of the second document.

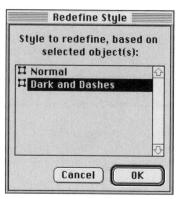

❻ *The* **Redefine Style dialog box** *lets you change a style to the attributes of the selected object or text.*

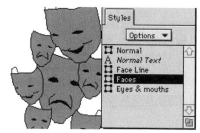

❼ *The style Faces was defined with a 50% black fill.*

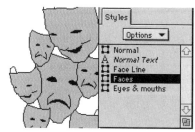

❽ **Redefining the style** *Faces to a lighter fill changed all the artwork without selecting any objects.*

❾ **Hide names** *changes the display of the Styles palette.*

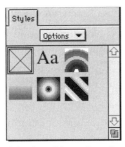

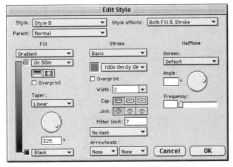

⑩ *The visual display of the Styles palette.*

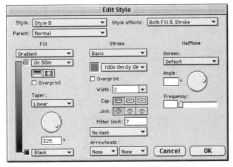

⑪ *The* **Edit Style dialog box for objects** *lets you change all the object attributes at once.*

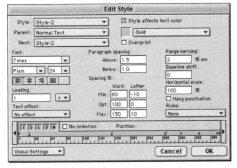

⑫ *The* **Edit Style dialog box for text** *lets you change all the text attributes at once.*

To change the Styles display:

Choose Hide names from the Options pop-up menu of the Styles palette **⑨**. The display of the Styles palette changes to show visual representations of both the object and text styles **⑩**.

You can also use the Edit Style dialog box to make changes to an object style.

To use the Edit Style dialog box:

1. Select a style in the Styles palette that you want to change.

2. Choose Edit Style from the Options pop-up menu of the Styles palette. The Edit Style dialog box appears.

    TIP If you select an object style, the dialog box reflects object attributes **⑪**. If you select a text style, the dialog box reflects text attributes **⑫**.

3. Use any of the settings in the dialog box to change the style attributes.

4. Click OK, and the style changes go into effect.

FreeHand also offers the ability to base one style on another. FreeHand calls the relationship between these styles *Parent* and *Child*.

To create Parent and Child styles:

1. Define two object styles or two text styles in the Styles palette.

TIP To make it easier to understand Parent/Child styles, define only one difference (for instance, stroke weight or point size) to the second style.

2. Select the second style and choose Set parent from the Options pop-up menu of the Styles panel. The Set Parent dialog box appears.

3. In the Set Parent dialog box, choose the first style as the parent. Click OK **⑬**. The two styles are now linked as Parent and Child.

TIP One Parent style can have many different Child styles based on it.

Once you have defined Parent and Child styles you will find it easy to make changes to many styles just by redefining the Parent.

To work with Parent and Child styles:

1. Select the Parent style and choose Edit style from the Options pop-up menu.

2. Make whatever changes you want to the Parent style attributes. Click OK.

3. Notice how the changes have been applied to the objects or paragraphs. Only those attributes that are shared by both the Parent and Child styles will change after editing the Parent style **⑭**.

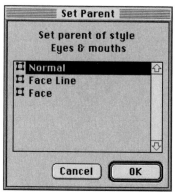

⑬ *The* **Set Parent dialog box** *allows you to base one style on another.*

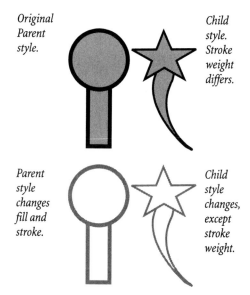

Original Parent style.

Child style. Stroke weight differs.

Parent style changes fill and stroke.

Child style changes, except stroke weight.

⑭ *An example of what happens in a* **Parent and Child relationship** *when one style is based on another and the Parent style is redefined.*

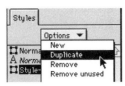

⑮ *Choose* **Duplicate** *from the Options pop-up menu of the Styles palette to make a copy of a style.*

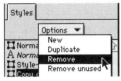

⑯ *The* **Remove** *command deletes a style from the Styles palette.*

To duplicate styles:

1. Choose the object or text style you want to copy.

2. Choose Duplicate from the Options pop-up menu of the Styles palette **⑮**. A new style with the preface *Copy of* appears.

To remove a style:

1. In the Styles palette, click the name of the style you want to delete.

2. Choose Remove from the Options pop-up menu. The style disappears from the palette **⑯**.

TIP If you delete a style that has been applied to objects or paragraphs, those objects or paragraphs keep their attributes.

As you have seen, styles let you make changes to many objects at once as long as you originally defined and applied the styles as you worked. There is another way, however, to quickly make changes to objects: the Find & Replace Graphics dialog box. Its Select feature allows you to select an object based on certain attributes.

To find objects by attribute:

1. Choose **Edit > Find & Replace > Graphics** to open the Find & Replace Graphics dialog box **⑰**.

TIP Make sure your document has various objects with different fills, strokes, colors, shapes, fonts, text effects, and attributes so you have lots of things to work with.

2. Click the Select tab to open that section of the dialog box.

3. Use the Attribute pop-up menu **⑱** to choose features you want selected.

4. Use the Search pop-up menu to limit the search to a selection, the active page, or the entire document.

5. Click Find. The objects that fit the search criteria are selected.

6. Click the Add to selection box to add the results of the search to the objects currently selected.

TIP The number of objects found in a search are listed at the bottom of the Find & Replace Graphics dialog box.

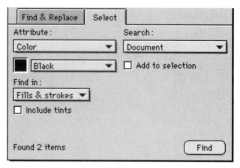

⑰ *The* **Select section** *of the Find & Replace Graphics dialog box.*

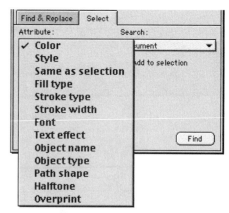

⑱ *The* **Attribute choices** *of the Find & Replace Graphics dialog box.*

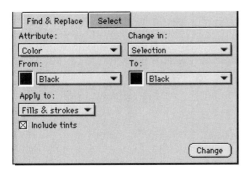

⑲ *The **Find & Replace section** of the Find & Replace Graphics dialog box.*

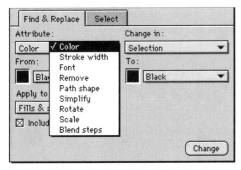

⑳ *The **Attribute choices** of the Find & Replace Graphics dialog box.*

The Find & Replace feature allows you to find all objects with a certain attribute and then change that attribute to something else. For instance, you can find all objects with a black fill and change them to a different color.

To find and change attributes:

1. In the Find & Replace Graphics dialog box, click the Find & Replace tab to open that section.

2. Use the Attribute pop-up menu **⑲** to select those features you want to find.

3. Use the From pop-up menu **⑳** in the left section of the box to select features of the objects you want to find.

4. Use the Change-in pop-up menu to limit the search to a selection, the active page, or the entire document.

5. Use the To pop-up menu in the right section of the box to select features you want to substitute.

6. Click Change. FreeHand automatically changes the objects from one set of attributes to another. The number of objects that change is listed at the bottom of the Find & Replace Graphics dialog box.

TIP Use the + sign before a number in the To field to increase all the stroke weights or point sizes by that amount. For instance, if you enter +2 pt, then all strokes will be increased by 2 points. So 2 points becomes 4; 3 points becomes 5; 4 points becomes 6; and so on.

Find & Replace Attributes

The Set Note command allows you to add a name to an object and write notes or information about that object.

To use the Set Note command:

1. Select one or more objects.

2. Choose **Xtras > Other > Set Note**. The Set Note dialog box appears ㉑.

3. Give your selection a name and type the notes you want to have associated with the object.

4. You must press Return or Enter to apply the note. You can then close the Set Note dialog box.

TIP To see a previously made note, select the object and choose Set Note from the Operations palette or from the Xtra Operations toolbar.

㉑ *The **Set Note dialog box** allows you to name an object and insert any information about that object.*

While not as powerful as styles or the Find & Replace Graphics dialog box, there is another way to make changes in graphic attributes quickly.

To use Copy and Paste Attributes:

1. Select an object with a set of attributes that you want to apply to another object.

2. Choose **Edit > Copy Attributes**.

3. Select the object or objects that you want to change.

4. Choose **Edit > Paste Attributes**. The second object does not change its shape but does change its attributes, such as fill and stroke, to match the first ㉒.

㉒ *The attributes of the hat in the left image were copied. The pants and shoes of the right image were then selected and **Paste Attributes** was applied.*

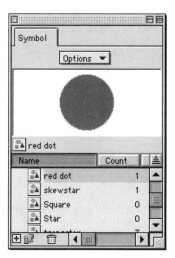

❷❸ *The **Symbol panel** allows you to place instances of symbols you create to save both time and file size.*

❷❹ *The **alert panel** opens if you drag an object onto the name of an existing symbol on the Symbol panel.*

Another powerful tool FreeHand provides is the Symbol panel. Symbols not only streamline the use of repetitive elements, they also help minimize the size of the files in which they are used. A single symbol can appear many times (each called an instance) in a document and each can be transformed using the tools on the Transform panel. Each instance refers back to the symbol and is affected by any changes made to the original, much like the Parent and Child relationship for styles.

Symbols can be made from paths with a variety of strokes and fills, groups, or text blocks.

To use a symbol to create an instance:

1. Select **Window > Panels > Symbols** from the menu. The Symbol panel opens ❷❸.

2. Select a symbol from the list. If you want to see it in the preview window, check Preview in the Options pop-up menu.

3. Drag the symbol from either the list or the preview window onto the page to create an instance.

TIP When you first install FreeHand, there are no symbols in the Symbol panel. You can create your own symbols or use the symbols that are provided on the FreeHand CD in the Symbols folder inside the Assets folder.

To create a new symbol by dragging:

1. Select the path, group, or text block you want to convert to a symbol.

2. Drag the object between existing names on the list of the Symbol panel so that no existing symbol is highlighted.

3. Double-click on the temporary name (Graphic-01, for example) and type in the name you want to give your new symbol.

TIP If you accidentally drag your new symbol onto the name of an existing one, click New Symbol in the alert box ❷❹ that opens.

To create a symbol using the menu commands:

1. Select the path, group, or text block you want to convert to a symbol.

2. Choose **Modify > Symbol > Convert to Symbol** from the menu bar **25**.

3. Double-click on the temporary name and type in the name you want to give your new symbol.

TIP Choose **Modify > Symbol > Copy to Symbol** if you do not want to change the original into an instance of the new symbol.

TIP You can also select an object and click the "+" icon at the bottom-left corner of the Symbol panel to create a new symbol.

Symbols created in one document can be exported as libraries that can then be opened for use in other documents.

To export symbols:

1. Choose Export from the Options pop-up menu on the Symbol panel. The Export Symbols dialog box opens **26**.

2. Select the symbols you want to export, holding down the Command/Ctrl key to pick more than one.

3. Click Export. The Save *(Mac)* Export Symbols *(Win)* dialog box opens **27**.

4. Assign a name to the library you are creating and click Save.

25 *Choose* **Modify > Symbol > Convert to Symbol** *to create a symbol from an object.*

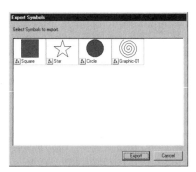

26 *The* **Export Symbols dialog box** *shows the symbols in your document. Make selections and click Export.*

27 *In the* **Save/Export Symbols dialog box** *, name the library of symbols you are exporting and save it.*

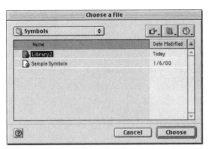

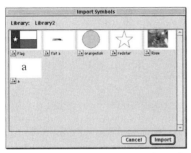

28 *The* **Choose a File dialog box** *shows the available symbol libraries. Select one and click Choose/Open.*

29 *The* **Import Symbols dialog box** *shows the available symbols. Select the ones you want and click Import.*

30 *Select an instance of the symbol you want to modify. Then release it from the symbol and modify it.*

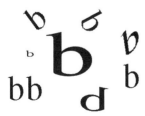

31 *Once you have replaced the old symbol with the modified one, all the instances are changed.*

To import symbols:

1. Choose Import from the Options pop-up menu on the Symbol panel. The Choose a File dialog box opens **28**.

2. Navigate to the symbol library you want and click Choose/Open. The Import Symbols dialog box opens **29**.

3. Select the symbols you want to import, using Command/Ctrl to select more than one.

4. Click Import to import the symbols into the symbol panel of the current document.

Repeated text or graphic elements placed as instances of a symbol can be all be changed in one fell swoop by modifying or replacing the symbol to which they all refer.

To modify a symbol:

1. Select an instance of the symbol you want to modify.

2. Choose **Modify > Symbol > Release Instance**. Modify the symbol to meet your new requirements **30**.

TIP You cannot change the attributes (fill, line weight, style, etc.) of an instance. If necessary, choose **Modify > Symbol > Release Instance**. The instance becomes a group and you can change it to meet your new requirements. You may need to ungroup the object to make the changes you want.

3. Drag the object back onto the name of the original symbol. The alert is displayed **24**.

4. Choose Replace. All instances of the symbol are now derived from the new symbol, but they retain whatever transformations were previously performed **31**.

   or

   Choose Convert to leave the instances as they were—they are converted to groups—and the symbol is replaced by the new one.

To delete a symbol:

1. Highlight the symbol you want to remove from the list on the Symbol panel.

2. Choose Remove from the Options pop-up menu. The alert window opens if there are instances of the symbol in the document **32**.

3. Click Convert *(Mac)* or Release *(Win)* to leave all the instances of the removed symbol in the document as groups.

   or

   Click Delete to remove the instances.

TIP You can replace a symbol by dragging an entirely new object onto its name in the Symbol panel.

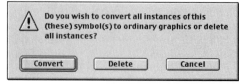

32 *Use the alert panel to control the fate of instances of the symbols you delete.*

PATH OPERATIONS 16

Once you have created paths using any of the creation tools, you can modify those paths in a wide variety of ways. These modifications are called *path operations*. Path operations are actions that start with one or more paths and combine or manipulate them into new shapes. This chapter looks at the majority of path operations. Some specialized path operations such as blends are covered in other chapters.

In this chapter, you will learn how to

Apply different path operations using the menus, toolbars, and panels.

Join objects into composite paths.

Paste Inside to create clipping paths.

Open and close paths.

Reverse the direction of paths.

Use the Knife tool to modify paths.

Remove the overlap between paths.

Simplify points on a path.

Add points to a path.

Use the Union, Divide, Intersect, Punch, Crop, and Transparency commands.

Use the Fractalize command.

Use the Emboss command.

Use the Expand Stroke command.

Use the Inset Path command.

Use the Envelope tools to modify objects.

Use the Envelope toolbar to apply and remove envelopes from graphics.

Paste a path as an envelope.

Reapply path operations commands using a keyboard shortcut.

Attach and release objects from the Perspective grid.

Set up a custom Perspective grid.

With the path operations you have three, sometimes four, different ways to choose the same command. Most of the exercises in this chapter activate the path operations by using the Xtras menu. There is an Operations palette that you can use to invoke the path operations.

To use the Operations palette:

Choose **Window > Toolbars > Xtra Operations**. This opens the Operations palette ❶.

TIP Hold the Command/Ctrl key as you click an icon in the Operations palette to apply the previous setting for that command.

Imagine you have created an illustration of a doughnut with a hole in the center. You need a special type of path to see through the hole. In FreeHand, these are called joined paths. In other programs they are called composite paths.

To create joined paths:

1. Use the Rectangle tool to create a closed object and fill it with a gradient fill to help you see the effects of the joined path.

2. Draw a closed object and fill it with a solid color for the outside of the joined path.

3. Draw a third closed object and position it inside the object created in Step 2.

4. Select the objects created in Steps 2 and 3 ❷.

5. Choose **Modify > Join**. This creates a hole in the object that you can see through ❸.

TIP If the second object is not completely contained inside the first, the hole will appear where both objects overlap.

TIP Hold the Option/Alt key to select an individual path of any joined paths.

TIP If you change the fill or stroke attributes of one of the paths, that change applies to all the paths of the composite.

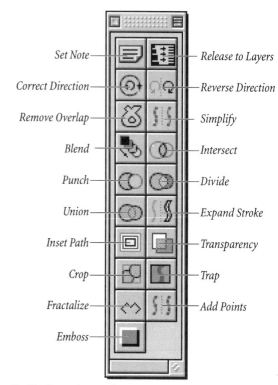

❶ *The* **Operations palette**.

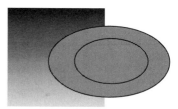

❷ *Two objects selected before they are joined to make a composite path.*

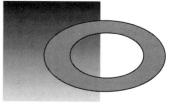

❸ *Two objects after they have been joined to make a* **joined or composite path**.

❹ *A* **clipping path** *is needed so that the rectangles are not visible outside the edges of the star.*

❺ *When the rectangles are* **pasted inside** *the star, the star acts as a clipping path.*

❻ *Drag the* **diamond control point** *(circled) to reposition the objects pasted inside a clipping path.*

To split joined objects:

1. Select the entire joined object.

2. Choose **Modify > Split**. This releases the paths into separate objects.

Pasting an object inside another allows you to fill objects so that anything outside the objects will not be seen. The object that is filled is called a clipping path or mask.

To use Paste Inside:

1. Draw several foreground objects that overlap one background object, such as the rectangles overlapping a star in the example **❹**.

2. Use the Pointer tool to select just the foreground objects, such as the rectangles, and choose **Edit > Cut**.

3. Select the background object and choose **Edit > Paste Inside**. The objects pasted will be visible only inside the background object **❺**.

TIP Hold the Option/Alt key to select objects pasted inside the clipping path.

To move objects pasted inside:

1. Select the clipping path; a diamond-shaped control point appears.

2. Drag the diamond-shaped control point, and release the mouse button when everything is where you want it **❻**.

TIP To release the pasted objects, select the clipping path and choose **Edit > Cut Contents**.

TIP To transform just the clipping path without affecting any of the objects pasted inside, make sure the Contents box in the Transform panel is not checked.

Split Joined Objects; Paste Inside

To close an open path:

1. Select the open path.
2. Click the Object Inspector.
3. Click the Closed box. The path closes with a line from one end point to the other ❼.

To close an open path using the mouse:

Drag one of the endpoints of the path onto the other endpoint. This closes the path ❽.

To open a closed path:

1. Select the closed path that you want to open.
2. Click the Object Inspector.
3. Click the Open box. The object opens by deleting the segment between the first and last points created on the path.

Ordinarily, you would not care about the direction of a path which is determined by the order in which you lay down the points as you draw. But you may want to reverse the direction of a path if text is aligned with it (*see pages 139–141*) or when the path is used in a blend.

To use the Reverse Direction command with blends:

1. Create a blend between two open, stroked paths. Make the number of steps a low number so that you can see the objects in the blend ❾.
2. Hold the Option/Alt key and select one of the original paths at the end of the blend.
3. Choose **Xtras > Cleanup > Reverse Direction**. Notice that the blend changes its shape. That is because the two paths have different directions ❿.

❼ *To close an open path, check the* **Closed box** *in the Object Inspector palette.*

❽ *Drag one endpoint onto another to close an object.*

❾ *When two objects with the same direction are blended, the blend follows a smooth look.*

❿ *When the direction of an object in a blend is reversed, the shape of the blend changes.*

⓫ *The* **Knife tool** *in the Toolbox.*

⓬ *The* **Knife tool dialog box.**

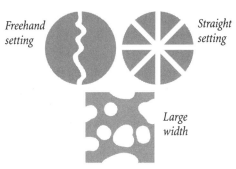

Freehand setting

Straight setting

Large width

⓭ *Different effects that can be created with the Knife tool.*

With the Knife tool, you can open paths, slice objects into parts, punch holes in objects, and even erase parts of objects.

To use the Knife tool:

1. Double-click the Knife tool ⓫ in the Toolbox to open the Knife Tool dialog box ⓬.

2. Click the Freehand radio button to make a curved or wavy line cut. Click the Straight radio button to make a straight-line cut.

TIP Hold the Option/Alt key as you drag with the Knife to temporarily set the Knife for straight cuts.

TIP As you draw at the straight setting, hold down the Shift key to constrain your cuts to 45° angles.

3. Set the width to control the space between the cuts.

TIP A width of 0 leaves no space between the objects created by the cuts.

TIP Setting the width to a very large size turns the Knife into an eraser that erases portions of the object.

4. Click Close cut paths so that the objects created by the Knife are closed paths.

5. Click Tight fit so that the Knife tool follows the movements of your mouse precisely.

6. Click OK and then drag with the Knife across an object or objects ⓭.

TIP The Knife tool cuts only selected objects.

To use the Remove Overlap command:

1. Use the Freehand tool (*see pages 38– 39*) to create an object that overlaps itself. Make sure that Auto Remove Overlap is not checked in the Freehand Tool dialog box.

2. Choose **Xtras > Cleanup > Remove Overlap**. Notice that the overlapping areas are eliminated ⓮.

Too many points on a path can cause problems when you print. The Simplify command lets you remove excess points.

To use the Simplify command:

1. Use the Freehand tool to create an intricate path with a number of points.

2. Choose **Xtras > Cleanup > Simplify**. The Simplify dialog box appears ⓯.

3. Drag the slider to change the value in the Amount field. The greater the number, the more points will be eliminated. This may change the shape of the original object ⓰.

Certain effects need additional points on the path to look good. For instance, the Add Points command lets you easily add extra points to a path.

To use the Add Points command:

1. Select an object.

2. Choose **Xtras > Distort > Add Points**.

3. Each time you choose the command, a new point will be added between each existing pair of points ⓱.

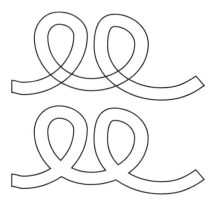

⓮ *The effects of applying the* **Remove Overlap** *command.*

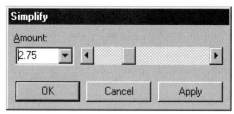

⓯ *The* **Simplify dialog box.**

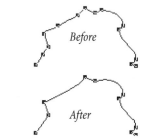

⓰ *The effects of the* **Simplify** *command.*

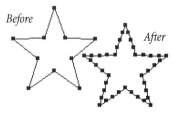

⓱ *The results of the* **Add Points** *command.*

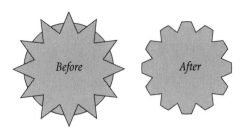

® *The effects of the* **Intersect** *command.*

Before

PUNCH

After

PUNCH

® *The effects of the* **Punch** *command.*

The Intersect command lets you create a new object from the shape where two objects overlap.

To use the Intersect command:

1. Select two or more paths that overlap each other.

2. Choose **Xtras > Path Operations > Intersect**.

3. A new path is created that is the shape of the overlapping area **®**.

TIP The Intersect command deletes from the selection any objects that do not overlap.

The Punch command allows you to use one object to punch holes in another.

To use the Punch command:

1. Select two or more objects that overlap each other.

TIP To have multiple objects such as text act as the punch, make those objects a joined path (*see page 170*).

2. Choose **Xtras > Path Operations > Punch**.

3. The top object punches through the bottom object **®**.

TIP The Intersect and Punch commands modify the original objects as they create the new paths. To save the original objects while creating new ones, hold the Shift key as you apply the Intersect or Punch commands.

or

TIP Change the Preferences setting (*see page 249*).

Intersect; Punch

The Union command allows you to take many objects and turn them into one path.

To use the Union command:

1. Create two or more objects so that they overlap one another.

2. Choose **Xtras > Path Operations > Union**.

3. The multiple paths join into one ⑳.

TIP If the selected objects for the Union, Intersect, or Punch commands have different attributes, the final object takes on the attributes of the backmost object.

⑳ *The effects of the* **Union** *command.*

The Divide command creates new paths from the overlapping areas of objects.

To use the Divide command:

1. Create two or more objects so that they overlap one another.

2. Choose **Xtras > Path Operations > Divide**.

3. The paths divide into new paths wherever they overlapped ㉑.

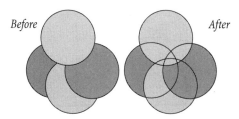

㉑ *The effects of the* **Divide** *command.*

The Transparency command lets you simulate a see through effect.

To use the Transparency command:

1. Create two or more overlapping objects filled with different colors.

2. Choose **Xtras > Path Operations > Transparency** to open the Transparency dialog box ㉒.

3. Set the amount of the transparency.

TIP If the amount is less than 50%, the front color is more obvious. If it is more than 50%, the back color looks more obvious.

4. Click OK to see the transparency effect ㉓.

TIP Unlike the transparency lens fills, this command creates a new path that simulates transparency.

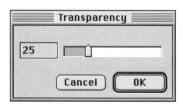

㉒ *The* **Transparency** *dialog box.*

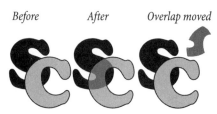

㉓ *The effects of the* **Transparency** *command.*

Before

After

㉔ *The effects of the* **Crop** *command.*

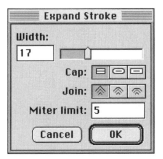

㉕ *The* **Expand Stroke** *dialog box.*

Before   *After*

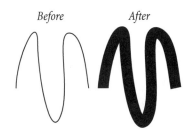

㉖ *The* **effects of the Expand Stroke** *command.*

The Crop command allows you to use the top object as a cookie cutter.

To use the Crop command:

1. Select various objects with one object on top.

2. Choose **Xtras > Path Operations > Crop**.

3. All the objects at the bottom are trimmed so that only those portions that were under the topmost object remain **㉔**.

TIP To use text that has been converted to paths as the crop, ungroup and then choose Join.

FreeHand offers you a way to convert lines or open paths to closed paths by using the Expand Stroke command. This allows you to convert strokes into closed paths that can have fills such as the Lens or Gradient fills.

To use the Expand Stroke command:

1. Select the path you wish to convert.

2. Choose **Xtras > Path Operations > Expand Stroke**. The Expand Stroke dialog box appears **㉕**.

3. Enter the width you want for the final object.

4. Set the Cap, Join, and Miter-limit settings. Note that while these settings are the same as the settings for a stroke, the final object will actually be a filled path.

5. Click OK to create a new filled path **㉖**.

To use the Inset Path command:

1. Create a closed path.

2. Choose **Xtras > Path Operations > Inset Path**. The Inset Path dialog box appears **㉗**.

3. In the Steps field, enter the number of copies you want to create.

4. If the number of steps is greater than 1, choose Uniform, Farther, or Nearer from the pop-up menu to control the distances between the inset objects **㉘**.

5. Use the slider to set the size of the new objects. Positive numbers place the new objects inside the original. Negative numbers place the new object outside the original.

6. When you are satisfied with your choices, click OK. This creates copies of the object inset from the original.

TIP Multiples created by the Inset Path command are created as grouped objects.

The Fractalize command allows you to distort an object for dramatic effects.

To use the Fractalize command:

1. Select the object to distort.

2. Make sure the Even/Odd fill box is checked in the Object Inspector.

3. Choose **Xtras > Distort > Fractalize**.

4. Repeat the command until you are satisfied with the effect **㉙**.

㉗ *The **Inset Path** dialog box.*

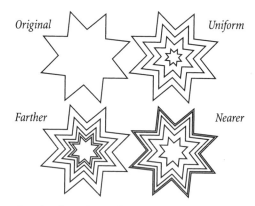

㉘ *The effects of the different **Inset Path settings.***

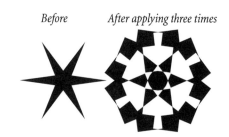

㉙ *The effects of the **Fractalize command.***

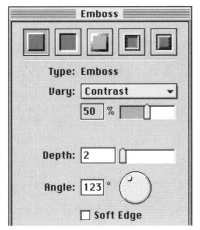

⊕ *The* **Emboss dialog box.**

⊕ *The effects of the* **Emboss options.**

The Emboss command allows you to create the look of raised or depressed areas on a background.

To use the Emboss command:

1. Select one or more objects. Choose **Xtras>Create>Emboss** to open the Emboss dialog box **⊕**.

2. Click one of the top icons to choose from the five types of embossing effects: emboss, deboss, chisel, ridge, or quilt **⊕**.

3. Use the Vary pop-up menu to choose between Contrast or Color.

4. Adjust the Vary slider to control how much the new objects differ from the original.

5. Set the Depth field for how obvious the embossing should be.

6. Set the angle to control where the light and dark areas of the emboss should be.

7. Click the Soft Edge box to make the transition less abrupt.

8. Click OK when you are satisfied and view the results.

To use the Repeat Xtra Command:

Although many path operations can be found under the Modify menu, you have an extra feature if you choose the commands via the Xtras menu. When you choose a command from the Xtras menu or the Operations toolbar, that command will be listed at the top of the Xtras menu as the Repeat [Xtra] command. This means that you do not have to go all the way to the submenu to choose the command, you can simply choose it at the top of the menu.

TIP You can work even faster by using the keystroke for the Repeat [Xtra] command. The Mac keystroke is **Command-Shift-+**. The Win keystroke is **Ctrl-Alt-Shift-X**.

The Envelope toolbar allows you to warp and distort graphics and text blocks and to store and reuse the "envelopes" you create as presets. It comes with 21 ready-made presets.

To apply a preset envelope to a graphic:

1. If the Envelope toolbar is not visible, choose **Window > Toolbars > Envelope** to open the Envelope toolbar **32**.
2. Select the path or text block you want to shape **33**.
3. Select the envelope preset you want from the pop-up menu.
4. Click the Create envelope icon to distort the selected object **34**.

To remove an envelope from a graphic:

1. Choose **Window > Toolbars > Envelope** to open the Envelope toolbar.
2. Select the path or text block you want to return to its standard form.
3. Click the Remove icon in the Envelope toolbar.

or

Click the Release icon to remove the envelope while leaving the distortion in place. A path will return to being a path; a text block will become a group and the individual letters will have been converted to paths **35**.

TIP To edit text within an envelope, Option/Alt double-click it to open the Text Editor. Make your changes and click OK to apply them. Unlike text changed to paths, text in an envelope remains editable.

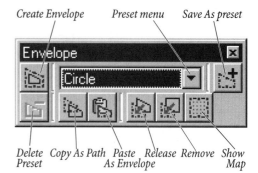

Create Envelope   Preset menu   Save As preset

Delete   Copy As Path Paste   Release Remove Show
Preset   As Envelope   Map

32 *The **Envelope toolbar** contains a number of preset shapes you can choose among to distort an object.*

33 *Envelope distortions can be applied to text blocks as well as to other vector objects.*

34 *Applying the circle envelope preset to an elongated object creates an elliptical text object.*

35 *Releasing the text block from the envelope leaves five separate paths.*

36 *Create a path you want to use as an envelope preset.*

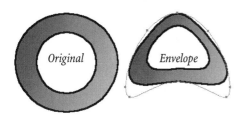

37 *Applying the custom envelope to a path creates an object somewhere between the original and the preset.*

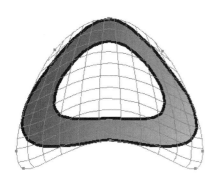

38 *The effect of selecting* **Show Map**.

You can also create custom envelope shapes from paths.

To use a path as an envelope:

1. Create a path using your choice of drawing tools.
2. Select the path **36**.
3. Choose **Edit > Copy** to copy the path to the clipboard.
4. Select the object to which you want to apply the envelope.
5. Choose **Modify > Envelope > Paste as Envelope** or click the Paste as Envelope icon on the Envelope toolbar. The envelope is applied to the object **37**.
6. As with any path, you can move, add or remove points on an envelope to control its shape.

Once you have a new envelope shape, you may want to save it to use it on other objects.

To save a custom envelope:

1. Select the envelope you wish to save.
2. Choose **Modify > Envelope > Save as Preset** or click the Save as Preset icon on the Envelope toolbar.

To delete an envelope preset:

1. Select the envelope you wish to remove from the pop-up menu on the Envelope toolbar.
2. Choose **Modify > Envelope > Delete Preset** or click the Delete Preset icon on the Envelope toolbar.

TIP Select Show Map from the Envelope toolbar or choose **Modify > Envelope > Show Map** to display a grid of lines in the envelope and help visualize the distortion created by the Envelope tool **38**.

After you have created an envelope to modify a path or a text block, you can convert it to a path for use in you document.

To paste an envelope as a path:

1. Select the envelope you want to copy **39**.

2. Choose **Modify > Envelope > Copy As Path** from the menu to copy the path to the clipboard.

3. Choose **Edit > Paste** to paste the shape into the document. You can then place it behind the original envelope if you wish **40**.

TIP Sometimes, when you paste a path as an envelope on a text block, the text runs the wrong way **41**. To correct this problem choose **Modify > Envelope > Remove** to release the text from the envelope. Then repeat the process of applying the envelope to the text block. The text should now run across the envelope as you wanted it to in the first place **39**.

39 *A text block with a custom envelope applied.*

40 *Copy the envelope as a path and put it behind the original envelope to put a fill behind the text.*

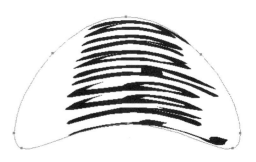

41 *The Paste As Envelope command sometimes gives unexpected results.*

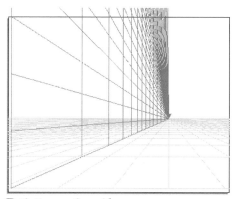

42 *The* **Perspective grid.**

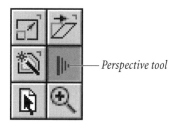

— *Perspective tool*

43 *The* **Perspective tool.**

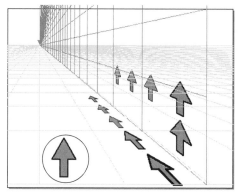

44 *The original arrow (circled) and as it appears attached to the floor and side grids.*

The Perspective grid is a very powerful tool for quickly and easily creating graphics that maintain a consistent perspective. Essentially, it allows you to create envelopes that adjust automatically as they are moved on the page.

To attach an object to the Perspective grid:

1. Choose **View > Perspective Grid > Show**. The grid appears on the page **42**.

2. Choose the Perspective tool **43** from the Toolbox and drag an object to the desired place on the grid.

3. Tap one of the cursor keys on the keyboard:

   Left to attach it to the left grid.

   Right to attach it to the right grid.

   Down to attach it to the floor grid oriented to the right vanishing point.

   Up to orient the object toward the left vanishing point and to attach it to the floor grid.

4. Release the mouse. The object is attached to the grid as an envelope **44**.

To move an object on the Perspective grid:

Drag an object with the Perspective tool. As it moves it changes shape to conform to the perspective grid.

TIP Hold down the Option/ Alt key to copy an object while dragging it on the grid with the Perspective tool. Hold down the Shift key to constrain its movement to the grid axes.

Attach Object to Perspective Grid; Move Object on Grid

To set up the Perspective grid:

1. Choose **View** > **Perspective Grid** > **Define Grids** to open the Define Grids dialog box ⑮.

2. Double click to change the name of the grid and set values for the number of vanishing points, grid cell size, and colors.

3. Click OK to accept the setting and return to the document. The grids you have defined can be selected from the bottom of the **View** > **Perspective Grid** submenu.

4. To move the vanishing points and the grids, drag them with the Perspective tool.

TIP To keep the objects attached to the grid, select the objects and hold down the Shift key as you as you move the vanishing points and the grids.

TIP As you make changes to a grid in a document, those changes are continuously saved. If you want to save a grid configuration, click Duplicate in the Define Grid dialog box to create a copy of the grid before you make your changes.

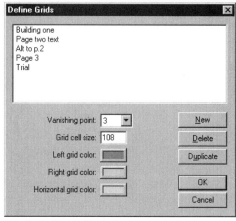

⑮ *The **Define Grids** dialog box sets the parameters for the Perspective grids used by the document.*

Grid objects are envelopes. As with other envelopes, you can release an object leaving it distorted.

To release objects from the grid:

Select the object you want to release leaving it distorted. Choose **View** > **Perspective Grid** > **Release with Perspective.**

You can also remove an object from the grid and return it to its original shape.

To remove objects from the grid:

Select the object you want to release and restore to its original shape. Choose **View** > **Perspective Grid** > **Remove Perspective**.

TIP You can use the commands **Modify** > **Envelope** > **Release** and **Modify** > **Envelope** > **Remove** as well as the Release and Remove buttons on the Envelope toolbar to release or remove objects from the grid.

Xtras are features that are added to the basic FreeHand program. When you install FreeHand, the program loads a set of built-in Xtras. These are the Xtras from Macromedia. You do not pay extra for them.

You can also buy Xtras from other companies. These are called third-party Xtras. Third-party Xtras are usually more sophisticated than the basic Xtras.

This chapter covers the details of working with most of the Xtras from Macromedia. Some of these Xtras, such as the Arc and Chart, are covered in other chapters.

In this chapter, you will learn how to

Open the Xtra Tools toolbar.

Use the 3D Rotation tool.

Use the Fisheye Lens tool.

Use the Smudge tool.

Use the Shadow tool.

Use the Roughen tool.

Use the Eyedropper.

Use the Mirror tool.

Use the Graphic Hose tool.

Use the Bend tool.

Manipulate colors using the Colors Xtras.

Use the Trap Xtra.

Use the Delete Empty Text Blocks and Delete Unused Named Colors Xtras.

Use third-party Xtras in FreeHand.

Use the Xtras Manager.

Use the Repeat Xtras command.

Xtras

You can find Xtras through the Xtras menu as well as in the Xtra Tools toolbar.

To use the Xtra Tools toolbar:

Choose **Window > Toolbars > Xtra Tools**. The Xtra Tools toolbar appears ❶.

The 3D Rotation tool applies a distortion to the perspective of an object as if it were rotated in space. Before you use the 3D Rotation tool, you must set its controls.

To set the 3D Rotation controls:

1. Double-click the 3D Rotation tool. The 3D Rotation controls appears ❷.

2. With the Easy radio button selected, use the Rotate from pop-up menu to select the point from which the rotation should occur.

   - Choose Mouse click to set the rotation pivot point by clicking in your document.

   - Choose Center of selection to make the point the physical center of the object.

   - Choose Center of gravity to have the point be the center of the object when adjusted for uneven shapes.

   - Choose Origin to have the rotation pivot point be the bottom-left corner of the bounding box that surrounds the selection.

3. Set a Distance amount for how much distortion occurs during the rotation. For the greatest distortion effect, enter small numbers.

TIP The Expert setting lets you enter the point of rotation as x, y coordinates.

TIP In the Expert mode, a plus sign (+) appears on the page as you drag. The (+) sign indicates the point from which the rotation is projected.

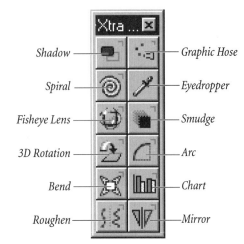

Shadow — Graphic Hose
Spiral — Eyedropper
Fisheye Lens — Smudge
3D Rotation — Arc
Bend — Chart
Roughen — Mirror

❶ *The* **Xtra Tools toolbar.**

❷ *The* **3D Rotation controls.**

3D Rotation Tool

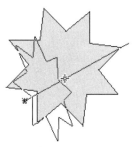

❸ *As you drag with the* **3D Rotation tool**, *a line extends from your starting point. Drag along the line to control the amount of distortion applied to the object.*

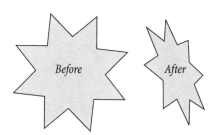

❹ *The results of applying the* **3D Rotation tool.**

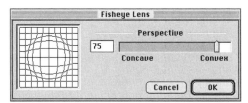

❺ *The* **Fisheye Lens dialog box.**

Before

GAINING WEIGHT?

After

GAINING WEIGHT?

❻ *The results of applying the* **Fisheye Lens tool.**

Once you have chosen settings for the 3D Rotation tool, you can then apply it to objects.

To use the 3D Rotation tool:

1. Select the object or objects you want to modify and choose the 3D Rotation tool.

2. If you chose Mouse click, press and drag the cursor over the spot on the object from which the rotation should occur.

3. Drag the cursor away from this spot. A line extends out. The farther along the line you drag, the greater the 3D rotation **❸**.

TIP As you press, a preview shows how the object is being modified.

4. When you are satisfied with the rotation, release the mouse button, and the object changes shape **❹**.

TIP In the Easy setting, the point of projection (the perspective vanishing point) will be the point where the mouse is clicked.

To use the Fisheye Lens tool:

1. Select the object you want to modify.

2. Double-click the Fisheye Lens tool in the Xtra Tools toolbar. The Fisheye Lens dialog box appears **❺**.

3. Drag the slider to enter the amount you want in the Perspective field. Convex or positive numbers cause the object to bulge. Concave or negative numbers cause the object to be pinched. Click OK.

4. Drag your cursor to create an oval over the area you want to distort.

5. Release the mouse button to apply the distortion **❻**.

TIP Hold the Option/Alt key to create a distortion from the center outward.

TIP Hold the Shift key to constrain the distortion to a circular shape.

The Smudge tool provides you with a quick and easy way to add a soft edge to an object.

To use the Smudge tool:

1. Select the object or objects you want to modify.

2. Choose the Smudge tool from the Xtra Tools toolbar. Your cursor changes into the Smudge fingers.

3. Drag the fingers along the direction the smudge should take. A line extends from the object. That is the length of the smudge ❼.

4. Release the mouse button to create the smudge ❽.

TIP Spot colors used in the Smudge tool do not separate correctly.

TIP Hold the Option/Alt key to create a smudge from the center outward.

TIP The number of steps in a smudge is governed by the printer resolution in the Document Inspector. If a smudge looks jagged, undo the smudge, increase the resolution, and then reapply the smudge.

❼ *Dragging with the* **Smudge fingers** *controls the length and direction of the effect.*

❽ *The results of applying the* **Smudge tool.**

If you are smudging objects over colors, the smudge should fade to those background colors. To do so, you change the smudge colors.

To change the smudge colors:

1. Double-click the Smudge tool in the Xtra Tools toolbar to display the Smudge dialog box ❾.

2. Drag colors from the Color Mixer or Color List into the Fill and the Stroke boxes.

3. Click OK and then apply the smudge as usual.

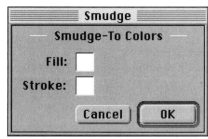

❾ *The* **Smudge dialog box** *lets you set the colors that the fill and stroke fade into.*

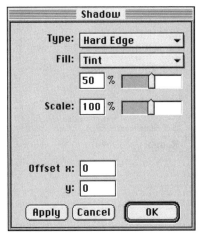

⑩ *The* **Shadow dialog box.**

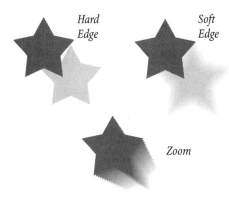

Hard
Edge

Soft
Edge

Zoom

⑪ *The three different* **types of shadows.**

A more sophisticated version of the Smudge tool is the Shadow tool.

To use the Shadow tool:

1. Select the object or objects you want to modify.

2. Double-click the Shadow tool in the Xtra Tools toolbar to open the Shadow dialog box **⑩**.

3. Set the type to Hard Edge, Soft Edge, or Zoom **⑪**.

4. Set the Fill color for the shadow using the pop-up menu. Use Color to set a specific color for the shadow. Use Shade to create a shadow color that is a darker color of the original object. Use Tint to create a shadow that is a lighter color of the original object.

5. Use the slider for the Color and Tint fills to adjust the lightness or darkness of the shadow.

6. Use the Scale slider to set the size of the shadow element. Less than 100% makes a shadow that is smaller than the original. Greater than 100% makes a shadow that is larger than the original.

7. Set the *x* and *y* offset amounts to position the shadow away from the original.

8. Click OK to apply the shadow to the object.

   TIP Once you have applied a shadow to an object, you can use the mouse to drag the shadow into new positions.

Shadow Tool

189

The Roughen tool takes clean, smooth paths and makes them irregular and ragged. This can be very useful in making artwork look hand-drawn, or less "perfect."

To use the Roughen tool:

1. Select the object or objects you want to modify.

2. Double-click the Roughen tool in the Xtra Tools toolbar to open the Roughen dialog box 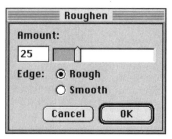.

3. Use the Amount field or slider to increase the number of segments per inch that are added using the tool.

4. Select the Rough radio button to create corner points. Select the Smooth radio button to create curved points.

5. Click OK. With the Roughen tool still selected, press the object and drag. The further you drag, the greater the distortion **13**.

12 *The* **Roughen** *dialog box.*

NERVOUS
20 points per inch

PANICKED
50 points per inch

13 *The results of* **applying the Roughen tool.**

The Eyedropper tool lets you copy colors between objects.

To use the Eyedropper tool:

1. Choose the Eyedropper tool from the Xtra Tools toolbar. The cursor changes to an eyedropper icon.

2. Position the eyedropper over the color you want to copy.

3. Press down with the eyedropper. Do not let go of the mouse. Your cursor turns into a little square of that color.

4. Drag that square onto the fill or stroke of another object to apply color **14**.

14 *Use the* **Eyedropper** *to transfer a color from one object to another.*

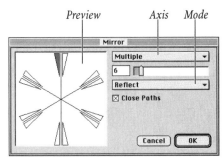

Preview   Axis   Mode

⑮ *The **Mirror dialog box** is where you set the different functions of the Mirror tool.*

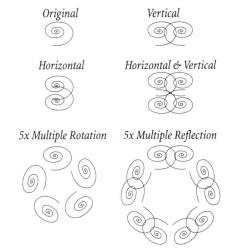

Original

Vertical

Horizontal

Horizontal & Vertical

5x Multiple Rotation

5x Multiple Reflection

⑯ *The various effects created with the **Mirror tool.***

⑰ *Using the Mirror tool shows the **line for the axis** and a preview of the effect.*

The Mirror tool gives you an interactive way to create multiple rotated and reflected objects.

To set the Mirror tool controls:

1. Double-click the Mirror tool in the Xtra Tools toolbar to open the Mirror dialog box **⑮**.

2. Use the Axis pop-up menu to choose the axis around which the objects should reflect. Horizontal reflects from top to bottom. Vertical reflects from left to right. Horizontal & Vertical reflects both ways at once. Multiple reflects around multiple axes **⑯**.

3. In the Multiple setting, use the slider to control the number of axes the object reflects around.

4. In the Multiple setting, choose the Reflect or Rotate mode.

5. Click OK to apply the settings.

To use the Mirror tool:

1. Select the object you want to reflect. Choose the Mirror tool in the Xtra Tools toolbar.

2. Move the cursor onto the page area and press on the point around which the reflection should occur. A line extends out showing the axis that the object is reflected around **⑰**. A preview of the reflection appears.

3. Drag the cursor until you are satisfied with the effect.

4. Release the mouse button to apply the Mirror tool effect.

TIP Tap the left- or right-arrow keys to decrease or increase the number of axes in the multiple setting.

TIP Tap the up- or down-arrow keys to change the Multiple setting from reflect to rotate.

TIP Hold the Option/Alt key to rotate the angle of the axis.

Mirror Tool

The Graphic Hose allows you to store objects (including bitmapped images, text, envelopes, and symbols) and then drag on the page to paint with those objects. There are two parts to using the Graphic Hose: storing the objects in the Graphics Hose panel and setting the options for painting with the hose.

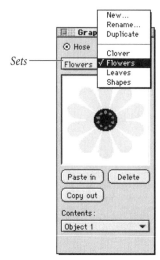

Objects for the Graphic Hose are stored as sets within the Graphic Hose panel.

To store objects in the Graphic Hose panel:

1. Double-click the Graphic Hose tool in the Xtra Tools toolbar to open the Graphic Hose panel.

2. Click the Hose radio button to display the Hose sets ⓲.

3. Choose New from the Sets pop-up menu to add a new set. A dialog box appears where you can name the new set.

4. Select artwork on the page and choose **Edit > Copy** or use the keystroke command to copy the artwork.

5. Click Paste in. The artwork appears in the preview window as an object in the Contents pop-up menu.

6. Copy and paste additional artwork into the set. The artwork is added as a new object to the Contents menu.

TIP There is a limit of 10 objects for each set.

TIP Graphic Hose sets are available for any document and other sessions of working with FreeHand.

TIP You can use symbols *(see page 165)* as the elements for the Graphic Hose. This allows you to modify the symbol element and all the objects created by the Graphic Hose update automatically.

⓲ *The **Graphic Hose panel** where you can store objects in the Hose sets.*

Graphic Hose

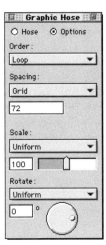

⑲ *The* **Graphic Hose Options** *controls let you change how the objects go on the page.*

⑳ *The* **original two stars** *(circled) were used to create the different sized and rotated stars.*

Once you have created Hose sets, you need to set the Options to control how the Graphic Hose applies objects on the page.

To use the Graphic Hose tool:

1. Double-click the Graphic Hose tool in the Xtra Tools toolbar to open the Graphic Hose panel **⑲**.

2. Click the Options radio button to display the Options controls.

3. Use the Order pop-up menu to control in what order the objects in the set are applied. Loop applies the objects in numerical order. Back and Forth applies the objects in forward then reverse order. Random applies the objects in no specific order.

4. Use the Spacing pop-up menu to control the distance between the objects. Grid applies the objects onto a grid with a size you set in the Grid field. Variable applies the objects in spacing that you set as Tight or Loose. Random applies the objects with no specific distance between them.

5. Use the Scale pop-up menu to control the size of the objects. Uniform sets a certain size for all the objects. Random applies the objects in no specific sizes.

6. Use the Rotate pop-up menu and angle wheel to control the rotation of the objects. Uniform sets a certain angle for all the objects. Incremental applies rotations that change in specific increments from one object to the next. Random rotates the objects without any order.

7. Once you have set all the options, drag the Graphic Hose on the page to apply the Hose artwork **⑳**.

Graphic Hose

The Bend tool applies a distortion to objects to warp the path segments in or out.

To use the Bend tool:

1. Double-click the Bend tool in the Xtra Tools toolbar to open the Bend dialog box **21**.

2. Adjust the slider or enter an amount in the field to increase or decrease the number of points per inch that are added. Click OK.

3. With the object selected, drag down to create a rounded bend **22**.

   or

   Drag up to create a spiked bend **22**.

   TIP The point where you start the drag is the center of the distortion.

   TIP The longer you drag, the greater the amount of the bend.

The Color Control Xtra allows you to adjust the colors in objects.

To use the Color Control dialog box:

1. Select the objects you want to adjust.

2. Choose **Xtras > Colors > Color Control** to open the Color Control dialog box **23**.

3. Choose CMYK, RGB, or HLS color.

4. Use the sliders or the fields to add or subtract color from the objects you have chosen. Positive numbers add color. Negative numbers subtract color.

5. Check the Preview box to see how your adjustments affect the selected objects without actually applying the changes.

6. When you are satisfied with the color changes, click OK. Your changes are applied to the objects.

   TIP The Color Control dialog box only works on objects that have been colored with process colors, not spot colors.

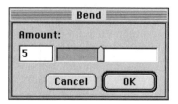

21 The **Bend dialog box** *allows you to control the number of points per inch that are added during a bend distortion.*

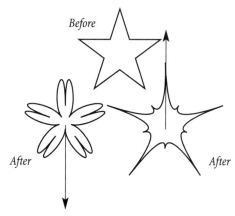

22 The **results of applying the Bend tool**. *The arrows indicate the point where the drag started and ended.*

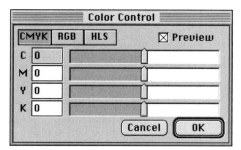

23 The **Color Control** *dialog box.*

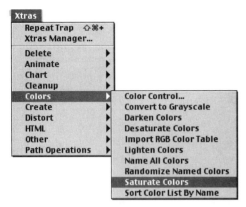

㉔ *The Xtras Color tools are selected from the menu.*

㉕ *The results of using the* **Darken Colors** *and* **Lighten Colors** *commands.*

FreeHand offers additional Xtras for working with color when you select **Xtras > Colors >** from the menu: Convert to Grayscale, Darken Colors, Lighten Colors, Import RGB Color Table, Saturate Colors, Desaturate Colors, Name All Colors, Randomize Named Colors, and Sort Color List By Name **㉔**.

To darken or lighten colors:

1. Select the object or objects you want to change.

2. Choose **Xtras > Colors > Darken Colors** or **Lighten Colors ㉕**.

   Darken Colors decreases the Lightness value of the color in 5% increments.

   Lighten Colors increases the Lightness value of the color in 5% increments.

3. To continue to darken or lighten the colors, repeat the command as many times as necessary (*see page 179*).

To saturate or desaturate colors:

1. Select the object or objects you want to change.

2. Choose **Xtras > Colors > Saturate Colors** or **Desaturate Colors**.

   Saturate Colors increases the saturation value of the color in 5% increments. This makes muted colors more vibrant.

   Desaturate Colors decreases the saturation value of the color in 5% increments. This makes colors less vibrant.

3. To continue to saturate or desaturate the colors, repeat the command as many times as necessary (*see page 179*).

To convert colors to grayscale:

1. Select the object or objects you want to change.

2. Choose **Xtras > Colors > Convert to Grayscale.** All colors are converted to grays with the equivalent tonal value.

FreeHand offers several Xtras that help you manage colors in the Color List and in your document.

To name all colors:

Choose **Xtras > Colors > Name All Colors**. All colors used by objects in your document that are not named appear on the Color List, with their names showing their CMYK percentages.

To sort the Color List by name:

Choose **Xtras > Colors > Sort Color List By Name**. This rearranges the Color List. The default colors appear first, followed by the colors named by their CMYK and RGB compositions, and then named colors **26**.

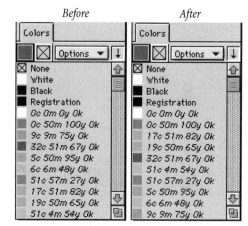

26 *The results of applying the* **Sort Color List by Name** *command.*

To delete unused named colors:

Choose **Xtras > Delete > Unused Named Colors**. Colors that are not applied to an object or a style are deleted. The default colors are not deleted even if they are not used.

TIP Delete unused colors before exporting artwork to layout programs such as Adobe PageMaker or QuarkXPress.

To use the Randomize Named Colors Xtra:

Choose **Xtras > Colors > Randomize Named Colors**. This command changes the values of the named colors in the Color List. All objects with named colors applied to them are changed **27**. This command creates interesting effects when applied to abstract illustrations.

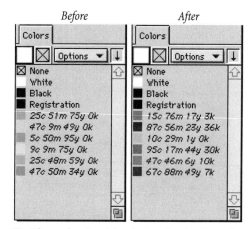

27 *The results of applying the* **Randomize Named Colors** *command.*

If you deselect the text block before typing in it, you leave an empty text block on the page.

To delete empty text blocks:

Choose **Xtras > Delete > Empty Text Blocks** to delete empty text blocks.

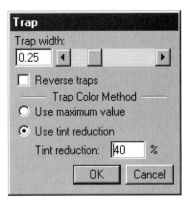

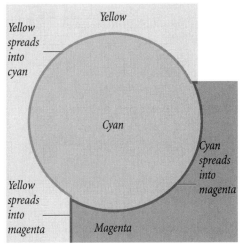

❷❽ *The **Trap** dialog box.*

❷❾ *The results of **applying the Trap command.***

Trapping is a technique printers use to compensate for misregistration of color plates in the printing process. FreeHand lets you create traps with the Trap Xtra. Although the Trap Xtra is very easy to apply, setting the proper values takes years of experience. If you do not understand trapping and you want to set traps, consult the print shop that will print your work.

To use the Trap Xtra:

1. Select two or more objects in your illustration that you want to trap.

2. Choose **Xtras > Create > Trap**. The Trap dialog box appears **❷❽**.

3. Use the sliders or type in the Trap width suggested by your print shop.

4. If your print shop agrees, choose Use maximum value to make the trap color the strongest available.

   or

   Choose the Use tint reduction setting and enter the reduction amount suggested by your print shop.

5. Check the Reverse traps box to change the direction of the trap. (Reverse traps are sometimes called *chokes*.) Consult your print shop as to when you should do this.

6. Click OK. The traps are created **❷❾**.

TIP When you create traps, you create new objects set to overprint between the original objects. If you move or delete objects later, be careful that you do not leave the trap objects behind.

Using third-party Xtras

In addition to the Macromedia Xtras, there are third-party Xtras that you can use within FreeHand. These Xtras allow you to do things you cannot ordinarily do in FreeHand. For instance, VectorTools from Extensis gives you far more control over color than you have using the FreeHand Xtras. Other popular Xtras are KPT Vector Effects from MetaCreations, 3D Invigorator from Zaxwerks, and MAPublisher from Avenza Software. Follow the instructions with the Xtras to install them. After you install them, third-party Xtras are listed either in their own menu or in one of the FreeHand Xtras categories.

If you install many third-party Xtras, the Xtras may conflict with each other. FreeHand comes with an Xtras Manager that allows you to turn the Xtras on or off. This can be helpful if you are trying to discover the source of an Xtras conflict or avoid conflicts.

To use the Xtras Manager:

1. Choose **Xtras>Xtras Manager**. The Xtras Manager dialog box appears ㉚ – ㉛.

2. Click next to each Xtra to make it active or inactive. Use the Options pop-up menu to turn all the Xtras on or off.

To use the Repeat Xtra command:

Once an Xtra is used from the Xtras menu, it appears as the Repeat [Xtra] command. This means that the Xtra can be reapplied via a keystroke.

The Mac keystroke is **Command-Shift-+**.

The Win keystroke is **Ctrl-Alt-Shift-X**.

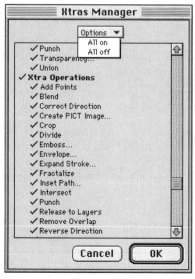

㉚ *Clicking the checkmarks next to each Xtra in the Xtras Manager makes the Xtras active or inactive.*

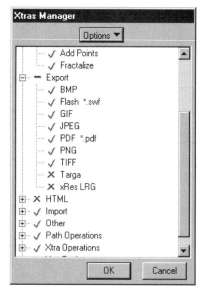

㉛ *On the Xtras Manager for Windows, the Xtra extensions that are turned off have an "x" in front of them.*

Third-party Xtras; Xtras Manager; Repeat Xtras

CHARTS AND GRAPHS 18

Here is where FreeHand really gets down to business — creating mathematically correct charts and graphs. Even if you do not understand the mathematics of graphs, you can still create exceptional graphs using FreeHand.

In this chapter, you will learn how to

Enter data into the FreeHand worksheet.

Use that data in different charts and graphs.

Modify the charts and graphs.

Create special pictographic elements to use in graphs.

To create a chart or graph, you need to open the worksheet and enter the data.

To open the worksheet:

1. Click the Chart tool in the Xtra Tools palette.

2. Drag the + sign cursor to create a rectangle on your work page. (The size of the rectangle determines the size of the chart.) The Chart worksheet appears ❶.

To enter data:

1. Type the data in the data entry area. This inserts the data into the currently active cell.

2. Press Return or Enter to apply the data to the cell and move to the cell below. Type the data for that cell.

3. Press Tab to apply the data to the cell and jump to the cell to the right.

4. Use the up, down, left, or right arrow keys to move to different cells.

5. Use the Import button to bring tab-delimited text directly into the worksheet.

Data entry area

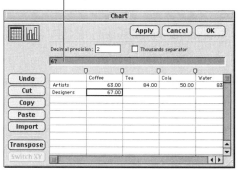

❶ *The* **chart worksheet** *is where you enter data for a chart or graph.*

Once you have entered the data, you need to choose the type of graph or chart you will create.

To style a graph or chart:

1. Click the chart style icon at the top of the Chart window. The worksheet disappears and the styling selections appears ❷.

2. Click one of the six chart type icons: grouped column, stacked column, line, pie, area, and scatter.

TIP To see the effects of changing the style and features of your graph, click Apply at the top of the Chart window.

When to use a grouped column graph

Use a grouped column graph ❸ to compare data using bars. Each bar represents one cell of data.

When to use a stacked column graph

Use a stacked column graph ❹ to compare the progress of data. Each stacked bar represents one row of data.

When to use a line graph

Use a line graph ❺ to compare the trend of data over a period of time. Each line represents a column of data.

When to use a pie chart

Use a pie chart ❻ to display data as percentages of the total. Each wedge represents one data cell. Each row of data creates a separate pie chart.

When to use an area graph

Use an area graph ❼ to compare the trend of data over a period of time. Each area represents a column of data. Each column's value is added to the previous column's total.

When to use a scatter graph

Use a scatter graph ❽ to plot data as paired sets of coordinates. Each coordinate represents a row of data containing two cells.

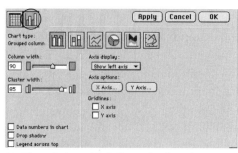

❷ *The* **Style icon** *(circled) switches from the worksheet to the controls for styling charts and graphs.*

❸ *The* **grouped column graph** *icon.*

❹ *The* **stacked column graph** *icon.*

❺ *The* **line graph** *icon.*

❻ *The* **pie chart** *icon.*

❼ *The* **area graph** *icon.*

❽ *The* **scatter graph** *icon.*

Styling Charts

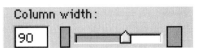

⑨ *The controls for* **Column width** *are available for grouped column and stacked column graphs.*

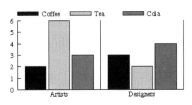

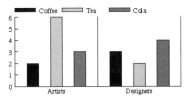

⑩ *A* **column width** *of 85 (top) and 50 (bottom).*

⑪ *The controls for* **Cluster width** *are available for only grouped column graphs.*

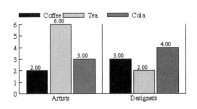

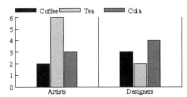

⑫ *A* **cluster width** *of 90 (top) and 50 (bottom).*

Once you have entered data in the worksheet and picked the style of the graph, you can still modify various elements of the graph. These controls change depending on the type of graph selected.

To change the column width:

1. Click the icon for grouped column or stacked column graphs.
2. To change the width that each column takes up within its cluster, drag the slider or enter the amount in the Column width field **⑨**.
3. Click Apply to see the effects on the graph **⑩**.

To change the cluster width:

1. Click the icon for a grouped column or stacked column graph.
2. To change the width of the cluster of the columns, drag the slider or enter the amount in the Cluster width field **⑪**.
3. Click Apply to see the effects on the chart **⑫**.

To show the data values:

All the graphs except area graphs let you display the data values in the graph itself **⑫**. Click the Data numbers in chart checkbox to see those values.

To add a drop shadow:

All the graphs except line and scatter graphs let you add a drop shadow behind the graph. Click the Drop shadow checkbox to see the effect.

To move the legend:

To move the legend from the side of the chart to the top, click the Legend across top checkbox.

TIP Charts are always created in grayscale. To add color, you can drag colors onto individual elements or subselect objects and change them through the Color List. Alternatively, choose **Edit > Find & Replace > Graphics** and change each gray to a color all at once.

All the graphs except the pie chart allow you to control whether or not gridlines are displayed along the *x* or *y* axis 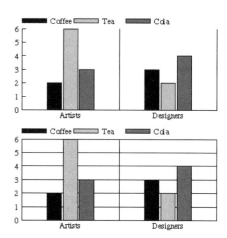.

To create gridlines:

1. Check the *x* axis box to display horizontal gridlines.

2. Check the *y* axis box to display vertical gridlines .

The most powerful part of modifying a column graph is in working with the *x* (horizontal) axis and the *y* (vertical) axis. You can modify how numerical values are displayed along an axis; if the axis has no numerical values, the options are grayed out.

To modify the axis values:

1. With a chart selected and the Chart dialog box open, click either the X axis or Y axis buttons under Axis options. The Options dialog box appears .

2. Under Axis values, click Calculate from data if you want the numbers along the axis to be calculated from the data entered in the worksheet.

   or

   Under Axis values, click Manual to enter your own values for the axis.

3. Choose from the Major Tick marks pop-up menu to control where the tick marks sit along the axis: Across the axis, Inside the axis, or Outside the axis.

4. Choose from the Minor Tick marks pop-up menu to show those added tick marks and how they sit along the axis.

5. Enter the number of minor tick marks in the Count field.

6. Use the Prefix and Suffix Axis value labels to add a prefix (such as *$*) in front of the data or a suffix (such as */hour*) after the data in the axis.

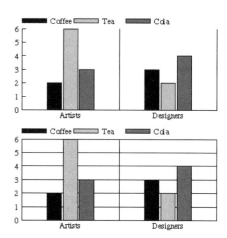

⓭ *X axis* **gridlines** *turned off (top) and turned on (bottom).*

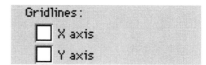

⓮ *The* **Gridlines** *boxes show and hide the* **x** *axis and* **y** *axis gridlines.*

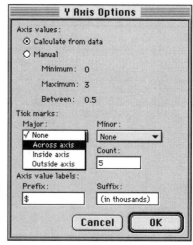

⓯ *The* **Y Axis Options** *dialog box.*

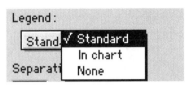

⑯ *The* **Legend options** *for a pie chart.*

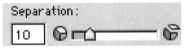

⑰ *The* **Separation controls** *for a pie chart.*

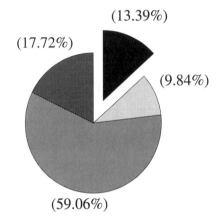

(13.39%)

(17.72%)

(9.84%)

(59.06%)

⑱ *A* **Separation amount** *of 23 has moved the black wedge away from the rest of the pie chart. The wedge that separates is the one representing the first cell of the worksheet row.*

Once you have created a chart, you can change it.

To modify an existing chart:

1. Select the chart you want to modify.

2. Double-click the Chart tool in the Xtra Tools palette.

   or

   Choose **Xtras > Chart > Edit**. The Chart worksheet opens and you can modify either the data in the worksheet or the display parameters in the chart type dialog box.

   TIP Do not ungroup a chart or graph, or you will lose the link to the worksheet information.

   TIP Because all charts and graphs are grouped items, you can Option/Alt-click to select an individual element.

When you create a pie chart, you have special controls for working with the wedges.

To change the pie chart legend:

1. Use the Legend pop-up menu in the chart type dialog box to display the choices for the pie chart's legend **⑯**.

2. To position the legend on the side of the chart, choose Standard from the pop-up menu.

3. To position the legend next to each wedge, choose In chart from the pop-up menu.

4. To not show the legend, choose None from the pop-up menu.

To change the wedge separation:

The first cell of data creates a wedge that can be moved away from the other segments. To move that wedge, drag the slider or enter an amount in the Separation field **⑰**. The first wedge moves away from the rest of the chart **⑱**.

TIP To enter numbers as labels, not graph data, insert quotation marks around the numbers. For example, the year 1997 would be entered as "1997."

FreeHand also lets you put graphics into the columns of your charts. These graphics, called pictographs, give visual representations of the type of data being shown.

To insert a pictograph in a chart:

1. Find the graphic that you would like to have in the chart. (This may be a FreeHand graphic or an imported file.)

2. Select the graphic and copy it.

3. Select one column of the series to which you want to apply the pictograph.

TIP Option/Alt-click to select an individual element of the chart.

4. Choose **Xtras> Chart> Pictograph**. The Pictograph dialog box appears.

5. Click Paste in. The copied graphic appears in the preview window **⑲**.

6. To repeat the graphic within the column, click the Repeating box. To stretch the graphic within the column, leave the box unchecked.

7. Click OK. The Pictograph replaces the column of the chart **⑳**.

On Using Pictographs

Programs such as FreeHand have given many people the tools to create pictographs in charts. Unfortunately, pictographs can easily distort the meaning of the data. For an excellent study on maintaining graphical integrity in charts, see T*he Visual Display of Quantitative Information* by Edward R. Tufte, published by Graphics Press.

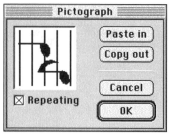

⑲ *The* **Pictograph** *box, where you can paste in the pictograph for a selected series.*

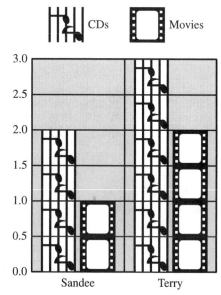

⑳ *An example of* **a chart that uses pictographs** *for the columns.*

OTHER APPLICATIONS 19

N o one program can do it all, so on occasion
you may need to work with other
applications along with FreeHand. This may
be to import files from other applications or to
export your FreeHand artwork so that it can be
opened or used by other applications.

As time goes on, designers are focusing more
and more on publishing to the Web as an
alternative to—or even a replacement for—
traditional publishing on paper. FreeHand 9 has
moved to accommodate them by creating a
direct route to HyperText Markup Language, the
lingua franca of the Internet.

In this chapter, you will learn how to

Import TIFF, PICT, and EPS files.

Change the size of imported images.

Colorize imported images.

Make an imported image transparent.

Change the lightness or contrast of imported
images.

Apply Photoshop filters to imported images.

Extract an embedded image from a file.

Export files.

Set options for exporting bitmapped files.

Use the Export Again command.

Rasterize vector images in your documents.

Convert files into Adobe Acrobat PDF files.

Prepare artwork for the Extensis Portfolio.

Setup the URL Editor.

Assign links to graphic and text objects.

Export FreeHand files as HTML.

You may want to add artwork, such as scans, to your file. This means importing artwork.

To import artwork using the File menu:

1. Choose **File > Import**.

2. Use the dialog box to find the image you want to import. If you are going to print your file, import TIFF or EPS artwork.

3. After you open the file, your cursor changes into a corner symbol ❶.

4. Click the corner symbol to import the file in its original size.

   or

   Drag the corner symbol to set the image to a specific size ❷.

TIP Unless you have changed the Import Preferences settings (*see page 251*), the placed image is only linked to the FreeHand file, not actually included. If you send the FreeHand file somewhere else, you must send the original image along with the FreeHand file for it to print properly.

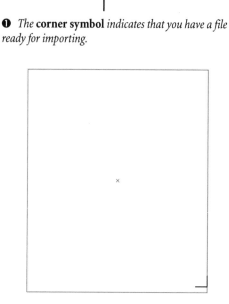

❶ *The* **corner symbol** *indicates that you have a file ready for importing.*

❷ **Dragging the corner symbol** *sizes the placed image.*

FreeHand allows you to drag artwork from some compatible applications directly onto the page. It is even possible in some cases to drag the image file onto the page and have it import automatically.

To import artwork by dragging and dropping (Mac):

1. Open the file from which you want to import artwork. Make sure the FreeHand document you are working in is also visible.

2. Select the artwork and drag it onto the FreeHand document. The artwork is imported as a group. Ungrouped, it becomes an embedded TIFF, regardless of its original format.

To import artwork by copying and pasting:

1. Open the file from which you want to import artwork.

2. Select the artwork you want to import and copy it to the clipboard.

3. Bring the FreeHand document to the front and choose **Edit > Paste** to import the image. As with dragging, artwork is imported as a group which becomes an embedded TIFF when ungrouped.

(Mac) You can scan artwork directly into FreeHand if you place the appropriate Photoshop image acquisition plug-in in the Xtras folder.

To scan artwork directly into FreeHand:

1. Select **Xtras > Acquire** and choose the scanner software. The scanner interface software dialog box opens.

2. Adjust the settings to your requirements and start the scan. The image is imported as an embedded TIFF.

Import Artwork

Once you have imported an image, there are many ways to modify that image.

To resize imported images by dragging:

1. Place the Pointer tool on one of the corner handles of the imported image.
2. Drag to change the size of the image ❸.

TIP Press Shift to retain the horizontal and vertical proportions of the image.

To resize imported images numerically:

1. With the imported image selected, open the Object Inspector ❹.
2. Use the Scale % *x* and *y* fields to change the size of the image.

    or

    Enter the dimensions in the *w* and *h* fields.
3. Press Return or Enter to apply the changes.

To transform an imported image:

1. Double-click the imported image.
2. Use the transformation handles to rotate, skew, or scale the image ❺.

    or

    Use any of the transformation tools (rotating, scaling, reflecting, skewing) to modify the image.

❸ *Drag a corner handle to* **change the size** *of an imported image.*

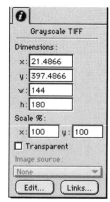

❹ *The* **Object Inspector** *lets you resize images.*

❺ *You can modify imported images with the transformation handles or any of the transformation tools.*

Resize Imported Artwork

❻ **Drag a color swatch** *onto black-and-white or grayscale TIFF or PICT files to colorize those images.*

FreeHand also lets you change the color of grayscale or black-and-white TIFF and PICT images.

To colorize an imported image:

1. Select a black-and-white or grayscale image.

2. Drag a color swatch from the Color List or Color Mixer onto the image ❻.

To make an image transparent:

1. Select a grayscale imported image.

2. Click Transparent in the Object Inspector. This converts the image to black (or some other color) and transparent and lets objects behind your image show through the clear areas ❼.

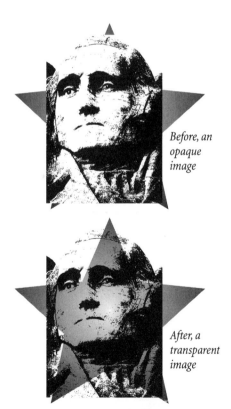

Before, an opaque image

After, a transparent image

❼ *The results of applying the* **Transparent option** *to a grayscale image.*

FreeHand also lets you change the shade, or lightness and contrast, of grayscale or black-and-white TIFF and PICT images.

To change the shade of an imported image:

1. Select a black-and-white or grayscale image.

2. Open the Object Inspector and click the Edit button. The Image dialog box appears ❽.

3. Click the controls for Lightness or Contrast or adjust the slider bars to change the image ❾-⓫.

TIP You can change the shade or color of a portion of an image by putting one of the transparent lens fills over an imported image (*see page 97*).

You can also use Photoshop-compatible plug-ins within FreeHand to modify imported images.

TIP Only those plug-ins written to the specifications of Photoshop version 3 will work within FreeHand.

To install Photoshop filters within FreeHand (Mac):

Move or copy the plug-ins (or an alias) into the FreeHand: English: Xtras folder.

To install Photoshop filters within FreeHand (Win):

Move or copy the plug-ins into the Program Files\Macromedia\FreeHand9\English\Xtras file.

TIP Photoshop filters appear in the FreeHand Xtras menu with [TIFF] before the name of the Xtra. For instance, a filter might be listed as *[TIFF] Solarize* (Mac) or *[TIFF] Texturizer* (Win). This indicates that the filter only works on bitmapped images.

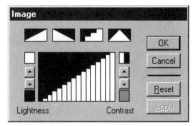

❽ *The Image dialog box allows you to adjust the lightness and contrast of the image.*

❾ *Inverting the ramp of the sliders in the Image dialog box creates a negative image.*

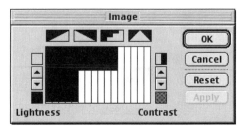

⓾ *Dragging the bars up or down allows you to create a number of different effects.*

⓫ *Setting the bars to only three levels as above creates a posterized image.*

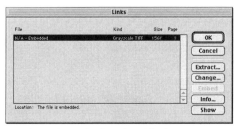

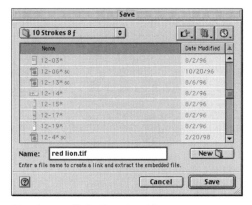

To apply a Photoshop filter to a TIFF image:

1. Select the placed TIFF image.

2. From the Xtras menu, choose the Photoshop filter you want to apply.

3. If a dialog box or a settings box appears, follow the steps necessary to adjust the settings for the filter.

4. The filter is applied to the image **⑫**.

When you use any Photoshop filters on TIFF images in FreeHand, the result is an embedded TIFF image. To keep the file size low, use the Extract feature of the Links dialog box.

To extract an embedded image:

1. Select the image that is embedded in the FreeHand file.

2. Click the Links button in the Object Inspector to open the Links dialog box **⑬**.

3. The Extract button opens the Save (Mac) **⑭** or Extract Import (Win) dialog box, which lets you choose a name and destination for the extracted image.

TIP To swap one imported image for another, click the Change button and then select a new file.

TIP You can also use the Show button to move to and select an image.

TIP Modified imported images may take a longer time to print. If possible, replicate the changes on the original image and then reimport the image.

⑫ *The* **KPT 3 Twirl filter** *applied to a placed image.*

⑬ *The* **Links dialog box** *(Mac) lets you extract an embedded image from the FreeHand file.*

⑭ *The* **Save dialog box** *(Mac) lets you extract an embedded image from the FreeHand file. In Windows, it is called Extract Import.*

Apply Photoshop Filters; Extract Embedded Image

You can use another application to edit the graphics in your FreeHand document.

To edit an image with an external application:

1. Select the image you want to edit.

2. Choose **Edit > External Editor** from the menu. This opens the image in the application specified in the Object preferences within the Preferences dialog box (**File > Preferences** on the menu).

   If you have not specified an external editing application for a particular file type, the Choose a File (Mac) **⑮** or Please select a valid external application (Win) **⑯** navigation dialog box opens so you can select one. Once you have chosen an application for a file type, that becomes the default until you change it in the Preferences dialog box.

3. When you have completed your edits, save your changes in the external application.

4. Return to your FreeHand document and click Done in the Editing in Progress dialog box **⑰** to implement your changes or click Cancel to leave the graphic as it was.

TIP You can activate the external editing function by holding down Option/Alt and double-clicking on a graphic.

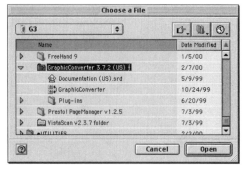

⑮ *The* **Choose a File** *(Mac) dialog box is where you select an application to edit your graphics.*

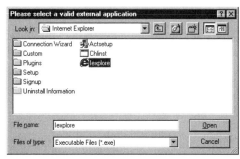

⑯ *Use the* **Please select a valid external application** *(Win) dialog box to navigate to an application for editing your graphic elements.*

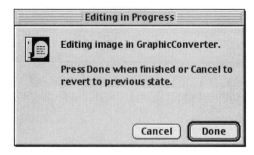

⑰ *When you have completed the editing process, click Done in the Editing in Progress dialog box.*

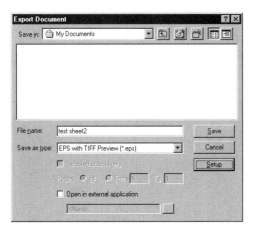

⑱ The **Export Document** *dialog box.*

⑲ The **Bitmap Export Defaults** *dialog box is the first step in specifying the parameters for bitmapped exports.*

FreeHand offers you many different ways to convert or export your FreeHand files into formats that can be read by other applications. Because some formats change the look of your file, pick your format according to your needs.

To export files:

1. With the file open, choose **File > Export**. The Export Document dialog box appears **⑱**.

2. In the middle of the box, note the name of the file. The name automatically includes a suffix that signals the file format.

3. If necessary, change the file format by making a choice from the Format (Mac) or Save as type (Win) pop-up menu.

4. Click the Selected objects only box to export only those objects that are currently selected.

5. Once you have selected a format, click Options (Mac) or Setup (Win) to choose attributes that are applicable to the format you have chosen.

If you choose to export a document in a bitmapped format such as TIFF, PNG, GIF, or JPEG, you need to set the bitmap options.

To set the bitmap options:

1. Once you have chosen a bitmapped format in the Export dialog box, click Options (Mac) or Setup (Win) to open the Bitmap Export Defaults dialog box **⑲**.

2. Make a choice from the Resolution pop-up menu, or enter the amount in the field.

3. Use the Anti-aliasing pop-up menu to choose the amount of smoothing, or softening, to apply to the image.

4. To create an alpha channel that can be used as a mask in programs such as Photoshop and Fractal Painter, click Include alpha channel. To make the alpha channel include the background, click Alpha includes background.

Once you have chosen the bitmap options, you still need to set additional bitmap options depending on the type of format.

To set the additional bitmap options:

In the Bitmap Export Defaults dialog box, click More to display the options for your specific format ⑳–㉓. Choose the Color Depth for the type of output you need. For instance, if you need to include the alpha channel with a PICT file, you would choose 32-bit with Alpha. (*See Chapter 20, "Web Art and Animations" to set GIF, JPEG, or PNG export options.*)

TIP To change the default settings for the Bitmap Export Defaults dialog box, change the settings in Import/Export Preferences (*see page 251*).

If you need to export many different files all with the same settings, it could be cumbersome to set the same export options over and over. Instead, you can use the Export Again command.

To use the Export Again command:

1. Choose **File > Export** on the first file and set all the export options.

2. Save that file as usual.

3. Open the next file and choose **File > Export Again**. The Export dialog box opens with all the settings the same as the previous file.

4. Save that file. Repeat for any other files that need to be exported.

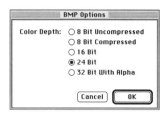

⑳ *The options for a* **BMP** *file.*

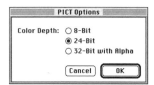

㉑ *The options for a* **PICT** *file (Mac).*

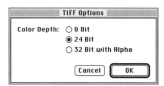

㉒ *The options for a* **TIFF** *file.*

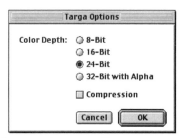

㉓ *The options for a* **Targa** *file.*

㉔ *The* **Rasterize** *dialog box controls how artwork is converted into a bitmapped PICT image.*

In addition to exporting a file as a rasterized format such as TIFF or PICT, you can also use the Rasterize command to convert the items you have selected into pixel-based art (TIFF) in the FreeHand document.

To rasterize an image:

1. Select the objects you want to convert.

2. Choose **Modify > Rasterize**. The Rasterize dialog box appears **㉔**.

3. Set the resolution to the amount you need. For instance, most print work uses a resolution of 300 dpi.

4. Set the anti-aliasing amount. This smooths lines or edges in the image with a slight blur.

5. Click OK. The objects turn into rasterized art **㉕** embedded in the file.

TIP If you are working with Adobe Photoshop, you can copy and paste, or drag and drop artwork directly from FreeHand into Photoshop. You have the option of pasting as pixels onto a Photoshop layer or pasting as a path onto the Photoshop paths layers.

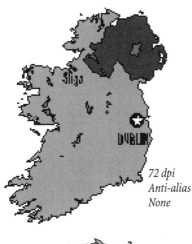

72 dpi
Anti-alias
None

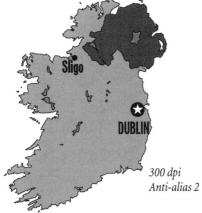

300 dpi
Anti-alias 2

㉕ *Using the* **Rasterize command** *at two different resolutions and anti-aliasing amounts.*

FreeHand also imports and exports text from other applications. Like graphics, text can be imported using the menu commands (*see page 125*) as well as by the copy and paste and drag and drop methods (from a limited number of applications).

To copy and paste text into a FreeHand document:

1. Open the file from which you want to import text.

2. Select the text you want to import and copy it to the clipboard.

3. Bring the FreeHand document to the front and choose **Edit > Paste** from the menu. The text is pasted in the middle of the screen.

TIP Copying text from an RTF file imports formatted text. Otherwise, it is imported and formatted in the style determined by the Text Inspector.

To drag and drop text into a FreeHand document:

1. Open the file from which you want to import text.

2. Select the text you want and drag it from the document onto the FreeHand page. The text is inserted in a new text block according to the settings in the Text Inspector.

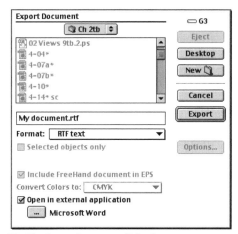

26 *The Export Document dialog box.*

27 *Dragging a text block from a FreeHand document into another application's window copies the text directly onto the page.*

To export text from a FreeHand document:

1. Select the text you want to export. If you select none or leave the Selected objects only box unchecked, FreeHand will export all the text in the document.

2. Choose **File > Export** to open the Export Document dialog box **26**. Name the file and specify a destination for it. If desired, check the open in external application box and select it from the navigation dialog box that opens.

3. Choose RTF text or ASCII text from the Format (Mac) or Save as type (Win) pop-up, and click Export (Mac) or Save (Win).

   Unlinked text blocks export in their stacking order from back to front, first page to last page.

Some applications are capable of copying text directly into FreeHand by dragging and dropping.

To drag text from a FreeHand document:

1. Select the text blocks you want to export.

2. Drag them onto the page of the destination document **27**.

   TIP (Mac) You can drag from FreeHand directly onto the desktop to create a clipping file.

To cut and paste text from a FreeHand document:

1. Select the text blocks you want to export.

2. Choose **Edit > Copy** or **Edit > Cut** from the menu.

3. In the destination document, paste the text where you want it to appear.

Export Text

FreeHand also lets you save documents as Adobe Acrobat PDF (portable document format) files.

To export an Acrobat PDF:

1. Choose PDF from the Format pop-up menu.

2. Click the Options button to open the PDF Export box **28**.

3. Choose All or the specific page range from the FreeHand document to export to the Acrobat file.

4. Use the Color Image Compression pop-up menu to choose the amount of compression applied to color images.

5. Use the Grayscale Image Compression pop-up menu to choose the amount of compression applied to grayscale images.

6. Use the Compatibility pop-up menu to select the version of Acrobat.

7. Check which options you want applied to the PDF.

8. Click OK to return to the Export dialog box where you can name the PDF file and then export it.

FreeHand also lets you add information that can be used when your artwork is part of an Extensis Portfolio image database. This makes it easier to find your artwork in large catalogs.

To add Portfolio information:

1. With the file open, choose **View > Portfolio Info**. The Portfolio Info dialog box appears **29**.

2. Type the keywords and description information you want for the file.

3. Click OK. The Portfolio information is included as part of the file and can be read by Portfolio.

TIP To add a preview to your FreeHand file so it can be seen in a Portfolio database, you need to check the Preferences settings for Import/Export (*see page 251*).

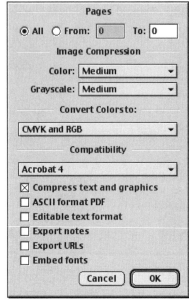

28 *The* **PDF Export dialog box** *allows you to set the attributes of an Acrobat file.*

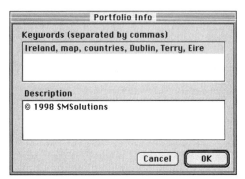

29 *The* **Portfolio Info dialog box** *allows you to create keywords and descriptions that can help you find the image in an Extensis Portfolio database.*

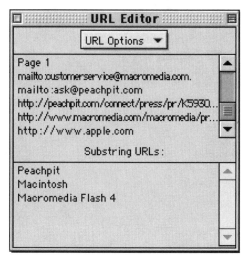

❸⓪ *The* **URL Editor** *shows the URLs and other links available for your document. The substring URLs appear when you select a text block containing links.*

❸❶ *Enter new links in the* **New URL dialog box.**

Designers are focusing more and more on publishing to the Web as an alternative to—or even a replacement for—traditional publishing on paper. FreeHand 9 has moved to accommodate them by creating a direct route to HyperText Markup Language, the *lingua franca* of the Internet.

One of the most important features of a page written in HTML is its ability to include links. Links let the reader click on a word or phrase or an image and go to another location, either on the current Web site or on a totally different site. Links also let the reader send e-mail or download files. In FreeHand you need to specify these links before you create the HTML file.

Links are created using the URL Editor. In order to assign links, you must first add them to the URL editor.

To add a URL to the URL Editor:

1. Choose **Window > Xtras > URL Editor**. The URL Editor opens **❸⓪**.
2. Use the URL options pop-up menu to choose New.
3. In the New URL dialog box that appears, type the URL **❸❶**.
4. Click OK to add the URL to the list.
5. Repeat steps 2–4 to add all the URL links you need.

URL link choices

The three most common URL links are http, mailto, and ftp.

http Stands for HyperText Transfer Protocol, used when you want to access a Web site. For example, http://www.macromedia.com is the Web address to the Macromedia home page.

mailto This URL is used to send e-mail. For example, mailto:sandeec@aol.com is the link you can use to send me e-mail.

ftp This stands for File Transfer Protocol. This URL lets people download files. Suppose you want someone to download a file called sandee.sit that is stored on your Web server in a folder called promo on the cohen.com Web site. The URL link would be ftp://ftp.cohen.com/promo/sandee.sit.

Once you have added all the URL links, you can then assign them to objects or text.

To assign URL links:

1. Select the object or objects.

TIP Text can be selected either as a text block or as highlighted text within the block.

2. Open the URL Editor and click the URL you want to link to the selected object.

   or

   Drag the address onto the object 😳-😳 (Mac). A white square appears as you drag. Release the mouse button when the square touches the object you want to link.

TIP Use page links to let people navigate from page to page in your document.

3. Repeat steps 1–2 to assign the URL links to all the objects you need.

TIP You can create "hotspots" in your document by creating paths with no stroke and a lens fill with the opacity set to 0. This will allow you to link to a specific area of an image.

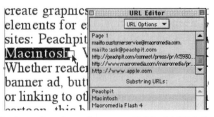

😳 *A word or phrase becomes a link by highlighting it and dragging the link onto it, or by clicking the URL in the URL Editor.*

😳 *You can select a graphic and click on a* **mailto** *URL to open an e-mail application.*

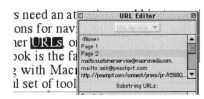

😳 *Page links help the reader navigate through a site.*

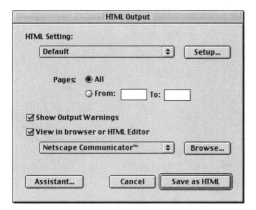

❸❺ The **HTML Output** *dialog box.*

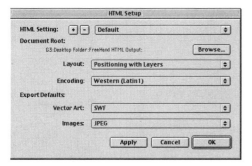

❸❻ The **HTML Setup** *dialog box.*

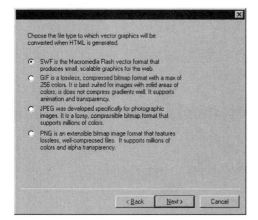

❸❼ The **HTML Export Output Wizard** *(Win) and the HTML Output Assistant (Mac) guide you through the process of setting up the creation of an HTML file.*

To set the HTML Output preferences:

1. Select **File > Publish as HTML** to open the HTML Output dialog box **❸❺**.

2. Choose from the settings in the pop-up menu or click Setup to create a new one. (*See below for HTML setup.*)

3. Check the Show Output Warnings checkbox if you want the HTML Output Warnings screen to display warnings of possible problems with the export of this file to HTML.

4. Check the View in browser or HTML Editor checkbox if you want the file to open immediately in an external application.

5. Select a browser or HTML editor from the pop-up menu or click the Browse button to choose one using the Select a browser navigation dialog box.

To create an HTML setting:

1. In the HTML Output dialog box, click Setup to open the HTML Setup dialog box **❸❻**.

2. Click the + button to create a new setting. Give it a name and click OK.

3. Then choose the folder/directory in which you want to save the HTML files.

4. In the Layout area, choose either Positioning with Layers or Positioning with tables as a layout option.

5. Leave Encoding set to Western (Latin 1) unless you have a very good reason to do otherwise.

6. Choose default settings for vector art and images from the two pop-up menus.

7. Click OK to accept all your preferences.

TIP Click the Assistant (Mac) or Wizard (Win) button to let FreeHand help you through the setup process with short explanations of the various alternatives **❸❼**.

To check the HTML Output Warnings:

1. Choose **Window > Xtras > HTML Output Warnings** to open the HTML Output Warnings window **38**.

2. Click either Scan Page or Scan Document. FreeHand displays a list of potential problems with the export to HTML.

TIP Some of the items listed as HTML output warnings may not have any impact on the Web page you create; experience will help you evaluate which ones need to be dealt with and which can be safely ignored.

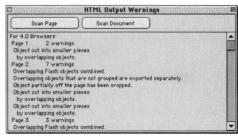

38 *The* **HTML Output Warnings** *window lists possible problems before you create an HTML version.*

Once you have set the preferences for your HTML output, you can create an HTML file directly from your FreeHand document.

To create HTML Output:

1. Select **Xtras > HTML > Publish as HTML** to open the HTML Output dialog box.

2. Choose from the settings on the pop-up menu.

3. Select the pages you want to export.

4. Click Save as HTML to save the document in HyperText Markup Language. FreeHand will put the HTML file in the file/directory selected as the document root in the HTML Setup dialog box. The images will be placed in a subfolder within that file/directory.

If you have checked the View in browser or HTML Editor checkbox in the HTML Output dialog box **35**, the file will open and you will be able to see what the exported HTML file looks like **39**.

Text links will be distinguished according to the preferences set in your browser. Usually, they are underlined and displayed in a specific color.

Graphic links will be indicated by the standard arrow cursor changing to the little pointing finger **40**.

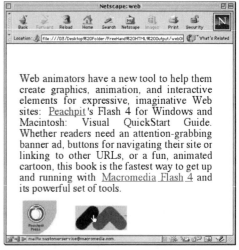

39 *The HTML file can be viewed in a browser or HTML editor.*

40 *Links are indicated by a distinctive style in text (above) or by the pointing finger icon below.*

WEB ART AND ANIMATIONS 20

More than any other illustration or layout program, FreeHand 9 provides a wealth of features for the World Wide Web. This includes URL links, Web graphics, and Web animations. These Web features come in the basic FreeHand 9 program. You do not need any extras to do everything in this chapter.

In this chapter you will learn how to

Import the Web-safe colors.

Create URL links for FreeHand elements.

Save files in the Flash 4 format.

Create Flash animations.

Create bitmapped Web graphics.

Set GIF attributes.

Set JPEG attributes.

Set PNG attributes.

TIP The technology for Web pages changes at a dramatic pace. Every month brings new features, techniques, and formats. If your Web page creation software provides new information on preparing Web graphics, follow its recommendations.

TIP For more information on designing Web graphics, see *Elements of Web Design* by Darcy DiNucci, et al., and *The Non-Designer's Web Book* by Robin Williams and John Tollett, both published by Peachpit Press.

When you create graphics for the Web, you need to consider the types of colors and number of colors in your document. The more colors in your art, the longer it takes to be displayed. Also, you may pick a color that is outside the range that a monitor can display. This can cause your colors to shift from what you intended, sometimes making the Web graphics illegible. Fortunately, FreeHand lets you limit your color palette to Web-safe colors.

To import Web-safe colors:

1. Use the Color List Options pop-up menu to choose the Web Safe Color Library. The library appears containing the 216 Web colors ❶.

2. Select the colors you want in your document (*see page 89*).

TIP Web pages take less time to display if you design with a small number of colors.

3. Click OK. The colors you have selected appear in the Color List ❷.

TIP The list of Web-safe colors show both their hexadecimal codes and their RGB values. The hexadecimal codes are the tags used by the HyperText Markup Language (HTML) to designate Web colors.

Once you have the Web-safe colors in the Color List, you must be careful that you do not do anything that creates colors outside the Web-safe colors.

To maintain the Web-safe colors:

- Use only the colors in the Color List to choose colors in the document.

- Do not use the Color Mixer or Tint palette to create new colors or modify colors.

- Avoid using blends and gradients unless you understand how they may change when exported as a Web graphic (*see page 233*).

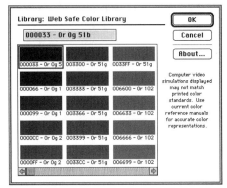

❶ *The* **Web Safe Color Library** *lets you choose up to 216 colors that can be used for Web graphics.*

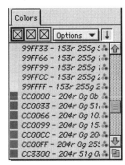

❷ *Web-safe colors are displayed in the Color List with their* **hexadecimal codes** *as well as their RGB values.*

❸ *The* **URL Editor** *stores the Web addresses for a document.*

❹ *The* **New URL dialog box** *allows you to type in a URL address for whatever link you would like to have in your Web graphic.*

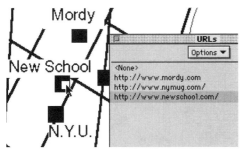

❺ *(Mac) To* **link an object to a URL,** *drag from the URLs panel and drop the white square onto the object you want to have linked.*

FreeHand lets you turn an object into a link for a Web URL. This means that when your graphic is viewed on the Web, someone can click the linked object and open a new Web page. Before you link objects to URLs, you need to enter the Web address in FreeHand's URLs panel.

To add addresses to the URLs panel:

1. Choose **Window > Xtras > URL Editor.** The URL Editor panel appears ❸.
2. Choose New from the Options pop-up menu to open the New URL dialog box ❹.
3. Type the link address in the Location field.
4. If you want to add more URLs, choose New from the URL Options pop-up menu and type in the additional addresses.

TIP Rather than retype long addresses with minor changes, use the Duplicate command in the URL Options pop-up menu and then choose Edit to make the changes.

TIP Use the Remove command in the URL Options pop-up menu to delete URLs that are no longer needed.

Once your URLs are in the URL Editor, you can then apply them to objects.

To apply a URL to an object:

1. Select the object or objects.
2. Click the URL in the URL Editor. This links the object to that address.

   or

   (Mac) Drag an address from the URLs panel onto the object. A white square appears as you drag. Release the mouse button when the square touches the object ❺.

Create URL; Apply URL

Once you have a FreeHand file you can save it as a Flash file, Macromedia's application for creating vector graphics for the Web. Flash files are much smaller than other Web graphics. They can also be magnified to see details. Flash files can be single-frame images or animations.

Features supported in Flash animations

- Basic strokes and fills
- Lens fills (Transparency Lens fills remain transparent upon export)
- Gradient fills
- CMYK or RGB TIFFs and embedded images (JPEG, GIF, PNG)
- Blended paths
- Composite paths, including text converted into paths
- Clipping paths containing vector path image files
- Text blocks
- Arrowheads

To export as a single-frame Flash file:

1. Choose **File > Export**. The Export Document dialog box appears ❻.
2. (Mac) Use the Format pop-up menu to choose the Macromedia Flash (SWF) format.

   or

   (Win) Choose Flash (*.swf) from the Save as type pop-up menu.
3. Follow the naming conventions for the type of server that will display the file.
4. If you check the Open in external application box, the Choose a File (Mac) or the Please select a valid application (Win) dialog box opens ❼.
5. Navigate to an application and click Choose (Mac) or Open (Win).
6. Click the Options button (Mac) or Setup button (Win) to open the Flash Export dialog box.

❻ *The **Export Document** dialog box for Flash files.*

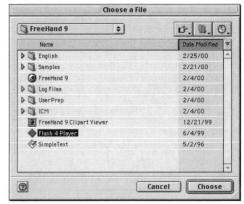

❼ *The **Choose a File** dialog box.*

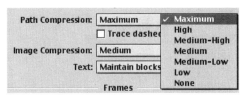

❽ *The* **Path Compression options** *for Flash files.*

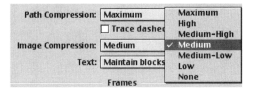

❾ *The* **Image Compression options** *for Flash files.*

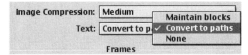

❿ *The* **Text block choices** *for Flash files.*

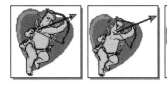

⓫ **Using multiple pages** *allows you to use each page as the frame of an animation.*

7. Use the Path Compression pop-up menu to control the precision used to convert FreeHand paths to Flash paths ❽. No compression is the most precise. Maximum compression creates the smallest files.

8. Use the Image Compression pop-up menu to control the compression of bitmapped images ❾. No compression creates the highest quality image. Maximum creates the smallest files.

9. Use the Text pop-up menu to control what happens to text blocks ❿. Maintain blocks keeps all the text for editing in Flash. Convert to Paths converts the text to artwork. None deletes the text from the file.

10. Set the animation pop-up to None.

11. In most cases, you can leave the compatibility set to Flash 4.

12. Click OK. Then click Export (Mac) or Save (Win). The file is exported and can be opened in Flash or used as part of a Web page.

You can also work within FreeHand to create Flash animations for the Web. Animations can be created by putting the art on multiple layers or by setting the art on multiple pages.

To create a page animation:

1. Create your first frame's artwork on a page.

2. Duplicate the page and modify the artwork on that duplicate page.

3. Continue to duplicate pages and modify the artwork. Each page of the document becomes a frame of the animation ⓫. You can then export the file as an animation.

TIP You can also draw all the animation cells on a single page, putting each on its own layer.

Page Animations

To create an animation from a blend:

1. Create a blend. (*See Chapter 11, "Blends"*)

2. Set the number of blend steps to control how many animation frames are created.

3. To control the movement, draw the path you want the animation to follow and choose **Modify > Combine > Join Blend to Path** .

4. Select the blend and choose **Xtras > Animate > Release to Layers**. This separates the blend so that each step is on its own layer ⑬.

Once you have created the artwork, either on separate layers or as multiple pages, use the animation options to control the look of the final animation.

To export as a multiframe Flash animation:

1. Choose **File > Export**. The Export Document dialog box appears ⑭.

2. (Mac) Use the Format pop-up menu to choose the Macromedia Flash (SWF) format.

   or

   (Win) Choose Flash (*.swf) from the Save as type pop-up menu.

3. Follow the naming conventions for the type of server that will display the file.

4. If you check the Open in external application box, the Choose a File (Mac) or the Please select a valid application (Win) dialog box opens.

5. Navigate to an application and click Choose (Mac) or Open (Win).

6. In the Export Document dialog box, click the Options button (Mac) or Setup button (Win) to open the Flash Export dialog box ⑮.

⑫ **Using a blend as an animation** *creates the effect of one object morphing into another. Placing the blend on a path controls the motion of the morphing effect.*

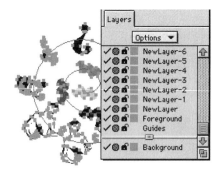

⑬ *The results of applying the* **Release to Layers** **command** *to a blend. Instead of one layer, the blend is divided onto many.*

Animation from a Blend; Export Flash Animation

⓮ *The* **Export Document dialog box** *allows you to set the Flash Player to open your exported file automatically.*

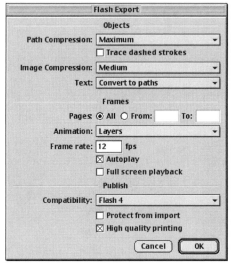

⓯ *The* **Flash Export** *dialog box.*

7. Use the Path Compression pop-up menu to control the precision used to convert FreeHand paths to Flash paths. No compression (None) is the most precise. Maximum compression creates the smallest files.

8. Use the Image Compression pop-up menu to control the compression of bitmapped images. No compression creates the highest quality image. Maximum creates the smallest files.

9. Use the Text pop-up menu to control what happens to text blocks. Maintain blocks keeps all the text for editing in Flash. Convert to paths converts the text to artwork. None deletes the text from the file.

10. Set the Animation pop-up menu to Pages if you have a multipage animation or Layers if you have all your frames on different layers on a single page. The Layers and Pages option collects the layers from all the pages as individual frames.

11. Set the Frame rate. The default is 12 and creates reasonably smooth movement.

12. Check the Autoplay and Full screen playback boxes to suit your requirements.

13. In most cases, you can leave the compatibility set to Flash 4.

14. Check Protect from import if you want to prevent the file from being used by others.

15. Check High quality printing to enable that.

16. Click OK to accept the settings. Then click Export (Mac) or Save (Win). The file is exported and can be opened in Flash or used as part of a Web page.

You can open and view your exported Flash animations in Flash 4. You can also view an animation using the Flash 4 Player that ships with FreeHand 9.

To play a Flash animation:

Drag the exported Flash file onto the icon for the Flash 4 Player **16**. The Player application will open and play the file.

or

Open the Flash Player and then choose **File > Open** to navigate to the file you want to play.

TIP If you check Open in external application and select Flash 4 Player in the Export Document dialog box, the exported file will open immediately.

TIP If you have the Flash plug-in installed in a Web browser, you can drag the animation icon directly onto the browser window to view the animation.

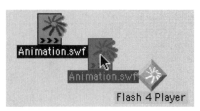

16 *Drag a Flash file onto the* **Flash 4 Player icon** *to play it.*

17 *The* **Bitmap Export Defaults dialog box** *allows you to set the overall options for exporting files into different Web formats.*

Two advantages of using a Flash file on the Web are the smaller file size and ability to magnify the image. However, because Flash files require a browser plug-in, you may want to save your artwork in a different file format for those who do not have it. FreeHand also lets you export your files in various bitmapped formats for use on the Web.

To save a file as a bitmap for the Web:

1. Create the artwork you want to turn into a bitmapped graphic.

2. Choose **File > Export**.

3. Choose GIF, JPEG, or PNG from the Format pop-up menu.

4. Click the Options (Mac) or Setup (Win) button (*for more information on exporting, see pages 213–214*). The Bitmap Export Defaults dialog box appears **17**.

5. Use the Resolution pop-up menu or enter the proper resolution in the field. For most Web graphics, this amount does not have to be higher than 72 dpi.

TIP Lowering the image quality reduces the size of the file.

6. Use the Anti-aliasing pop-up menu to control how much softening of the image is applied. (*For more information on anti-aliasing, see page 215.*)

7. To create an alpha channel that can be used as a mask for your image, check Include alpha channel.

8. To include the background area in the alpha channel, check Alpha includes background.

9. Use the More button to open the options for each of the bitmapped formats. Set the options and then save the file.

TIP While Windows and Macintosh allow a file name with spaces and upper- and lowercase letters, UNIX systems require all lowercase letters and no spaces.

TIP Lowering the image quality reduces the size of the file.

Once you have set the bitmapped attributes, you then need to set the options for the specific file format you have chosen. One of the most common formats for Web graphics is the GIF (pronounced as either "Gif" or "Jif") format.

To set the GIF options:

1. Click More in the Bitmap Export Defaults dialog box. The GIF Options dialog box opens ⓲.

2. Use the Palette pop-up menu to choose the Web palette. This limits the colors in the GIF image to only the Web-safe colors.

3. Select Dither to allow colors to mix together to form additional colors. Select None if you want colors to change into the closest color in the palette.

TIP Turn off the Dither option if you have detailed artwork or text that needs to be clearly visible.

4. Click Interlaced to create an image that appears almost immediately in a rough form and then gradually becomes clearer.

TIP Interlaced images give your viewers a quick idea of what the image is. They can then decide whether to wait for the full image or skip to another part of your Web site.

5. Click Transparent Background to create an image which has a transparent background when viewed on the Web ⓳.

6. Click to select the square for the color that you want to be transparent. An image on a white background would then have the white square of the GIF colors selected.

TIP If you choose a transparent background color, make sure the color is not used inside the image or that part of the image will also be transparent.

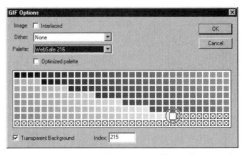

⓲ *The* **GIF Options** *let you control how the image is displayed on the Web. The* **selected color square** *(circled) and the number in the Index box indicate which color in the image becomes transparent.*

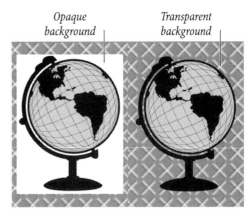

Opaque background   *Transparent background*

⓳ *The difference between an image without a transparent background (left) and one with a transparent background (right).*

⓴ *A* **blend between two Web-safe colors** *creates other colors between the original Web colors.*

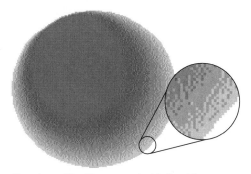

㉑ *When a blend is converted with the* **Dither option turned on***, the area between the original Web colors has a speckled look as the colors mix many Web-safe colors together.*

㉒ *When a blend is converted with the* **Dither option turned off***, the area between the original Web colors has a banded look as the colors abruptly change from one Web-safe color to another.*

The best way to limit the number of colors in a Web graphic is to choose only from the list of Web-safe colors and not create any blends or gradients. What happens then if you *do* choose a color that is not in the Web-safe palette or create a gradient or blend? In those cases, you create colors outside the range of the Web-safe colors. You then need to understand how those colors are converted **⓴–㉒**.

Dithered colors

Dithering is the process that makes a few colors look like more. For instance, the dither between red and yellow means that dots of red are next to dots of yellow. An even mix between the red and yellow dots appears orange. More red than yellow appears red-orange. More yellow than red appears yellow-orange.

Dithering is the best way to preserve the look of blends in Web graphics **㉑**. Dithering is usually not acceptable for flat areas of color and should be turned off when exporting those graphics.

Nondithered colors

When colors are not dithered, they are converted to the closest Web-safe color. This may mean that a deep red turns brown or a light green turns dark. When you are working with flat colors, this is acceptable unless the color shift causes two colors you intend to be distinct to resemble each other too closely.

When blends or gradients are not dithered, there are abrupt changes in each step of the blend **㉒**. This usually looks unacceptable; turn dithering on when exporting graphics with gradients or blends.

Another format used on the Web is the JPEG (pronounced "Jay-peg") format.

To set the JPEG options:

1. Choose **File > Export**.

2. Select JPEG in the Format pop-up menu of the Export Document dialog box.

3. Click Options in the Export Document dialog box to open the Bitmap Export Defaults dialog box.

4. Click More to open the JPEG Options dialog box **23**.

5. Enter a percentage for Image Quality.

6. Click Progressive JPEG to create an effect similar to the Interlaced GIF, which displays nearly instantly in rough form and gradually becomes clear.

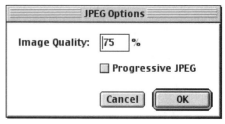

23 **JPEG Options** *let you control the quality of your image and how that image is displayed on the Web.*

The last format is the PNG (pronounced Ping) format. This format has applications in both Web graphics and printing.

TIP PNG files require a plug-in to be viewed in most Web browsers. They are used in applications such as Microsoft PowerPoint.

To set the PNG options:

1. Make sure that PNG is selected in the Format pop-up menu of the Export Document dialog box.

2. Click More in the Bitmap Export Defaults dialog box. The PNG Options dialog box appears **24**.

3. Choose the options for the color bit depth. High bit depths are for print work.

4. Click Interlaced PNG to create an effect similar to the Interlaced GIF, which displays nearly instantly in rough form and gradually becomes clear.

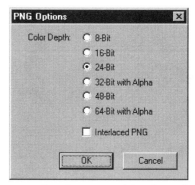

24 **PNG Options** *let you control the color quality of your image and how that image is displayed on the Web.*

PRINTING

Once you have finished your illustration onscreen, you will probably want to print it. This chapter is divided into two parts. The first part, Basic Printing, covers the print options for printing to a simple desktop printer. The second part, Advanced Printing, covers the print options for printing to high-resolution imagesetters.

In Basic Printing you will learn how to

Print a certain number of copies.

Print certain pages.

Choose the the paper source.

Set the tiling options.

Scale the illustration or make it automatically fit the size of the page.

Choose between separations or composite proof.

In Advanced Printing you will learn how to

Add marks and labels around the artwork.

Set the imaging options.

Set the Output options.

Set global trapping.

Select and set the proper PostScript Printer Description file (PPD).

Set halftone screens.

Set the transfer function.

Set the inks that need to knockout or overprint.

Set the screen angles.

Use the Collect for Output feature and create a report about your document.

Printing

BASIC PRINTING

Before you print your document, determine what kind of printer you will be using. If your printer is not a PostScript device, the Custom, Textured, and PostScript fills and strokes do not print. If you are in doubt as to the type of printer you have, check the documentation that came with the printer.

To set the print range and output options (Mac):

1. Choose **File > Print**. The Printer dialog box appears ❶.
2. In the Copies field, enter the number of copies you want to print.
3. In the Pages section, choose All if you want all the pages in your document to print.

   or

   Enter the range of pages. If you want to print only one page, type that page number in both the From and To fields.
4. Set the Paper Source options.

   TIP The Mac Print dialog box may look different if you have different printer software.

To set the print range and output options (Win):

1. Choose **File > Print**. The Print dialog box appears ❷.
2. In the Output section, enter the number of copies you want to print.
3. In the Print Range options, choose All if you want all the pages in your document to print.

   or

   Choose Current page to print the active page in the document window.

   or

   Choose Pages and enter specific page numbers to print only certain pages.
4. Click the Properties button to access the Paper options.

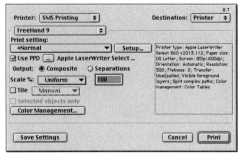

❶ *The* **page and copies options** *for the Macintosh platform.*

❷ *The* **page and copies options** *for the Windows platform.*

Print Range and Output Options

Scale %: [Uniform ▼] [100]

❸ *The* **Scale choices** *for the Macintosh platform in the Printer dialog box.*

┌─ Scale % ──────────────┐
│ [Uniform ▼]   │
│ [100]   │
└────────────────────────┘

❹ *The* **Scale choices** *for the Windows platform in the Printer dialog box.*

☒ Selected objects only

[☐ Selected objects]

❺ *The* **Selected objects choices** *for the Macintosh platform (top) and the Windows platform (bottom) in the Printer dialog box.*

Output: ⦿ Composite ○ Separations

[⦿ Composite   ○ Separations]

❻ *The* **Composite or Separations choices** *for the Macintosh platform (top) and the Windows platform (bottom) in the Printer dialog box.*

To set the scale options:

1. In the Printer dialog box, use the Scale pop-up menu ❸-❹ to choose one of the three Scale options.

Choose Uniform to scale the artwork without distorting it.

or

Choose Variable to scale the artwork with different amounts for the x and y dimensions.

or

Choose Fit on paper to change the size of your illustration so that it fits on the paper.

2. If you have chosen Uniform or Variable, enter the amounts in the percentage field.

To print selected objects:

Click Selected objects only ❺ to print only those objects that are currently selected.

To set the basic separations options:

If your illustration has color in it, choose Composite or Separations ❻.

TIP If you are printing to an ordinary desktop printer, you will most likely want to print your job as a composite, which prints all colors on a single printout. However, if you are testing to make sure you have set your document up properly for different color plates, print separations.

If your artwork is bigger than the paper in your printer, you cannot print the entire illustration at actual size on one page. FreeHand lets you *tile* your illustration onto many pieces of paper that you can assemble to form the larger illustration.

To set the tile options:

If you want to tile your illustration, click Tile and choose Manual or Automatic from the Tile options ❼.

To tile an oversized illustration:

1. In the Printer dialog box, choose Manual or Automatic from the Tile options. If you choose Automatic, FreeHand automatically prints the artwork onto different pages. Manual lets you determine what part of the artwork to print, one page at a time.

2. If you choose Auto, choose how much overlap you want between each page.

3. If you choose Manual, move the zero point from the ruler down onto the artwork ❽. This means that whatever artwork is above and to the right of that point will print.

4. Choose Print. If you have chosen Manual, repeat step 3 as many times as necessary to print the entire art.

FreeHand uses the PPD (PostScript Printer Description) information for the page setup. To set choices such as paper size and orientation, select the correct PPD for your printer.

To select the PPD:

1. In either the Printer dialog box or the Print Setup dialog box, click on Use PPD ❾.

2. Click the ellipsis (…) button to find the list of PPDs that are installed.

3. Find the PPD for your printer and click Open. The information from that PPD is shown in the Print Setup box.

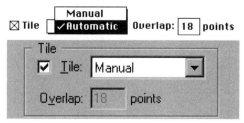

❼ *The* **Tile choices** *for the Macintosh platform (top) and the Windows platform (bottom) in the Printer dialog box*

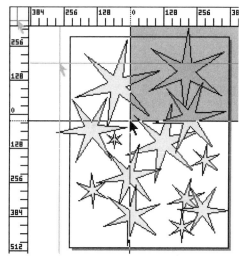

❽ **Drag the zero point** *from the ruler to set the position of the page for Manual tiling. (The shaded area shows the portion of the page that prints.)*

⊠ **Use PPD** (…) **Apple Personal LaserWrite…**

❾ *The* **Use PPD box and the ellipsis button** *allow you to select the proper PPD for the printer.*

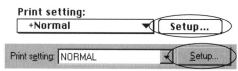

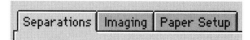

⑩ *The* **Setup button** *for the Macintosh (top) and Windows (bottom) opens the Print Setup options.*

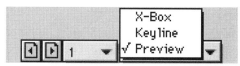

⑪ *The* **three tabs in the Print Setup dialog box** *let you control Separations, Imaging, and Paper Setup.*

⑫ *The* **Preview pop-up menu** *controls how the artwork is viewed in the Print Setup dialog box.*

⑬ *Print Setup in* **Preview mode.**

⑭ *Print Setup in* **Keyline mode.**

⑮ *Print Setup in* **X-Box mode.**

ADVANCED PRINTING

To change the print setup:

1. With the Printer dialog box open, click the Setup button **⑩**. This opens the Print Setup dialog box.

2. Click one of the three tabs at the top right of the box to reach controls for Imaging, Separations, or Paper Setup **⑪**.

The left side of the Print Setup box shows a preview of the artwork to be printed.

To control the Print Setup preview:

1. In the Print Setup dialog box, use the page number pop-up menu to control which pages are visible.

2. Use the preview pop-up menu to choose one of the three preview options **⑫**. Choose Preview to see the artwork with all the fills, colors, and so on **⑬**. Choose Keyline from the pop-up menu to see the paths that define each of the objects of your artwork without the fills, colors, and so on **⑭**. Choose X-Box to fill the area of each page with an *X* **⑮**.

   TIP If your artwork is extremely detailed, you may find it faster to view the print preview in the Keyline or X-Box modes.

3. Drag to move the artwork to different positions in the Print Preview area.

   TIP If you have moved the preview artwork, click the area just outside the print preview to restore it to the original position.

Print Setup: Print Setup Preview

When you print a file, the print shop that will be printing the job may ask you to add certain labels and marks around your artwork. Rather than create these marks manually, FreeHand can automatically add them.

To add labels and marks:

1. In the Print Setup dialog box, click the tab for Imaging. The Labels & Marks options appear on the right side of the dialog box 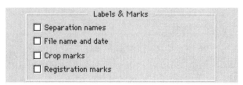.

2. Click Separation names to add a label with the name of the color plate that is printed.

3. Click File name and date to add the name of the file, page number, and date and time that the file is printed.

4. Click Crop marks to add the marks that indicate the trim size of the artwork.

5. Click Registration marks to add registration marks and color bars that are necessary for printing multiple colors.

TIP The labels and marks appear in the Print Setup preview ⑰ only if the page size for the FreeHand document is smaller than the paper size selected in the print setup.

The imaging options control the look and direction of the images when printed.

To choose the imaging options:

1. Click the tab for Imaging. The Imaging Options appear on the right side of the Print Setup dialog box ⑱.

2. Choose between Emulsion up or Emulsion down depending on the requirements of your print shop. This matters only when preparing to print film.

3. Choose Positive image for printing to paper.

TIP Negative image is the usual choice when printing to film separations, but check with your printer to be sure.

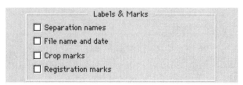

⑯ *Click the boxes for each of the* **Labels & Marks** *to have those marks printed around the artwork.*

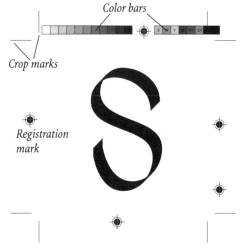

⑰ *Artwork printed with* **Crop marks and Registration marks** *selected.*

⑱ *The four* **Imaging Options.**

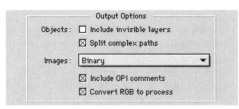

⑲ *The* **Output Options** *dialog box.*

Default ▼ Maximum color steps

⑳ *The* **Maximum color steps** *pop-up menu.*

Default ▼ Flatness

㉑ *The* **Flatness** *pop-up menu.*

FreeHand offers various options for printing to a PostScript device. These options stay with the file when it is saved or exported as an EPS file (*see page 11 or 213*).

To set the Output Options:

1. In the Print Setup dialog box, click the tab for Imaging. The Output Options appear on the right side of the dialog box **⑲**.

TIP You can also set the Output Options by choosing **File > Output Options**.

2. Check Include invisible layers to print objects that are on hidden layers.

3. Check Split complex paths, so that FreeHand automatically splits up paths that could cause printing errors.

4. Use the Images pop-up menu to choose how placed images should be processed. Choose Binary or Binary (Macintosh) to print on the Macintosh platform. Choose Binary (Cross Platform) for both Macintosh and Windows platforms. Choose ASCII only to output to the Windows platform or if you have trouble outputting on the Macintosh platform. Choose None if you use an OPI system when outputting your file.

5. Click Include OPI comments if your TIFF images will be replaced by a high-resolution version at a color electronic prepress system.

6. Click Convert RGB to process if you have RGB TIFF images that need to be converted to CMYK plates.

To set the Maximum Color Steps:

Leave this field set for Default. If you have trouble printing, use the pop-up menu to set a lower number in the Maximum color steps field **⑳**.

To set the Flatness:

Leave this field set for Default. If you get a limitcheck error when printing, enter a number from 1 to 100 in the Flatness field **㉑**.

Output Options

The Separations options **22** control how the colors of your file print when outputting your work to separate pieces of film.

To choose the Separations options:

1. If you want all the colors to print together, click the Composite radio button.

2. To separate the colors to different plates, click the Separations radio button.

3. Click Print spot colors as process to override the settings for spot colors.

4. To prevent a color from printing, click its checkmark in the *P* column to delete the checkmark for that color.

5. To set a color to overprint, click the *O* column. The Overprint Ink dialog box appears **23**. Click On to set all instances of that color to overprint. Click Threshold and enter an amount in the field to specify what tint of that color will overprint.

TIP A checkmark in the *O* column of the Separations controls indicates that the ink is set to overprint. A diamond indicates that the ink is set to overprint at a threshold amount.

6. To set the screen angle for a color, click the angle column for that color. The Screen Angle dialog box appears **24**. Enter the angle you want for that color and click OK. Repeat for each color.

TIP Do not adjust the screen angles, screen frequency, or overprinting options unless you know exactly what you are doing. Consult with the print shop that will be printing your job.

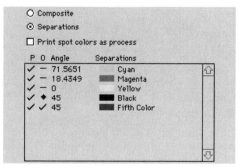

22 *The* **Separations** *controls.*

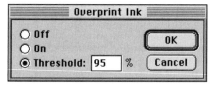

23 *The* **Overprint Ink** *dialog box.*

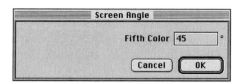

24 *The* **Screen Angle** *dialog box lets you set the angle at which a color's screens will be printed.*

㉕ *The* **Halftone screen pop-up menu** *for a typical laser printer.*

If your artwork has any screened objects, you may want to set the halftone screen.

To set the halftone screen:

1. Select the printer's PPD.
2. Open the Separations options.
3. Use the Halftone screen pop-up menu in the Separations options ㉕ to choose from the list of common screens for your output device.
4. To override any halftone screens set for individual objects, click Override objects.

TIP If you print to a laser printer and find banding in your blends, lower the screen frequency to around 35 lpi (lines per inch) or 40 lpi. While the screened artwork may look a little "dotty," this should reduce the banding.

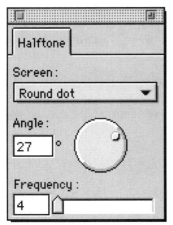

㉖ *The* **Halftone panel** *lets you change the halftone screen for individual objects.*

In addition to setting the halftone screen for the entire illustration, you can set the halftone screen for individual objects.

To set the halftone screen for individual objects:

1. Select the object whose halftone screen you want to set.
2. Choose **Window > Panels > Halftone**. The Halftone panel appears ㉖.
3. Choose the shape of the screen dot from the Screen pop-up menu.
4. Enter the angle of the screen in the Angle field or rotate the wheel to set the screen angle. If no value is set, the default is 45°.
5. Enter the frequency (lines per inch) of the screen in the Frequency field or use the slider to set the number. If no value is set, the default of the output device is used.

The Transfer function controls the dot gain for screened images.

To set the Transfer function:

1. With the Separations tab selected in the Print Setup dialog box, use the pop-up menu for the Transfer function **㉗**.

2. Choose Unadjusted if you are printing to a specially calibrated output device.

3. Choose Normalize if you are printing to an ordinary laser printer.

4. Choose Posterize if you want to speed the printing and do not mind sacrificing quality. This reduces the number of levels of screens.

㉗ *The **Transfer function** choices.*

In addition to the Trap Xtra (*see page 197*), FreeHand has a trapping option called *spread*.

To choose the spread size:

In the Spread size field **㉘**, enter the amount that you want basic fills and strokes to expand. This compensates for misregistrations in the printing. Before you enter any amount, talk to the print shop where the artwork will be printed.

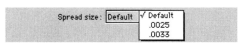

㉘ *The **Spread size field** sets all artwork to expand a certain amount to compensate for misregistrations in the final printing. It is an alternate to trapping.*

Once you have set all your print options, you can then save them as a Print Setting file.

To save and apply print settings:

1. Set all the print options the way you want the file to print.

2. Click the + sign next to the Print Settings pop-up menu **㉙**.

3. Use the Save dialog box to name and save the file in the PrintSet directory. This adds the preset to the pop-up menu.

4. Use the Print Settings pop-up menu to apply the settings to future files.

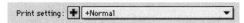

㉙ *The **Print setting controls** allow you to save and apply preset print options.*

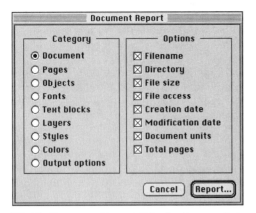

③ *The* **Document Report** *dialog box lets you select the information to be included in the document report.*

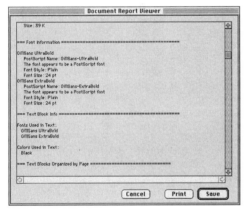

③ *The* **Document Report Viewer** *lets you read the report onscreen, save it as a text file, or print it.*

Sometimes you want a record or report of all the information about your FreeHand file. FreeHand provides you with a very sophisticated report for all your documents.

To create a document report:

1. With the document open, choose **File > Report**. The Document Report dialog box appears **③**.

2. Click the categories listed on the left side of the Document Report dialog box. Each one of these categories then displays a different set of Options.

3. Click each of the Options for each category to indicate which information you want listed.

4. Click Report (Mac) or OK (Win) to see the Document Report Viewer **③**, where you can read the complete document report.

5. Click Save to create a permanent text file of your report.

Information in each report category

Document File name, Directory, File size, File access, Creation date, Modification date, Document units, Total pages

Pages Page location, Dimensions, Bleed size, Orientation, Page type

Objects Set Note, Halftone, Place file

Fonts Font name, Font PS name, Font file format, Font style, Font size

Text Blocks Fonts used, Color used, Bounding box, Line count, Paragraph count, First line

Layers Foreground layers, Background layers, Visibility, Editing color, Access, Preview status

Styles Graphics styles, Text styles

Colors Named colors, Separations

Output Options Invisible layers, Split paths, Image date, Convert image, Max color steps, Fatness

Document Report

Unless you have your own high-resolution imagesetter, you must transfer your work onto a floppy disk or some type of removable media such as a Zip disk. You then send the disk or cartridge to a service bureau that will output the file. You must send certain files along with your FreeHand file. Rather than collect these files manually, the Collect For Output feature automates the process.

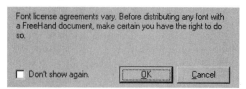

㉜ *The alert box that appears as part of the* **Collect For Output** *process.*

To use the Collect For Output command:

1. Choose **File > Collect For Output**. An alert box appears warning you that you should find out whether or not you have the rights to distribute fonts **㉜**. Click OK.

TIP Click Don't show again to stop the alert from appearing.

2. The Document Report dialog box appears (*see previous page*). Click each of the Options for each category to indicate which information you want listed. Click OK.

3. Choose a destination for the report and files, such as a folder on the current drive or a removable cartridge. Click Save.

4. FreeHand collects all the files necessary to print the document **㉝**. This includes the original FreeHand file, any linked graphics, the document report, fonts, the printer user prep, and printer driver (Mac).

㉝ *The files assembled by the Collect For Output command.*

CUSTOMIZING FREEHAND

Just because FreeHand installs with certain settings does not mean you have to keep them the way you found them. FreeHand gives you a wealth of choices as to how your application operates.

In this chapter, you will learn how to

Set the application preferences.

Customize the toolbars.

Customize the keyboard shortcuts.

Change the default settings for new documents.

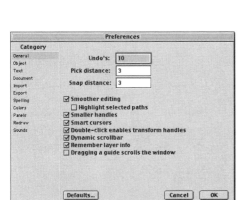

① *The* **Macintosh Preferences** *settings.*

Preferences control the entire application. This means that any changes you make to the Preferences settings will be applied to all documents — past, present, and future.

To change the preferences (Mac):

1. Choose **File > Preferences**. The Preferences dialog box appears **①**.

2. The preferences settings are divided into 11 categories on the left side of the Preferences dialog box.

3. Click the category you want to control and change the settings as needed.

To change the preferences (Win):

1. Choose **File > Preferences**. The Preferences dialog box appears **②**.

2. The preferences settings are divided into 10 categories shown as tab settings at the top of the Preferences dialog box.

3. Click the category you want to control and change the settings to suit the way you work.

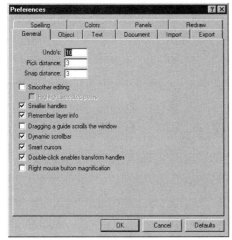

② *The* **Windows Preferences** *settings.*

Preferences

General preferences

Undo's lets you set the number of actions that can be reversed.

Pick distance controls, in pixels, how close the cursor has to come to manipulate a point.

Snap distance controls how close the cursor has to come when snapping one object to another.

Smoother editing allows faster screen redraw of objects on the page but uses more memory ❸.

Highlight selected paths displays paths and points in the color of the layer they are on ❸.

Smaller handles changes how the control handles of points are displayed ❹.

Smart cursors changes how the cursors for the tools are displayed ❺.

Double-click enables transform handles gives you the transformation handles when you double-click on an object (*see page 78*).

Dynamic scrollbar lets you see your artwork as you drag the scrollbars of the window.

Remember layer info means an object copied and pasted from one document to another will be pasted onto the same layer it originally had.

Dragging a guide scrolls the window means that if you drag a guide into a ruler, you move to a different section of the artwork.

Right mouse button magnification (Win) allows you to click-drag with the right mouse button pressed to define an area to be enlarged.

Object preferences

Changing object changes defaults means that if you change an object's fill or stroke, the next object has those attributes.

Groups transform as unit by default means that all items in a group transform together, but this may result in unwanted distortions.

Join non-touching paths means that when you choose Join for non-touching objects, FreeHand draws a line between the two nearest points.

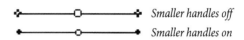

Smoother editing off   *Smoother editing on*   *Highlight selected paths on*

❸ *How the* **Smoother editing** *and* **Highlight** *preferences affect the display of points and paths.*

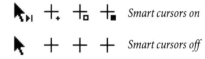

Smaller handles off
Smaller handles on

❹ *The* **Smaller handles** *choices.*

Smart cursors on

Smart cursors off

❺ *The* **Smart cursors** *choices.*

General Preferences; Object Preferences

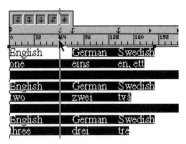

❻ *A line extends through the text to mark the tab location when* **Track tab movement with vertical line** *is turned on.*

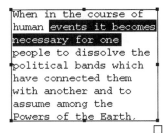

❼ *Working in a text block with the* **Show text handles when text ruler is off** *option turned on.*

❽ *Turning on* **Display Font Preview** *lets you see a representation of the font when the cursor passes over the font name.*

Path operations consume original paths means that when you apply path operations commands, the original paths are deleted.

Option/Alt-drag copies paths controls whether holding the Option/Alt key while dragging or transforming creates a duplicate of the object.

Show fill for new open paths allows you to see the fill in open paths. Only those paths drawn after changing this preference display the fills.

Warn before launch and edit controls whether the External Editor automatically opens when you double-click imported files.

Edit Locked Objects allows the stroke and fill attributes of locked objects to be modified. Also text within a locked text block can be modified.

External Editor menu selects the application that opens when you double-click imported files.

Default line weights field controls the sizes, in points, in the Stroke Widths submenu.

Auto-apply style to selected objects controls how an object is used to define a new style.

Define style based on selection means that a style takes its attributes from the selected object.

Text preferences

Always use Text Editor means that the Text Editor appears when you click with the Text tool.

Track tab movement with vertical line means a line extends through the text when tab stops are placed on the ruler **❻**.

Show text handles when text ruler is off lets you see the text block handles even if the text ruler is turned off **❼**.

New text containers auto-expand means that if you click to create a text block, the text block will expand as you type.

Text tool reverts to Pointer causes the Text tool to change to the Pointer tool when it is moved outside the text block **❽**.

Display Font Preview shows a representation of the font when you choose it in the font menus **❽**.

"**Smart quotes**" and its pop-up menu allows you to have FreeHand substitute typographer quotes or guillemets instead of plain tick marks ❾.

Build paragraph styles based on controls whether styles are defined by the first paragraph or the shared attributes of the text block.

Dragging a paragraph style changes controls whether the whole text block or a single paragraph changes when you drag a style icon.

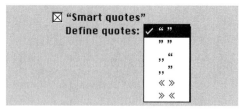

❾ *The various choices for* **Smart Quotes.**

Document preferences

Restore last view when opening document prompts FreeHand to remember the last view of a document before it was closed.

Remember window size and location prompts FreeHand to remember the size and position of the window that holds the file.

New document template lets you change the file that FreeHand uses for the defaults file.

Changing the view sets the active page means that as you scroll or change pages, the page that comes into view will be the active page.

Using tools sets the active page means that if you use a tool on a page, that page is active.

Always review unsaved documents upon Quit means that you will be presented with a dialog box prompting you to save each unsaved document when you quit ❿.

Search for missing links (Mac) lets you set which folder to search through for graphics that have lost their links to the original image.

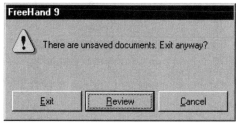

❿ *The* **unsaved documents** *dialog box.*

Import preferences

Convert editable EPS when imported means that, when possible, placed EPS files are converted to objects that you can select.

Embed images and EPS upon import means that the information necessary to print those graphics is embedded directly in the FreeHand document — not linked.

Convert PICT patterns to grays (Mac) converts the bitmapped patterns from MacDraw Pro and Canvas into a gray color.

DXF import options (Mac) control how objects are converted from the DXF format when they are imported into FreeHand.

PDF import options control how objects are converted from the PDF format when they are imported into FreeHand.

Clipboard paste format (Win) controls which formats FreeHand imports from the clipboard.

Export preferences

Save file thumbnails creates a preview of the artwork, visible in the **File > Open** dialog box.

Bitmap export lets you set the default attributes for exporting files in bitmapped format.

Bitmap PICT previews (Mac) changes the preview of files exported to programs such as QuarkXPress or Adobe PageMaker. This means faster redraw.

(Mac) Include Portfolio preview means that a preview is created for the program Extensis Portfolio.

UserPrep file field lets you choose the file FreeHand looks for when printing a document.

Override Output Options when printing (Mac) lets you choose between binary and ASCII image data. Your files print faster if you choose binary.

Clipboard output/copy formats controls the information on the Clipboard when you switch to another application.

Convert Colors/EPS color space lets you save your colors in the Photoshop 4/5, RGB, or CMYK formats.

Spelling preferences

Find duplicate words controls whether the checker finds errors such as "the the."

Find capitalization errors controls whether the checker finds mistakes such as "Really? how did that happen?"

Add words to dictionary exactly as typed means that case-sensitive words such as "FreeHand" or "QuickStart" are entered with capitalization intact.

Add words to dictionary all lowercase means the words are not case sensitive.

Colors preferences

The boxes for **Guide color or Grid color** open color pickers where you can choose the colors for guides and grid dots.

Color List shows Container color means that when a text block is selected, the Fill color shows the color of the text block.

Color List shows Text color means that when a text block is selected, the Fill color in the Color List shows the fill color of the text, not the block.

Auto-rename [changed] colors means that the names of colors automatically change when their CMYK or RGB values change.

Color Mixer/Tints panel uses split color well allows you to compare any changes to a color in the Color Mixer with the original color.

Dither 8-bit colors (Mac) improves how colors are displayed onscreen if you are working on a monitor with only 256 colors.

Color management gives you options for how colors are displayed onscreen.

⓫ *Showing the* **Tool Tips.**

Better Display on   *Better Display off*

⓬ *The* **Better Display** *choices.*

High-resolution on   *High-resolution off*

⓭ *The* **High-resolution display** *choices.*

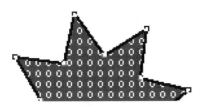

①④ *The Os indicate that the fill overprints.*

Panels preferences

Remember location of zipped panels allows a panel to occupy one location when zipped, and a different, unzipped location.

Show Tool Tips shows explanations of what the icons in the toolbars mean when your cursor passes over them **①①**.

Clicking on a layer name moves selected objects means you do not have to use the options pop-up on the Layer panel to change the layer an object inhabits.

①⑤ *An example of* **Greeked text** *(top) and visible text (bottom).*

Redraw preferences

Better display means that Graduated and Radial fills are displayed in smoother blends **①②**.

Display text effects means that special effects such as Inline and Zoom are visible.

Redraw while scrolling means that you see your artwork as you scroll instead of after you finish scrolling.

High-resolution image display means that TIFF images will have a better display **①③**.

Display overprinting objects means that *Os* are displayed when an object is set to overprint **①④**.

Image RAM cache (Win) controls the amount of RAM set aside for the import of images from other applications.

①⑥ *Dragging* **without a preview.**

Greek type below controls the size at which text is *Greeked* or displayed as a gray band **①⑤**.

Preview drag field controls how many items are displayed as a preview as they are moved or transformed **①⑥–①⑦**.

TIP Press and release the Option/Alt key as you drag to see a preview of all the items regardless of how the preferences are set.

①⑦ *Dragging* **with a preview.**

Sounds preferences (Mac)

FreeHand lets you hear sounds when you snap to different objects such as grids, points, and guides. The pop-up menu next to each action lets you choose the sound for that action.

None turns off the sound.

Play lets you preview the sound.

Snap sounds enabled turns on the sounds for all the choices.

Play sounds when mouse is up plays the sound whenever the cursor passes over the object, even if the mouse button is not pressed. (Very noisy!)

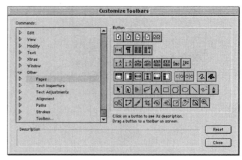

⑱ *The* **Customize Toolbars** *dialog box.*

TIP While most changes you make to the Preferences settings take effect in your document immediately, they are not saved to your hard disk until you quit FreeHand.

FreeHand lets you customize the Toolbox, Text toolbar, and Main toolbar. This allows you to add or delete icons for commands or change the tools in the Toolbox.

To add icons to the toolbars:

1. Choose **File > Customize > Toolbars**. The Customize Toolbars dialog box appears **⑱**.
2. Use the categories on the left side of the dialog box to find the command that you want to add to a toolbar.
3. Click the command. The icon for the command highlights on the right side of the dialog box.
4. Drag the icon for the command onto one of the toolbars.

To delete icons from the toolbars:

With the Customize Toolbars dialog box open, drag an icon off any toolbar.

TIP Hold the Command/Alt key and drag an icon off a toolbar at any time without opening the Customize Toolbars dialog box.

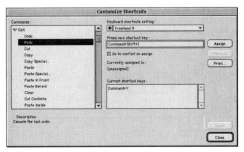

⑲ *The* **Customize Shortcuts** *dialog box.*

FreeHand lets you customize the keyboard shortcuts that are assigned to commands. This allows you to add shortcuts to commands or to change the shortcuts so they match other programs.

To customize keyboard shortcuts:

1. Choose **File > Customize > Shortcuts**. The Customize Shortcuts dialog box appears **⑲**.

2. Use the categories on the left side of the dialog box to find the command that you want to customize.

3. Click the command. The current shortcut keys, if any, appear in the Current shortcut keys area.

4. Type the keyboard shortcut that you want for the command.

5. If the shortcut is assigned to another command, that command appears after the words *Currently Assigned to*. Type a new command or change the conflicting shortcut.

6. Click Assign to set the shortcut.

7. Repeat the steps to assign additional commands or click the Close button to return to the work page.

8. Use the Print button to print the shortcuts for later reference or save the shortcuts as a file.

TIP In Windows, click the tabs at the top of the dialog boxes to switch between the Customize Toolbars and Customize Shortcuts dialog boxes.

If you are used to working in other programs, you can change the FreeHand shortcuts to match the keystrokes of other programs.

To apply the preset shortcuts:

1. In the Customize Shortcuts dialog box, use the Keyboard shortcut setting pop-up menu to display the list of preset shortcuts.

2. Choose from the list of presets and then click Assign.

Keyboard Shortcuts

FreeHand also lets you change the default settings for your documents. Defaults are the settings that you have when you open a new FreeHand document. Default settings include such things as all the preferences already covered in this chapter, units of measurement, which colors are listed in the Color List, if the rulers are visible, page sizes and how many pages a new document should have, grid and perspective settings, and the settings of all the panels, inspectors, and toolbars. To change the defaults, you work with the FreeHand Defaults template.

To set the FreeHand Defaults file:

1. With FreeHand open, choose **File > New**. An untitled file opens.

2. Create a new document, changing the preferences and settings to your specifications ⑳.

3. Choose **File > Save As.** The Save dialog box opens.

4. Navigate to the folder/directory English within the FreeHand folder/directory.

5. Select FreeHand Template as the format or type and name the file FreeHand Defaults (Mac) ㉑ or Defaults (Win). Click Save.

6. Respond to the alert asking if you want to replace the existing file by clicking Replace or Yes ㉒.

TIP Before you make any changes to the defaults file, make a copy of the original file and save it in a separate place in case you need to restore the original defaults.

TIP The name of the file used as the default for new documents is controlled in the Document preferences.

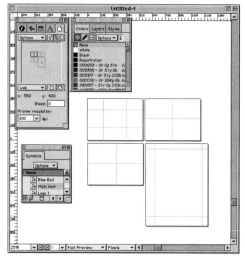

⑳ *Any changes you make to the FreeHand Defaults file become the* **default settings for all new files***.*

㉑ *Saving a new document as the FreeHand Defaults template changes the way a new file opens.*

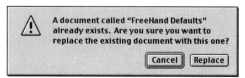

㉒ *Click Replace or Yes to confirm that you want to make a change to the default template.*

Defaults

ONSCREEN ELEMENTS

Onscreen elements include the windows, toolbars, panels, and other parts of the software that you work with onscreen. One of the important features of FreeHand is the ability to customize some of these onscreen elements (*see Chapter 22, "Customizing FreeHand"*).

That means that if you are working on a copy of FreeHand that has been modified, your toolbars and menus may not match the ones shown here. However, if you have installed FreeHand fresh from the box, all your menus and onscreen elements should match the ones shown here.

There are minor differences between the Macintosh and Windows platforms and the appearance of the interfaces. However, those differences do not affect the use of the elements.

In Appendix A you will learn

The elements of the document window.

The elements in a sample dialog box.

The default elements of the Toolbox.

The default settings for the toolbars.

The settings for the Inspector panels.

The settings for the Transform panel.

The settings for the tabbed panels.

The settings for the Xtra Tools and Operations panels.

The settings for the Align panel.

The settings for the Find & Replace Graphics and Find Text panels.

The keyboard commands to display the tools and panels.

FreeHand document window

The document window is the main window where your artwork is actually created. There are slight differences between the Macintosh version and Windows versions.

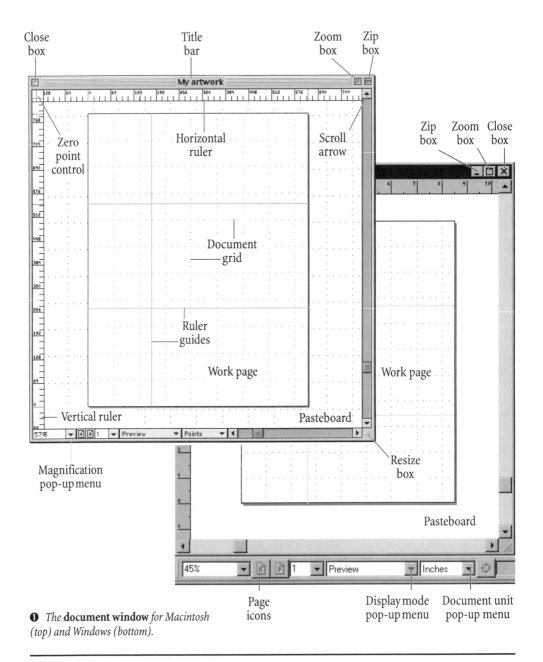

❶ *The* **document window** *for Macintosh (top) and Windows (bottom).*

Sample dialog box

Many of FreeHand's features are set using dialog boxes. Though each dialog box differs, they all use similar setting devices: pop-up menus, fields in which to enter numbers, sliders, wheels, color drop boxes, check boxes, icons, radio buttons and buttons. There are some differences between the Macintosh and the Windows devices.

Drag to set **slider**

Drag colors in or out of a **color drop box**

Type in a **field**

Drag to rotate a **wheel**

Click to select an **icon**

Click in a **check box**

Click a **radio button**

Press to access choices in a **pop-up menu**

Click to activate a **button**

Sample Dialog Box

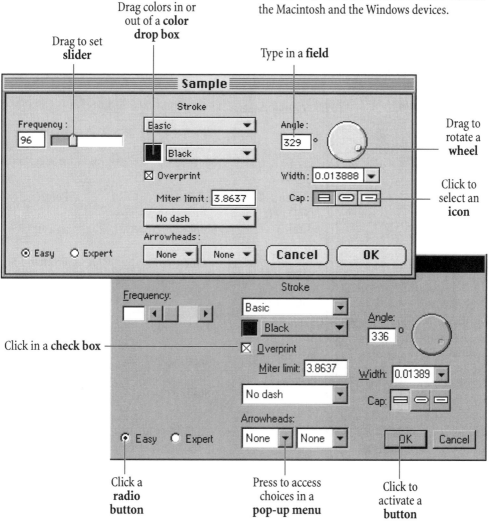

❷ *A* **sample dialog box** *for Macintosh (top) and Windows (bottom).*

Toolbox

The Toolbox contains 22 different tools that perform selection, creation, text, transformation, and magnification functions.

Click to select each tool or use the keyboard commands to access the tools. The keyboard commands listed are the default settings for FreeHand 9. The tools in the Toolbox and keyboard commands can be changed using the Customize Shortcuts dialog box.

TIP The keyboard shortcuts can be typed by simply pressing the key listed. No modifier key is needed.

Double-click tools with a corner symbol to access their dialog box settings. Changing the settings for the Freehand and Freeform tools changes the icons for those tools.

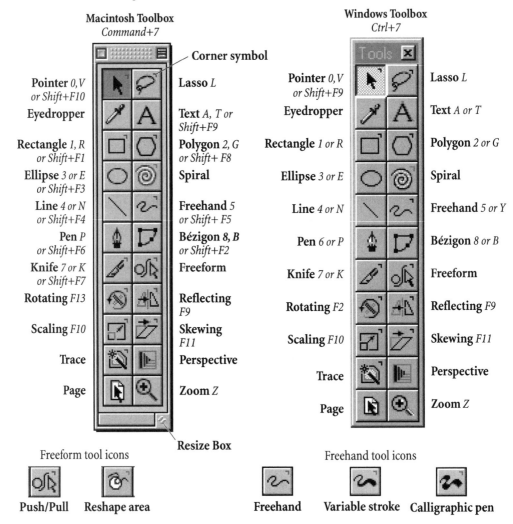

Macintosh Toolbox
Command+7

Windows Toolbox
Ctrl+7

Corner symbol

Pointer *0,V or Shift+F10* — Lasso *L*
Eyedropper — Text *A, T or Shift+F9*
Rectangle *1, R or Shift+F1* — Polygon *2, G or Shift+ F8*
Ellipse *3 or E or Shift+F3* — Spiral
Line *4 or N or Shift+F4* — Freehand *5 or Shift+ F5*
Pen *P or Shift+F6* — Bézigon *8, B or Shift+F2*
Knife *7 or K or Shift+F7* — Freeform
Rotating *F13* — Reflecting *F9*
Scaling *F10* — Skewing *F11*
Trace — Perspective
Page — Zoom *Z*

Pointer *0,V or Shift+F9* — Lasso *L*
Eyedropper — Text *A or T*
Rectangle *1 or R* — Polygon *2 or G*
Ellipse *3 or E* — Spiral
Line *4 or N* — Freehand *5 or Y*
Pen *6 or P* — Bézigon *8 or B*
Knife *7 or K* — Freeform
Rotating *F2* — Reflecting *F9*
Scaling *F10* — Skewing *F11*
Trace — Perspective
Page — Zoom *Z*

Resize Box

Freeform tool icons
Push/Pull   Reshape area

Freehand tool icons
Freehand   Variable stroke   Calligraphic pen

❸ *The* **Toolbox and keyboard commands** *for the Macintosh and Windows platforms.*

Toolbars

In addition to the Toolbox, FreeHand has four other toolbars that can be aligned to the screen or used as floating palettes: the Envelope Toolbar, the Main Toolbar, Text Toolbar, and Info Toolbar. The keyboard commands show or hide the toolbars. The icons in the toolbars and keyboard commands can be changed using the Customize Shortcuts dialog box.

In addition, the Status Toolbar for Windows can be moved as a floating palette.

❹ *The* **Envelope Toolbar**.

❺ *The* **Main Toolbar**. *Show/Hide Win: Ctrl+Alt+T.*

❻ *The* **Text Toolbar**. *Show/Hide Mac: Command+Option+T; Win: Ctrl+Alt+T.*

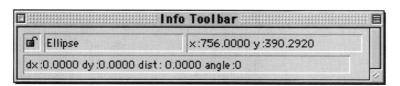

❼ *The* **Info Toolbar**. *Show/Hide Win: Ctrl+Alt+T.*

❽ *The* **Status Toolbar**. *Show/Hide Win: Ctrl+Alt+T.*

Toolbars

Inspector panels

The five different Inspector panels change depending on the icons that are selected and what type of object is select. The keyboard commands show or hide the panels.

Object Inspector
Cmd+I (Mac)
Ctrl+I (Win)

Fill Inspector
Cmd+Opt+F (Mac)
Ctrl+Alt+F (Win)

Stroke Inspector
Cmd+Opt+L (Mac)
Ctrl+Alt+L (Win)

Document Inspector
Cmd+Opt+D (Mac)
Ctrl+Alt+D (Win)

Text Inspector
Cmd+T (Mac)
Ctrl+T (Win)

Paragraph Inspector
Cmd+Opt+P (Mac)
Ctrl+Alt+P (Win)

Spacing Inspector
Cmd+Opt+K (Mac)
Ctrl+Alt+K (Win)

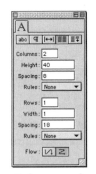

Columns and Rows Inspector
Cmd+Opt+R (Mac)
Ctrl+Alt+R (Win)

Adjust Columns Inspector
Cmd+Opt+C (Mac)
Ctrl+Alt+C (Win)

❾ *The* **Inspector panels** *and keyboard shortcuts.*

Symbols panel

The Tabbed panels

In addition to the Toolbox and Inspector panels, FreeHand has seven other panels. The tabs for these panels allow them to be shown together or individually. The keyboard commands show or hide the panels.

Color List
Cmd+9 (Mac)
Ctrl+9 (Win)

Styles panel
Cmd+3 (Mac)
Ctrl+3 (Win)

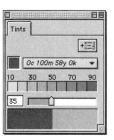

Tints panel
Cmd+Shift+Z (Mac)
Ctrl+Shift+3 (Win)

Color Mixer
Cmd+Shift+C (Mac)
Ctrl+Shift+9 (Win)

Halftones panel
Cmd+H (Mac)
Ctrl+H (Win)

Layers panel
Cmd+6 (Mac)
Ctrl+6 (Win)

⑩ *The **tabbed panels** and keyboard shortcuts.*

The Transform panels

The Transform panels allow you to move or transform selected objects by numerical input. The Transform panel settings change depending on which of the transform icons are selected. The Transform panels can be displayed by the keyboard commands or by double-clicking each of the transformation tools in the Toolbox.

Move panel
Cmd+E (Mac)
Ctrl+E (Win)

Rotate panel
Cmd+F13 (Mac)
Ctrl+F2 (Win)

Scale panel
Cmd+F10 (Mac)
Ctrl+F10 (Win)

Skew panel
Cmd+F11 (Mac)
Ctrl+F11 (Win)

Reflect panel
Cmd+F9 (Mac)
Ctrl+F9 (Win)

⑪ *The* **Transform panels** *and keyboard shortcuts.*

Xtra Operations and Xtra Tools toolbars

The Xtra Operations toolbar lets you apply operations to objects. The Xtra Tools toolbar contains additional drawing and modification tools. The toolbars may be displayed via the **Window > Toolbars** menu or via the keyboard shortcuts.

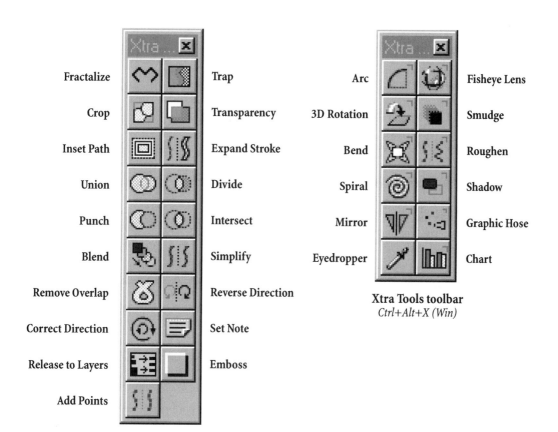

Fractalize		Trap	Arc		Fisheye Lens
Crop		Transparency	3D Rotation		Smudge
Inset Path		Expand Stroke	Bend		Roughen
Union		Divide	Spiral		Shadow
Punch		Intersect	Mirror		Graphic Hose
Blend		Simplify	Eyedropper		Chart
Remove Overlap		Reverse Direction			
Correct Direction		Set Note			
Release to Layers		Emboss			
Add Points					

Xtra Tools toolbar
Ctrl+Alt+X (Win)

Xtra Operations toolbar
Ctrl+Alt+O (Win)

Xtra Tools and Xtra Operations Toolbars

⑫ *The* **Xtra Operations** *and* **Xtra Tools toolbars** *and keyboard shortcuts (Win).*

The Align Panel

The Align panel is used to line up selected objects in different ways. It is displayed via the **Window > Panels** menu or via the keyboard commands. Because it has no tab, it cannot be joined to the panels with tabs.

Align panel
Cmd+Opt+A (Mac)
Ctrl+Alt+A (Win)

⓭ *The* **Align panel** *and keyboard shortcuts.*

Find & Replace Graphics and Find Text panels

The Find & Replace Graphics panel has two different settings: one for Find & Replace, the other for Select. It is used for making global changes to graphic objects.

The Find Text panel allows you to search for certain text strings and replace them with others.

The panels are displayed via the **Edit > Find & Replace** menu or via the keyboard commands.

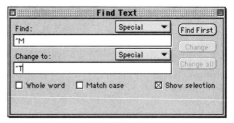

Find Text
Cmd+Shift+F (Mac)
Ctrl+Shift+F (Win)

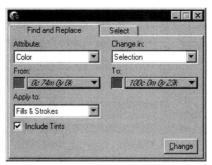

Find & Replace Graphics
Cmd+Opt+E (Mac)
Ctrl+Alt+E (Win)

⓮ *The* **Find & Replace Graphics** *and* **Find Text** **panels** *and keyboard shortcuts.*

KEYBOARD SHORTCUTS

Working with keyboard shortcuts is probably the fastest way to work on a computer in any application. FreeHand offers a wealth of keyboard shortcuts for almost all the menu commands as well as many non-menu items.

As explained in Chapter 22, you can change the keyboard shortcuts to fit your own particular work habits. This may be to make FreeHand work similarly to another program that you are used to. It may be to add a shortcut to a command that does not have a shortcut.

If you change your keyboard shortcuts, you can print a copy of those changes to use as a reference.

This appendix lists the default keyboard shortcuts in FreeHand. If you have not made any changes to your settings, you will find that this list matches how FreeHand works on your computer. If you have changed your settings, you can use the Print command in the Customize dialog box to print your own list.

In Appendix B you have

A list of all the default keyboard shortcuts for the Macintosh platform on pages 268–270.

A list of all the default keyboard shortcuts for the Windows platform on pages 270–272.

Keyboard Shortcuts

MACINTOSH KEYBOARD COMMANDS

The following are many of the default keyboard shortcuts. The abbreviations used are:

Cmd	=	Command key
Opt	=	Option key
Left	=	Left arrow key
Right	=	Right arrow key
Down	=	Down arrow key
Up	=	Up arrow key
Space	=	Spacebar
Num	=	Keypad number

File menu commands (Mac)

New . . . . Cmd+N
Open . . . . Cmd+O
Close . . . . Cmd+W
Save . . . . Cmd+S
Save As . . . . Cmd+Shift+S
Import . . . . Cmd+R
Export . . . . Cmd+Shift+R
Print . . . . Cmd+P
Preferences . . . . Cmd+Shift+D
Quit . . . . Cmd+Q

Edit menu commands (Mac)

Undo . . . . F1, Cmd+Z
Redo . . . . Cmd+Y
Cut . . . . F2, Cmd+X
Copy . . . . F3, Cmd+C
Paste . . . . F4, Cmd+V
Cut Contents . . . . Cmd+Shift+X
Paste Inside . . . . Cmd+Shift+V
Copy Attributes . . . . Cmd+Shift+Opt+C
Paste Attributes . . . . Cmd+Shift+Opt+V
Duplicate . . . . Cmd+D
Clone . . . . Cmd+=
Select All . . . . Cmd+A
Select All In Document . . . . Cmd+Shift+A

Find & Replace Text . . . . Cmd+Shift+F
Find & Replace Graphics . . . . Cmd+Opt+E

View menu commands (Mac)

Fit Selection . . . . Cmd+0
Fit To Page . . . . Cmd+Shift+W
Fit All . . . . Cmd+Opt+0
50% magnification . . . . Cmd+5
100% magnification . . . . Cmd+1
200% magnification . . . . Cmd+2
400% magnification . . . . Cmd+4
800% magnification . . . . Cmd+8
Previous custom view . . . . Cmd+Opt+1
Preview . . . . Cmd+K
Fast Mode . . . . Cmd+Shift+K
Flash Anti-alias . . . . Cmd+Shift+Opt+G
Toolbars . . . . Cmd+Opt+T
Panels . . . . F12, Cmd+Shift+H
Page Rulers . . . . Cmd+Opt+M
Text Rulers . . . . Cmd+/
Snap To Point . . . . Cmd+'
Snap To Guides . . . . Cmd+\
Snap To Grid . . . . Cmd+;

Modify menu commands (Mac)

Object Inspector . . . . Cmd+I
Stroke Inspector . . . . Cmd+Opt+L
Fill Inspector . . . . Cmd+Opt+F
Text Inspector . . . . Cmd+T
Document Inspector . . . . Cmd+Opt+D
Transform Scale . . . . Cmd+F10
Transform Move . . . . Cmd+E
Transform Rotate . . . . Cmd+F13
Transform Reflect . . . . Cmd+F9
Transform Skew . . . . Cmd+F11
Transform Again . . . . Cmd+,
Bring To Front . . . . Cmd+F

Move Forward . . . . Cmd+[

Move Backward. Cmd+]

Send To Back . . . . Cmd+B

Align Again . . . . Cmd+Shift+Opt+A

Join . . . . Cmd+J

Split. . . . . Cmd+Shift+J

Blend . . . . Cmd+Shift+B

Join Blend To Path. . . . . Cmd+Shift+Opt+B

Rasterize . . . . Cmd+Shift+Opt+Z

Lock. . . . . Cmd+L

Unlock . . . . Cmd+Shift+L

Group . . . . Cmd+G

Ungroup . . . . Cmd+U

Text menu commands (Mac)

Size > Smaller . . . . Cmd+Shift+<

Size > Larger . . . . Cmd+Shift+>

Style > Plain. . . . . F5, Cmd+Shift+Opt+P

Style > Bold . . . . F6, Cmd+Opt+B

Style > Italic . . . . F7, Cmd+Opt+I

Style > Bold Italic . . . . . . F8, Cmd+Shift+Opt+O

Highlight . . . . Cmd+Shift+Opt+H

Strikethrough. . . . . Cmd+Shift+Opt+S

Underline. . . . . Cmd+Shift+Opt+U

Align > Left . . . . Cmd+Shift+Opt+L

Align > Right . . . . Cmd+Shift+Opt+R

Align > Center . . . . Cmd+Shift+Opt+M

Align > Justified . . . . Cmd+Shift+Opt+J

Em Space . . . . Cmd+Shift+M

En Space . . . . Cmd+Shift+N

Thin Space. . . . . Cmd+Shift+T

Discretionary Hyphen . . . . Cmd+-

Text Editor. . . . . Cmd+Shift+E

Spelling . . . . Cmd+Shift+G

Run Around Selection . . . . Cmd+Opt+W

Flow Inside Path. . . . . Cmd+Shift+U

Attach To Path. . . . . Cmd+Shift+Y

Convert To Paths. . . . . Cmd+Shift+P

Xtras menu commands (Mac)

Repeat Last Xtra . . . . Cmd++

Window menu commands (Mac)

New Window . . . . Cmd+Opt+N

Text Toolbars. . . . . Cmd+Opt+T

Toolbox . . . . Cmd+7

Object Inspector . . . . Cmd+I

Stroke Inspector . . . . Cmd+Opt+L

Fill Inspector. . . . . Cmd+Opt+F

Text Inspectors. Cmd+T

Document Inspector . . . . Cmd+Opt+D

Layers Panel . . . . Cmd+6

Styles Panel . . . . Cmd+3

Color List. . . . . Cmd+9

Color Mixer . . . . Cmd+Shift+C

Tints Panel. . . . . Cmd+Shift+Z

Halftones Panel . . . . Cmd+H

Align Panel . . . . Cmd+Opt+A

Transform Panel . . . . Cmd+M

Other commands (Mac)

Previous Page . . . . Cmd+Page Up

Next Page . . . . Cmd+Page Down

Character Inspector. . . . . Cmd+T

Paragraph Inspector . . . . Cmd+Opt+P

Spacing Inspector . . . . Cmd+Opt+K

Columns & Rows Inspector . . . . . . Cmd+Opt+R

Adjust Columns Inspector . . . . Cmd+Opt+C

Text commands (Mac)

Increase Leading . . . . Cmd+Num +

Decrease Leading . . . . Cmd+Num -

Increase Kerning 1% . . . . Cmd+Opt+Right

Decrease Kerning 1% . . . . Cmd+Opt+Left

Increase Kerning 10% . . Cmd+Shift+Opt+Right

Decrease Kerning 10% . . . Cmd+Shift+Opt+Left

Increase Baseline Shift . . . . Cmd+Opt+Up

Decrease Baseline Shift . . . . . . Cmd+Opt+Down

Alignment commands (Mac)

Top . . . . Cmd+Opt+8

Right . . . . Cmd+Opt+6

Center Horizontal . . . . Cmd+Opt+7

Center Vertical . . . . Cmd+Opt+9

Bottom . . . . Cmd+Opt+5

Left . . . . Cmd+Opt+4

Stroke commands (Mac)

Thinner . . . . Cmd+Opt+Shift+<

Thicker . . . . Cmd+Opt+Shift+>

Toolbox commands (Mac)

Select . . . . Shift+F10, V

Text . . . . Shift+F9, A, T

Rectangle . . . . Shift+F1, 1, R

Polygon . . . . Shift+F8, 2, G

Ellipse . . . . Shift+F3, 3, E

Line . . . . Shift+F4, 4, N

Freehand . . . . Shift+F5, 5, Y

Pen . . . . Shift+F6, 6, P

Knife . . . . Shift+F7, 7, K

Bézigon . . . . Shift+F2, 8, B

Rotate F13

Reflect F9

Scale F10

Skew F11

Magnify . . . . Z

WINDOWS KEYBOARD COMMANDS

The following are many of the default keyboard shortcuts. The abbreviations used are:

Ctrl = Control (Win) key
Alt = Alt (Win) key
Left = Left arrow key
Right = Right arrow key
Down = Down arrow key
Up = Up arrow key
Space = Spacebar
Num = Keypad number

File menu commands (Win)

New . . . . Ctrl+N

Open . . . . Ctrl+O

Close . . . . Ctrl+F4

Save . . . . Ctrl+S

Save As . . . . Ctrl+Shift+S

Import . . . . Ctrl+R

Export . . . . Ctrl+Shift+R

Print . . . . Ctrl+P

Preferences . . . . Ctrl+Shift+D

Exit . . . . Alt+F4

Edit menu commands (Win)

Undo . . . . Ctrl+Z, Alt+Backspace

Redo . . . . Ctrl+Y, Ctrl+Alt+Backspace

Cut . . . . Ctrl+X, Shift+Del

Copy . . . . Ctrl+C, Ctrl+Ins

Paste . . . . Ctrl+V, Shift+Ins

Cut Contents . . . . Ctrl+Shift+X

Paste Inside . . . . Ctrl+Shift+V

Copy Attributes . . . . Ctrl+Alt+Shift+C

Paste Attributes . . . . Ctrl+Alt+Shift+V

Duplicate . . . . Ctrl+D

Clone . . . . Ctrl+Shift+C

Select: All . . . . Ctrl+A

Select: All In Document . . . . Ctrl+Shift+A

Find & Replace: Text. . . . . Ctrl+Shift+F

Find & Replace: Graphics . . . . Ctrl+Alt+E

View menu commands (Win)

Fit Selection . . . . Ctrl+0

Fit To Page . . . . Ctrl+Shift+W

Fit All. . . . . Ctrl+Alt+0

50% magnification . . . . Ctrl+5

100% magnification . . . . Ctrl+1

200% magnification . . . . Ctrl+2

400% magnification . . . . Ctrl+4

800% magnification . . . . Ctrl+8

Previous custom view . . . . Ctrl+Alt+Shift+1

Preview. . . . . Ctrl+K

Fast Mode . . . . Ctrl+Shift+K

Flash Anti-alias . . . . Ctrl+Alt+Shift+G

Toolbars . . . . Ctrl+Alt+T

Panels . . . . Ctrl+Alt+H, F12

Page Rulers . . . . Ctrl+Alt+M

Text Rulers . . . . Ctrl+Alt+Shift+T

Snap To Point . . . . Ctrl+Shift+Z

Snap To Guides . . . . Ctrl+Alt+G

Modify menu commands (Win)

Object Inspector . . . . Ctrl+I

Stroke Inspector. . . . . Ctrl+Alt+L

Fill Inspector . . . . Ctrl+Alt+F

Text Inspector . . . . Ctrl+T

Document Inspector . . . . Ctrl+Alt+D

Transform Scale . . . . Ctrl+F10

Transform Move. . . . . Ctrl+E

Transform Rotate. . . . . Ctrl+F2

Transform Reflect . . . . Ctrl+F9

Transform Skew. . . . . Ctrl+F11

Transform Again . . . . Ctrl+Shift+G

Bring To Front . . . . Ctrl+F

Move Forward. . . . . Ctrl+Alt+Shift+F

Move Backward. . . . . Ctrl+Alt+Shift+K

Send To Back . . . . Ctrl+B

Align Again. . . . . Ctrl+Alt+Shift+A

Join . . . . Ctrl+J

Split. . . . . Ctrl+Shift+J

Blend . . . . Ctrl+Shift+B

Join Blend To Path . . . . Ctrl+Alt+Shift+B

Rasterize . . . . Ctrl+Alt+Shift+Z

Lock . . . . Ctrl+L

Unlock . . . . Ctrl+Shift+L

Group . . . . Ctrl+G

Ungroup . . . . Ctrl+U

Text menu commands (Win)

Size > Smaller . . . . Ctrl+Alt+1, Ctrl+Alt+Num 1
Ctrl+Alt+Shift+Down

Size > Larger. . . . . Ctrl+Alt+2, Ctrl+Alt+Num 2
Ctrl+Alt+Shift+Up

Style > Plain. . . . . Ctrl+Alt+Shift+P, F5

Style > Bold . . . . Ctrl+Alt+B, F6

Style > Italic . . . . Ctrl+Alt+I, F7

Style > Bold Italic . . . . Ctrl+Alt+Shift+O, F8

Highlight. . . . . Ctrl+Alt+Shift+H

Strikethrough. . . . . Ctrl+Alt+Shift+S

Underline . . . . Ctrl+Alt+U

Align > Left . . . . Ctrl+Alt+Shift+L

Align > Right . . . . Ctrl+Alt+Shift+R

Align > Center . . . . Ctrl+Alt+Shift+M

Align > Justified. . . . . Ctrl+Alt+Shift+J

Non-Breaking Space . . . . Ctrl+Shift+H

Em Space . . . . Ctrl+Shift+M

En Space . . . . Ctrl+Shift+N

Thin Space . . . . Ctrl+Shift+T

Text > Editor. . . . . Ctrl+Shift+E

Spelling . . . . Ctrl+Alt+S

Run Around Selection . . . . Ctrl+Alt+W

Flow Inside Path . . . . Ctrl+Shift+U

Attach To Path. . . . . Ctrl+Shift+Y

Convert To Paths. . . . . Ctrl+Shift+P

Xtras menu commands (Win)

Xtras: Repeat . . . . Ctrl+Alt+Shift+X

Window menu commands (Win)

New Window . . . . Ctrl+Alt+N
Toolbox . . . . Ctrl+7
Layers Panel . . . . Ctrl+6
Styles Panel. . . . . Ctrl+3
Color List. . . . . Ctrl+9
Color Mixer. . . . . Ctrl+Shift+9
Tints Panel . . . . Ctrl+Shift+3
Halftones Panel . . . . Ctrl+H
Align Panel . . . . Ctrl+Alt+A
Transform Panel . . . . Ctrl+M
Operations Xtras. . . . . Ctrl+Alt+O
Xtra Tools. . . . . Ctrl+Alt+X
Cascade Windows . . . . Shift+F5
Tile Windows Vertically. . . . . Shift+F4

Other commands (Win)

Previous Page . . . . Ctrl+Page Up
Next Page. . . . . Ctrl+Page Down
Paragraph Inspector . . . . Ctrl+Alt+P
Spacing Inspector . . . . Ctrl+Alt+K
Columns & Rows Inspector . . . . Ctrl+Alt+R
Adjust Columns Inspector . . . . Ctrl+Alt+C

Text commands (Win)

Increase Leading . . . . Ctrl+Num +
Decrease Leading . . . . Ctrl+Num -
Increase Kerning By 1% em . . . . Ctrl+Alt+Right
Decrease Kerning By 1% em . . . . . Ctrl+Alt+Left
Increase Kerning By 10% em. . . . .
. . . . Ctrl+Alt+Shift+Right
Decrease Kerning By 10% em . . . .
. . . . Ctrl+Alt+Shift+Left
Increase Baseline Shift . . . . Ctrl+Alt+Up
Decrease Baseline Shift . . . . Ctrl+Alt+Down

Alignment commands (Win)

Top . . . . Ctrl+Alt+Num 8
Right . . . . Ctrl+Alt+Num 6
Center Horizontal. . . . . Ctrl+Alt+Num 7
Center Vertical . . . . Ctrl+Alt+Num 9
Bottom. Ctrl+Alt+Num 5
Left. . . . . Ctrl+Alt+Num 4

Strokes commands (Win)

Thinner . . . . Ctrl+Shift+1
Thicker. . . . . Ctrl+Shift+2

Toolbox commands (Win)

Pointer. . . . . Shift+F9, 0, V
Text. . . . . A, T
Rectangle . . . . 1, R
Polygon. . . . . 2, G
Ellipse . . . . 3, E
Line. . . . . 4, N
Freehand. . . . . 5, Y
Pen. . . . . 6, P
Knife . . . . 7, K
Bézigon . . . . 8, B
Rotate F2
Reflect. F9
Scale F10
Skew F11
Magnify . . . . Z

FILLS & STROKES

As explained in Chapters 9 and 10, FreeHand features several different types of fills and strokes. Some of these, such as the Custom fills, Textured fills, and Custom strokes, do not appear onscreen. Others, such as the Pattern fills, display onscreen as they will print.

You may find it helpful to mark these pages so you can refer to them as you work with the Custom fills, Textured fills, and Custom strokes.

In Appendix C you will see

Printouts of the Custom fills at their default settings.

Transparent and opaque areas for each Custom fill.

Printouts of the Textured fills at their default settings.

The effects of applying a color or tint to a Textured fill.

Printouts of the Pattern fills at their default settings.

Printouts of the Custom strokes.

How the Custom strokes react with their background.

Fills and Strokes

Custom fills

The ten Custom fills appear onscreen as a series of *Cs* in the artwork. The examples below show how each Custom fill prints at its default settings. The gray circles show which of the Custom fills allow background objects to show through their transparent areas.

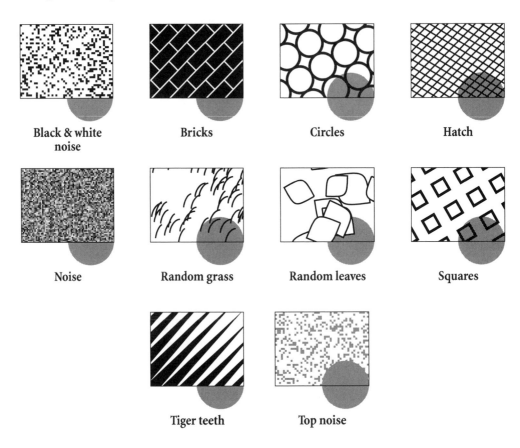

Black & white noise   Bricks   Circles   Hatch

Noise   Random grass   Random leaves   Squares

Tiger teeth   Top noise

Custom Fills

❶ *The* **ten Custom fills** *at their default settings.*

Textured fills

The nine Textured fills appear onscreen as a series of *Cs* in the artwork. The examples below show how each Textured fill prints at its default settings. The final example shows how only the fill responds to a change in color.

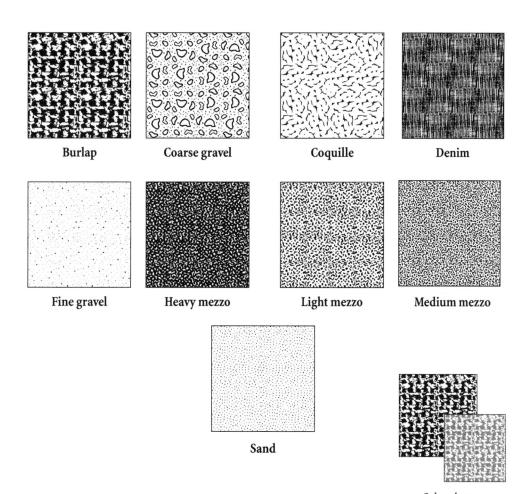

Burlap

Coarse gravel

Coquille

Denim

Fine gravel

Heavy mezzo

Light mezzo

Medium mezzo

Sand

Color change

❷ *The* **nine Textured fills** *at their default settings, and an example of a color change*

Pattern fills and strokes

The Pattern fills and strokes are bitmapped patterns that appear onscreen and print as shown below. In addition to these default settings, each of the patterns either may be inverted or have its pixels edited one by one.

❸ *The* **64 Pattern fills and strokes** *at their default settings.*

Custom strokes

The 23 Custom strokes appear onscreen as solid strokes. The examples below show how each of the fills will print at its default settings. The gray circles show how the white areas react with backgrounds — either staying white or becoming transparent.

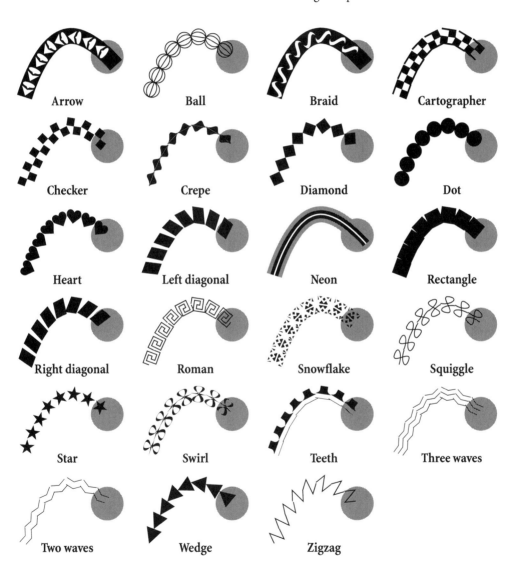

| Arrow | Ball | Braid | Cartographer |

| Checker | Crepe | Diamond | Dot |

| Heart | Left diagonal | Neon | Rectangle |

| Right diagonal | Roman | Snowflake | Squiggle |

| Star | Swirl | Teeth | Three waves |

| Two waves | Wedge | Zigzag |

Custom Strokes

❹ *The* **23 Custom strokes** *at their default settings.*

INDEX

Index

E

Index

G

General preferences, 248
GIF Options dialog box, 232
gradient fills, 94–96
    adding colors to, 96
    deleting colors from, 96
    linear, 94–95
    radial, 95–96
    See also fills
Graphic Hose palette, 192
    Options button, 193
    Order pop-up menu, 193
    Rotate pop-up menu, 193
    Scale pop-up menu, 193
    Sets pop-up menu, 192
    Spacing pop-up menu, 193
Graphic Hose tool, 192–193
    defined, 192
    double-clicking, 192
    sets, 192
    symbols and, 192
    using, 193
graphs. *See* Chart dialog box; charts and graphs
grayscale, converting colors to, 195
Greys library, 89
gridlines, chart, 202
grouped column graph, 200
grouped objects
    anchor points, 56
    moving, numerically, 55
    point selection in, 56
    resizing, 56
    selecting, 56
    sizing, numerically, 59
    transforming, as unit, 248
    working with, 56
grouping, 56
Guide Position dialog box, 17
guides
    adding, precisely, 16
    creating, by dragging, 15
    deleting, 16
    horizontal, 15, 16
    locking, 17
    moving, 16
    multiple, selecting, 17
    page range for, 16

repositioning, 17
snapping to, 18
turning paths into, 15
vertical, 15, 16
Guides dialog box, 16–17
    deleting guides from, 17
    illustrated, 16
    Release button, 17
Guides layer, 16, 27

H

halftone screen
    angle, 243
    frequency, 243
    for individual objects, 243
    setting, 243
Halftones panel, 243, 263
    illustrated, 243, 263
    keyboard shortcuts, 263
    opening, 243
hanging punctuation, 130
Highlight effect, 142
    edit dialog box, 143
    illustrated, 142
    See also text effects
HLS mode
    color definition, 83
    defined, 81
    tricolored icon, 87
hotspots, 220
HTML
    editor, 221, 222
    file, viewing, 222
    output creation, 222
    output preferences, 221
    output warnings, 222
    setting creation, 221
HTML Export dialog box, 221
HTML Output dialog box, 221, 222
HTML Output Warnings window, 222
HTML Picker, 83
HTML Setup dialog box, 221
http (HyperText Transfer Protocol) links, 220
hyphenation, 131

Index

M

Index

Y

Z